THE COMPLETE GUIDE TO OPTION PRICING FORMULAS

THE COMPLETE GUIDE TO OPTION PRICING FORMULAS

ESPEN GAARDER HAUG

McGraw-Hill
New York   Chicago   San Francisco   Washington, D.C.
Auckland   Bogotá   Caracas   Lisbon   London   Madrid
Mexico City   Milan   Montreal   New Delhi   San Juan
Singapore   Sydney   Tokyo   Toronto

Library of Congress Cataloging-in-Publication Data

Haug, Espen Gaarder.
   The complete guide to options pricing formulas / Espen Gaarder
Haug.
     p. cm.
   ISBN 0-7863-1240-8
   1. Options (Finance)—Prices. I. Title.
HG6024.A3H38 1997
332.63′228—dc21   97–8665
                                                  CIP

McGraw-Hill

*A Division of The **McGraw·Hill** Companies*

   11 12 13 14 15   DOC/DOC   0 9 8 7 6 5 4

ISBN 0-7863-1240-8

The sponsoring editor for this book was Stephen Isaacs, the managing editor was Kevin Thornton, the editing supervisor was John M. Morriss, and the production supervisor was Suzanne W. B. Rapcavage. It was set in New Century Schoolbook by Publication Services, Inc.

Printed and bound by R. R. Donnelley & Sons Company.

McGraw-Hill books are available at special quantity discounts to use as premiums and sales
promotions, or for use in corporate training programs. For more information, please write to the
Director of Special Sales, McGraw-Hill, Professional Publishing, Two Penn Plaza, New York, NY
10121-2298. Or contact your local bookstore.

 This book is printed on recycled, acid-free paper containing a
minimum of 50% recycled de-inked fiber.

INTRODUCTION

Some people collect stamps; others collect coins, matchboxes, butterflies, or cars. I collect options pricing formulas. The book you have before you is a copy of this collection. As opposed to cars, one can easily share a collection of options pricing formulas with others. A collection like this would naturally not have been possible if it weren't for all the excellent researchers both in academia and in the industry who willingly share their knowledge in various publications.

Persons who collect stamps usually arrange their stamps under some kind of system—their issue year, what country they come from, and so on. I have organized my collection of options pricing formulas in a similar fashion. Each formula is given a reference and the year when it was first published. With a few exceptions, I have also included a numerical example or a table with values for each option pricing formula. This should make it easier to understand the various options pricing models, as well as be of value to anyone who wants to check his or her computer implementation of an option pricing formula.

To better illustrate the use and implementation of options pricing formulas, I have included examples of programming codes for several of them. Programming codes for most of the formulas, together with ready-to-use spreadsheets, are included on the accompanying floppy disk. By using this computer code in combination with the book, options pricing should no longer seem like a black box. The book differs from other texts on options pricing in the way I have tried to cut accompanying text to the bone. Text is included to illuminate the essence of implementing and applying the options pricing formulas. This should make it easy and efficient to find the formula you need, whether it is to close a multimillion dollar options contract (without being ripped off) or to see if someone has already solved your problem of finding the value of some exotic options.

This collection of options pricing formulas is not intended as a textbook in options pricing theory but rather as a reference book for those who are already familiar with basic finance theory. However, if you think that a collection of options pricing formulas is useful only to theoreticians, you are wrong. The collection does not contain lengthy deductions of options pricing formulas[1] but rather the essence of options pricing. Most of these formulas are used daily by some of the best talent on Wall Street and by traders in financial centers worldwide. The collection of options pricing formulas is an ideal supplement for quant traders, financial engineers, students taking courses in options pricing theory, or anyone else working with financial options.

The collection came out of my work as head of options trading and derivatives research at the Chase Manhattan Bank Norway. Over several years, I collected everything I came across on the valuation of options. My collection of articles and books on the subject has increased every year. In order to see the large picture of the various options pricing models, as well as to avoid carrying around a heap of books and papers, I decided to compile the most central options pricing formulas into a small, compact book: *The Complete Guide to Option Pricing Formulas.*

Few, if any, financial markets have seen such explosive growth and new developments as the options markets. Continuously, new products are under development. With a few exceptions, I have chosen to collect options pricing models that can be used by practitioners. In a collection of formulas such as this, errors are particularly destructive. A great deal of effort has been put into minimizing typing errors. I hope that readers who find any remaining errors will call them to my attention so that they may be purged from any future editions.

The Complete Guide to Option Pricing Formulas is divided into six chapters. Chapter 1 begins with the breakthrough in options valuation, the Black–Scholes formula. It concentrates on analytical formulas and analytical approximations for pricing European and American standard or plain vanilla options. The chapter ends with a recent development in option pricing, a very interesting three-factor Black–Scholes type model for valuation of commodity options. Chapter 2 deals with a wide range of analytical solutions for so-called exotic options, in the Black–Scholes economy. Chapter 3 is concerned with numerical methods in options pricing: the binomial and trinomial model, three dimensional binomial trees, Monte Carlo simulation, and implied tree models. Chapter 4 presents interest-rate options, simple analytical models as well as more advanced yield-based models. I have chosen to limit coverage to one-factor term-structure models. Chapter 5 deals with different formulas for the estimation of volatility and correlation. Chapter 6 is on interpolation and simple interest-rate calculations.

A table of all the options pricing formulas is included following the table of contents, giving an overview for easy reference. The table gives a short description of the key characteristics of all the options pricing formulas in-

---

1. All material contains references to the originators, in case you wish to have all the details.

cluded in this book. If you are working with an option pricing problem, this table should be a natural starting point. Definitions of symbols are naturally important in a collection such as this. I have tried to define symbols in accordance with the modern literature. Currently, use of symbols in the theory of options pricing is far from standardized. Following the Options Pricing Overview is thus a Glossary of Notations, which will be useful when using this collection.

Several colleges and individuals have helped improve the quality and completeness of the book. I was fortunate to get the opportunity to discuss questions with several experts in the field. I appreciate the suggestions and help contributed by Hans-Peter Bermin, Petter Bjerksund, Jørgen Haug, Kristian Miltersen, Michael Ross, and Gunnar Stensland.

It has been a pleasure to work with the people at McGraw-Hill. In particular, I'm grateful for many helpful suggestions and assistance from Stephen Isaacs and Kevin Thornton. Needless to say, I remain solely responsible for any errors that still remain.

Espen Gaarder Haug, February 1997

CONTENTS

OPTIONS PRICING FORMULAS
OVERVIEW

The table on the next few pages offers an overview of the options pricing formulas presented in this book. For easy reference, each formula in the table is accompanied by a set of letters signifying key characteristics.

Type of formula:

C: Closed-form solution.
P: Closed-form approximation.
N: Numerical method.
E: European option.
A: American option.

Type of underlying asset:

S: Stock.
I: Stock/index paying a dividend yield.
F: Futures or forward contract.
C: Currency.
R: Interest rate or debt.

In the column "Computer code," a bullet (•) indicates that computer code for the formula is included in the book or on the accompanying floppy disk.

Option Pricing Formula	Type of Formula	Type of Underlying Asset	Distribution of Underlying Asset	Computer Code	Short Description
Plain Vanilla Options: Chapter 1					
Black–Scholes (1973)	C, E	S	Lognormal	•	The breakthrough in option pricing.
Merton (1973)	C, E	S, I	Lognormal	•	Extension of Black–Scholes formula including a dividend yield.
Black (1976)	C, E	F	Lognormal	•	Modified Black–Scholes for options on forward or futures.
Garman and Kohlhagen (1983)	C, E	C	Lognormal	•	Modified Black–Scholes for options on currencies.
Generalized Black–Scholes	C, E	S, I, F, C	Lognormal	•	Combines all the models above into one formula.
Merton (1976) Jump Diffusion	C, E	S	Jump diffusion[1]	•	Example of a model with a process different from Brownian motion.
Roll, Geske, and Whaley	P, A	S	Lognormal		American call option with single cash dividend.
Barone-Adesi and Whaley (1987)	P, A	S, I, F, C	Lognormal	•	Approximation much used in practice.
Bjerksund and Stensland (1993b)	P, A	S, I, F, C	Lognormal	•	Extremely computer efficient.
Miltersen and Schwartz (1997) commodity option model.	C, E	F	Lognormal[2]	•	Three-factor model with stochastic term structures of convenience yields and forward interest rates.
Exotic Options: Chapter 2					
Executive stock option	C, E	S, I	Lognormal	•	Take into account the probability that the executive will stay with the firm until the option expires.
Forward start option	C, E	S, I, F, C	Lognormal	•	Starts at-the-money or proportionally in- or out-of-the-money after a known elapsed time into the future.
Ratchet option (Cliquet option)	C, E	S, I, F, C	Lognormal		A series of forward starting options.
Discrete time-switch option	C, E	S, I, F, C	Lognormal	•	Accumulates cash for every time unit the option is in-the-money.
Simple chooser option (as-you-like-it option)	C, E	S, I, F, C	Lognormal	•	Gives the right to choose between a call and put option.
Complex chooser option	C, E	S, I, F, C	Lognormal	•	Offers more flexibility than a simple chooser option.

1. The model assumes that the underlying asset follows a jump-diffusion process.
2. Lognormal futures price and normal distributed convenience yields and interest rates.

Option Pricing Formula	Type of Formula	Type of Underlying Asset	Distribution of Underlying Asset	Computer Code	Short Description
Options on options (compound options)	C, E	S, I, F, C	Lognormal	•	Option on a plain vanilla option: call on call, call on put, put on call, and put on put.
Buyer-extendible option	C, E	S, I, F, C	Lognormal		Option that can be extended by the option holder.
Writer-extendible option	C, E	S, I, F, C	Lognormal	•	Option that will be extended by the writer if the option is out-of-the-money.
Two-asset correlation option	C, E	S, I, F, C	Lognormal	•	One asset decides if the option is in or out-of-the-money. Another asset with its own strike decides the payoff.
Exchange one asset for another option	C, E, A	S, I, F, C	Lognormal	•	Option to exchange one asset for another.
Exchange option on exchange option	C, E	S, I, F, C	Lognormal	•	Can be used to value sequential exchange opportunities.
Option on the maximum or minimum of two assets	C, E	S, I, F, C	Lognormal	•	Call or put options on the maximum or minimum of two assets.
Spread option	P, E	F	Lognormal	•	Option on the difference between two assets.
Floating strike look-back option (no-regrets option)	C, E	S, I, C	Lognormal	•	Options to sell at maximum or buy at minimum observed price.
Fixed strike look-back option (hindsight option)	C, E	S, I, C	Lognormal	•	An observed maximum or minimum asset price against a fixed strike.
Partial-time floating strike look-back option	C, E	S, I, C	Lognormal	•	Same as floating strike look-back except look-back monitoring only in parts of the option's lifetime.
Partial-time fixed strike lookback option	C, E	S, I, C	Lognormal	•	Same as fixed strike lookback except look-back monitoring only in parts of the option's lifetime.
Extreme spread option	C, E	S, I, C	Lognormal	•	Option on the difference between the observed maximum or minimum from two different time periods.
Standard barrier option (inside barrier option)	C, E	S, I, F, C	Lognormal	•	Options where existence is dependent whenever the asset price hits a barrier level before expiration.
Double barrier option	C, E	S, I, F, C	Lognormal	•	Options with two barriers, one above and one below the current asset price.
Partial-time single-asset barrier option	C, E	S, I, F, C	Lognormal	•	Barrier hits are only monitored in a part of the options' lifetime.

Option Pricing Formula	Type of Formula	Type of Underlying Asset	Distribution of Underlying Asset	Computer Code	Short Description
Two-asset barrier option (outside barrier option)	C, E	S, I, F, C	Lognormal	•	One asset decides barrier hits; the other asset decides payoff.
Partial-time two-asset barrier option	C, E	S, I, F, C	Lognormal	•	Barrier hits are only monitored in a part of the option's lifetime.
Discrete barrier option	C, E	S, I, F, C	Lognormal	•	Adjustment that can be used for pricing barrier options with discrete barrier monitoring.
Look-barrier option	C, E	S, I, C	Lognormal	•	Combination of a partial time barrier option and a forward start fixed strike look-back option.
Soft-barrier option	C, E	S, I, C	Lognormal	•	The option has a barrier range and is knocked in or out partially.
Gap option (pay-later option)	C, E	S, I, F, C	Lognormal	•	One strike decides if the option is in or out-of-the-money; another strike decides the size of the payoff.
Cash-or-nothing option	C, E	S, I, F, C	Lognormal	•	Pays out cash if in-the-money and zero if out-of-the-money.
Two-asset cash-or-nothing option	C, E	S, I, F, C	Lognormal	•	Two asset and two strikes decides if the option pays out a cash amount or nothing.
Asset-or-nothing option	C, E	S, I, F, C	Lognormal	•	Pays out asset if in-the-money; otherwise pays zero.
Supershare option	C, E	S, I, F, C	Lognormal	•	Pays out $\frac{\text{Asset}}{\text{Low strike}}$ if the asset falls between a lower and higher strike.
Binary barrier options (digital option)	C, E	S, I, F, C	Lognormal	•	Can price 28 different binary barrier options.
Geometric average option (Asian option)	C, E	S, I, F, C	Lognormal	•	Option on a geometric average: $(x_1 \cdots x_n)^{1/n}$.
Arithmetic average option (Asian option)	P, A	S, I, F, C	Lognormal	•	Options on an arithmetic average: $\frac{x_1 + \cdots + x_n}{n}$.
Foreign equity option stuck in domestic currency	C, E	S and C	Lognormal	•	Options on foreign equity in domestic currency.
Fixed exchange rate foreign equity option (Quantos)	C, E	S and C	Lognormal	•	Foreign equity option with fixed exchange rate.
Equity linked foreign exchange option	C, E	S and C	Lognormal	•	FX option where quantity depends on foreign equity price.
Takeover foreign exchange option	C, E	S and C	Lognormal	•	FX option that only can be exercised if takeover is successful.

Option Pricing Formula	Type of Formula	Type of Underlying Asset	Distribution of Underlying Asset	Computer Code	Short Description
Numerical Methods in Options Pricing: Chapter 3					
Binomial trees	N, E, and A	S, I, F, C	Lognormal	•	Can be used to value most types of single asset options.
Barrier option in binomial trees	N, E, and A	S, I, F, C	Lognormal	•	A "standard" binomial tree where the number of time steps is adjusted so the barrier falls on the nodes.
Convertible bonds in binomial trees	N, E, and A	Stock and bond	Lognormal Stock	•	Convertible bond valuation with variable credit adjusted discount rate.
Trinomial trees	N, E, and A	S, I, F, C	Lognormal	•	More computer efficient and gives better flexibility than binomial trees.
Three-dimensional binomial trees	N, E, and A	S, I, F, C	Lognormal	•	Can be used for valuation of most options on two correlated asset.
Implied binomial trees	N, E, and A	S, I, F, C	Implied distribution from market data		Especially useful for valuation of exotic options consistent with more liquid plain vanilla European options.
Implied trinomial trees	N, E, and A	S, I, F, C	Implied distribution from market data	•	Offers more flexibility than implied binomial trees.
Monte Carlo simulation	N, E[3]	S, I, F, C, R	Dependent on the simulated process	•	Very flexible but relatively slow in computer time.
Interest Rate Options: Chapter 4					
Black-76 cap and floor model	C, E	Implied forward rates	Lognormal forward rates		A whole series of options on implied forward rates.
Modified Black-76 swaption model	C, E	Swap rate	Lognormal swap rate	•	Options on interest-rate swaps: payer and receiver swaptions.
Black-76 for options on bonds	C, E	Forward price of bond	Lognormal bond forward price	•	Often used when time to maturity on the option is short relative to the time to maturity on the underlying bond.
Schaefer and Schwartz (1987) adjusted Black–Scholes model.	C, E	Bond price	Lognormal		Allows the price volatility of the bond to be a function of the bond duration.
Rendleman and Bartter (1980)	N, E, and A	R	Lognormal interest rate		No arbitrage-free equilibrium model.
Vasicek (1977)	C, E N, A	R	Normal interest rate mean reversion	•	No arbitrage-free equilibrium model.

3. With use of different techniques, it is possible to use Monte Carlo simulation for pricing American options as well. However, we will limit ourselves to looking at Monte Carlo simulation for European options.

Option Pricing Formula	Type of Formula	Type of Underlying Asset	Distribution of Underlying Asset	Computer Code	Short Description
Ho and Lee (1986)	C, E N, A	R	Normal interest rate		Arbitrage-free with respect to underlying zero coupon rates.
Hull and White (1990)	C, E N, A	R	Normal interest rate mean reversion		Arbitrage-free with respect to underlying zero coupon rates.
Black, Derman, and Toy (1990)	N, E, and A	R	Lognormal interest rate		Arbitrage-free with respect to underlying zero coupon rates.

GLOSSARY OF NOTATIONS

List is in alphabetical order, ending with non-Latin symbols.

A	Accumulated amount in time-switch options.
b	Cost of carry rate.
	(i.e., the cost of interest plus any additional costs).
	In every formula, it is continuously compounded.
c	Price of European call option.
C	Price of American call option.
d	The size of the downward movement of the underlying asset in a binomial or trinomial tree.
D	Cash dividend.
E	Spot exchange rate of a currency.
F	Forward price or futures price.
H	Barrier (only used for barrier options).
K	Predetermined cash payoff.
L	Lower barrier in a barrier option.
$M(a,b;\rho)$	The cumulative bivariate normal distribution function.
n	Number of time steps in lattice or tree model.
$n(x)$	The standardized normal density function.
$N(x)$	The cumulative normal distribution function.
p	Price of European put option.
	Up probability in tree or lattice models.
P	Price of American put option.
	Also used as bond price.
q	Instantaneous proportional dividend yield rate of the underlying asset.
	Down probability in implied trinomial tree.
Q	Fixed quantity of asset.
r	Risk-free interest rate. In general, this is a continuously compounded rate. An exception is the Black–Derman–Toy model in Chapter 4 and some of the formulas in the section on interest rates in Chapter 6.

r_f	Foreign risk-free interest rate.
S	Price of underlying asset.
T	Time to expiration of an option or other derivative security in number of years.
u	The size of the up movement of the underlying asset in a binomial or trinomial tree.
U	Upper barrier in barrier option.
w	Value of European option.
W	Value of American option.
X	Strike price of option.
y	Bond or swap yield.
γ	Percentage of the total volatility explained by the jump in the jump-diffusion model.
Γ	Gamma of option.
Δ	Delta of option.
Δt	Size of time step in a tree model.
θ	Mean reversion level.
Θ	Theta of option.
κ	Speed of mean reversion ("gravity").
λ	Arrow-Debreu prices in the implied tree model. Expected number of jumps per year in the jump-diffusion model.
Λ	Elasticity of a plain vanilla European option (options sensitivity in percent with respect to a percent movement in the underlying asset).
μ	Drift of underlying asset (also used in other contexts).
π	The constant Pi ≈ 3.14159265359.
ρ	Correlation coefficient.
σ	Volatility of the relative price change of the underlying asset.

THE COMPLETE GUIDE TO OPTION PRICING FORMULAS

1

⑥ PLAIN VANILLA OPTIONS

Plain vanilla options are standard call and put options without any special properties attached. (For example, a barrier, floating strike price, and extendible maturity are characteristics of exotic options, covered in Chapter 2.)

This chapter begins with analytical formulas for plain vanilla European options on stocks, stock indexes, futures, and currencies. It also covers the put–call parity for Black–Scholes type European options, as well as the option formulas' partial derivatives or option sensitivities. The next section of the chapter deals with analytical solutions for American options.[1] The last section introduces some of the latest developments in the valuation of commodity options.

1.1 ANALYTICAL FORMULAS FOR EUROPEAN OPTIONS

European options can only be exercised at maturity. This restriction makes it possible, in most cases, to find closed-form solutions.

1.1.1 The Black–Scholes Option Pricing Formula

The breakthrough in option pricing theory came with the famous Black and Scholes paper in 1973. Black and Scholes where the first to show that options could be priced by constructing a risk-free hedge by dynamically managing a simple portfolio consisting of the underlying asset and cash. The same principle is the foundation for almost any option pricing formula used in today's financial markets. The Black and Scholes (1973) formula can be used to value European stock options on a stock that does not pay dividends.[2] Letting c and p denote the price of European call and put options respectively, the formula states that

---

1. Valuation of American options using numerical techniques will be covered in Chapter 3.
2. The Black–Scholes formula can also be used to price American call options on a nondividend-paying stock since it will never be optimal to exercise the option before expiration.

$$c = SN(d_1) - Xe^{-rT}N(d_2) \tag{1.1}$$

$$p = Xe^{-rT}N(-d_2) - SN(-d_1), \tag{1.2}$$

where

$$d_1 = \frac{\ln(S/X) + (r + \sigma^2/2)T}{\sigma\sqrt{T}}$$

$$d_2 = \frac{\ln(S/X) + (r - \sigma^2/2)T}{\sigma\sqrt{T}} = d_1 - \sigma\sqrt{T}$$

$S = $ Stock price.
$X = $ Strike price of option.
$r = $ Risk-free interest rate.
$T = $ Time to expiration in years.
$\sigma = $ Volatility of the relative price change
    of the underlying stock price.
$N(x) = $ The cumulative normal distribution function,
    described in Appendix A.

Example
Consider a European call option with three months to expiry. The stock price is 60, the strike price is 65, the risk-free interest rate is 8% per annum, and the volatility is 30% per annum. Thus, $S = 60$, $X = 65$, $T = 0.25$, $r = 0.08$, $\sigma = 0.30$.

$$d_1 = \frac{\ln(60/65) + (0.08 + 0.30^2/2)0.25}{0.30\sqrt{0.25}} = -0.3253$$

$$d_2 = d_1 - 0.30\sqrt{0.25} = -0.4753$$

The value of the cumulative normal distribution $N(\cdot)$ can be found using the approximation function in Appendix A or Tables A-1 and A-2 in the same appendix.

$$N(d_1) = N(-0.3253) = 0.3725, \qquad N(d_2) = N(-0.4753) = 0.3173$$

$$c = 60N(d_1) - 65e^{-0.08 \times 0.25}N(d_2) = 2.1334$$

Computer algorithm

The *BlackScholes*$(\cdot)$ function returns the call price if the *CallPutFlag* is set equal to "c" or the put price when set equal to "p." In the computer code $v = \sigma$.

```
Function BlackScholes(CallPutFlag As String, S As Double, X As Double, _
       T As Double, r As Double, v As Double) As Double

     Dim d1 As Double, d2 As Double

     d1 = (Log(S/X) + (r + v^2/2) * T)/(v * Sqr(T))
     d2 = d1 - v * Sqr(T)
     If CallPutFlag = "c" Then
         BlackScholes = S * CND(d1) - X * Exp(-r * T) * CND(d2)
     ElseIf CallPutFlag = "p" Then
             BlackScholes = X * Exp(-r * T) * CND(-d2) - S * CND(-d1)
     End If
End Function
```

where $CND(\cdot)$ is the cumulative normal distribution function described in Appendix A. Example: *BlackScholes*("c", 60, 65, 0.25, 0.08, 0.30) will return a call price of 2.1334 as in the numerical example above.

1.1.2 European Option on a Stock with Cash Dividends

European option on a stock that pays out one or more cash dividends (lump sum) during the option's lifetime can be priced by using the Black–Scholes formula, by replacing S with S minus the present value of the dividends. In general, the stock price minus the present value of the dividends can be written as

$$S - D_1 e^{-rt_1} - D_2 e^{-rt_2} \cdots - D_n e^{-rt_n}, \qquad (t_n < T),$$

where D_1 is dividend payout one, t_1 is time to dividend payout, and T is the time to maturity of the option.

Example

Consider a European call option on a stock that will pay out a dividend of two, three and six months from now. The current stock price is 100, the strike price is 90, the time to maturity on the option is nine months, the risk-free rate is 10%, and the volatility is 25%. Hence, $S = 100$, $X = 90$, $T = 0.75$, $r = 0.10$, $\sigma = 0.25$, $D_1 = D_2 = 2$, $t_1 = 0.25$, $t_2 = 0.5$. The stock price minus the net present value of the cash dividends is

$$100 - 2e^{-0.10 \times 0.25} - 2e^{-0.10 \times 0.5} = 96.1469$$

Next, use the Black–Scholes formula:

$$d_1 = \frac{\ln(96.1469/90) + (0.10 + 0.25^2/2)0.75}{0.25\sqrt{0.75}} = 0.7598$$

$$d_2 = d_1 - 0.25\sqrt{0.75} = 0.5433$$

$$N(d_1) = N(0.7598) = 0.7763, \qquad N(d_2) = N(0.5433) = 0.7065$$

$$c = 96.1469N(d_1) - 90e^{-0.10 \times 0.75}N(d_2) = 15.6465$$

1.1.3   Options on Stock Indexes

Merton (1973) extended the Black–Scholes model to allow for a dividend yield. The model can be used to price European call and put options on a stock or stock index paying a known dividend yield equal to q.

$$c = Se^{-qT}N(d_1) - Xe^{-rT}N(d_2) \tag{1.3}$$

$$p = Xe^{-rT}N(-d_2) - Se^{-qT}N(-d_1), \tag{1.4}$$

where

$$d_1 = \frac{\ln(S/X) + (r - q + \sigma^2/2)T}{\sigma\sqrt{T}}$$

$$d_2 = \frac{\ln(S/X) + (r - q - \sigma^2/2)T}{\sigma\sqrt{T}} = d_1 - \sigma\sqrt{T}.$$

Example

Consider a European put option with six months to expiry. The stock index is 100, the strike price is 95, the risk-free interest rate is 10% per annum, the dividend yield is 5% per annum, and the volatility is 20% per annum. $S = 100, X = 95, T = 0.5, r = 0.10, q = 0.05, \sigma = 0.20$.

$$d_1 = \frac{\ln(100/95) + (0.10 - 0.05 + 0.20^2/2)0.5}{0.20\sqrt{0.5}} = 0.6102$$

$$d_2 = d_1 - 0.20\sqrt{0.5} = 0.4688$$

$$N(d_1) = N(0.6102) = 0.7291, \qquad N(d_2) = N(0.4688) = 0.6804$$

$$N(-d_1) = N(-0.6102) = 0.2709, \qquad N(-d_2) = N(-0.4688) = 0.3196$$

$$p = 95e^{-0.10 \times 0.5} N(-d_2) - 100e^{-0.05 \times 0.5} N(-d_1) = 2.4648$$

1.1.4 Options on Futures

The Black (1976) formula can be used to price European options when the underlying security is a forward or futures contract with initial price F:

$$c = e^{-rT} [FN(d_1) - XN(d_2)] \tag{1.5}$$

$$p = e^{-rT} [XN(-d_2) - FN(-d_1)], \tag{1.6}$$

where

$$d_1 = \frac{\ln(F/X) + (\sigma^2/2)T}{\sigma\sqrt{T}}$$

$$d_2 = \frac{\ln(F/X) - (\sigma^2/2)T}{\sigma\sqrt{T}} = d_1 - \sigma\sqrt{T}.$$

Example

Consider a European option on the brent blend futures with nine months to expiry. The futures price is USD 19, the strike price is USD 19, the risk-free interest rate is 10% per annum, and the volatility is 28% per annum. $F = 19$, $X = 19$, $T = 0.75$, $r = 0.10$, $\sigma = 0.28$.

$$d_1 = \frac{\ln(19/19) + (0.28^2/2)0.75}{0.28\sqrt{0.75}} = 0.1212$$

$$d_2 = d_1 - 0.28\sqrt{0.75} = -0.1212$$

$$N(d_1) = N(0.1212) = 0.5483, \qquad N(d_2) = N(-0.1212) = 0.4517$$

$$N(-d_1) = N(-0.1212) = 0.4517, \qquad N(-d_2) = N(0.1212) = 0.5483$$

$$c = e^{-0.10 \times 0.75}[19N(d_1) - 19N(d_2)] = 1.7011$$

$$p = e^{-0.10 \times 0.75}[19N(-d_2) - 19N(-d_1)] = 1.7011$$

1.1.5 Currency Options

The Garman and Kohlhagen (1983) modified Black–Scholes model can be used to price European currency options. The model is equal to the Merton (1973) model presented earlier. The only difference is that the dividend yield is replaced by the risk-free rate of the foreign currency r_f.

$$c = Se^{-r_f T}N(d_1) - Xe^{-rT}N(d_2) \tag{1.7}$$

$$p = Xe^{-rT}N(-d_2) - Se^{-r_f T}N(-d_1), \tag{1.8}$$

where

$$d_1 = \frac{\ln(S/X) + (r - r_f + \sigma^2/2)T}{\sigma\sqrt{T}}$$

$$d_2 = \frac{\ln(S/X) + (r - r_f - \sigma^2/2)T}{\sigma\sqrt{T}} = d_1 - \sigma\sqrt{T}.$$

Example
Consider a European call USD put DEM option with six months to expiry. The USD/DEM exchange rate is 1.56, the strike is 1.60, the domestic risk-free interest rate in Germany is 6% per annum, the foreign risk-free interest rate in the United States is 8% per annum, and the volatility is 12% per annum. $S = 1.56$, $X = 1.60$, $T = 0.5$, $r = 0.06$, $r_f = 0.08$, $\sigma = 0.12$.

$$d_1 = \frac{\ln(1.56/1.60) + (0.06 - 0.08 + 0.12^2/2)0.5}{0.12\sqrt{0.5}} = -0.3738$$

$$d_2 = d_1 - 0.12\sqrt{0.5} = -0.4587$$

$$N(d_1) = N(-0.3738) = 0.3543, \qquad N(d_2) = N(-0.4587) = 0.3232$$

$$c = 1.56e^{-0.08 \times 0.5}N(d_1) - 1.60e^{-0.06 \times 0.5}N(d_2) = 0.0291$$

1.1.6 The Generalized Black–Scholes Option Pricing Formula

The general version of the Black–Scholes model incorporates the cost-of-carry term b. It can be used to price European options on stocks, stocks paying a continuous dividend yield, options on futures, and currency options:

$$c_{GBS} = Se^{(b-r)T}N(d_1) - Xe^{-rT}N(d_2) \tag{1.9}$$

$$p_{GBS} = Xe^{-rT}N(-d_2) - Se^{(b-r)T}N(-d_1), \tag{1.10}$$

where

$$d_1 = \frac{\ln(S/X) + (b + \sigma^2/2)T}{\sigma\sqrt{T}}$$

$$d_2 = \frac{\ln(S/X) + (b - \sigma^2/2)T}{\sigma\sqrt{T}} = d_1 - \sigma\sqrt{T},$$

and b is the cost-of-carry rate of holding the underlying security.

$b = r$ gives the Black and Scholes (1973) stock option model.

$b = r - q$ gives the Merton (1973) stock option model with continuous dividend yield q.

$b = 0$ gives the Black (1976) futures option model.

$b = r - r_f$ gives the Garman and Kohlhagen (1983) currency option model.

Computer algorithm

The *GBlackScholes*($\cdot$) function returns the call price if the *CallPutFlag* is set equal to "c" or the put price when set equal to "p."

```
Function GBlackScholes(CallPutFlag As String, S As Double, X As Double, _
           T As Double, r As Double, b As Double, v As Double) As Double

    Dim d1 As Double, d2 As Double

    d1 = (Log(S/X) + (b + v^2/2) * T)/(v * Sqr(T))
    d2 = d1 − v * Sqr(T)
    If CallPutFlag = "c" Then
        GBlackScholes = S * Exp((b − r) * T) * CND(d1) − X * Exp(−r * T) * CND(d2)
    ElseIf CallPutFlag = "p" Then
        GBlackScholes = X * Exp(−r * T) * CND(−d2) − S * Exp((b − r) * T) * CND(−d1)
    End If
End Function
```

where $CND(\cdot)$ is the cumulative normal distribution function described in Appendix A. Example: *GBlackScholes*("p," 75, 70, 0.5, 0.10, 0.05, 0.35) returns a put price of 4.0870.

1.1.7 The Jump-Diffusion Model

Almost any option pricing formula presented in this book will be based on the assumption that the underlying asset is lognormally distributed (i.e., it follows a geometric Brownian motion). The valuation of options on assets that are assumed to follow stochastic processes other than Brownian motion has received attention mainly by academics. However, few of these alternative processes are used. One explanation is that most of these models require additional input parameters that not are directly observable in the financial markets. They must thus be estimated using various statistical techniques. The additional accuracy offered by several of these models is outweighed by the complexity of estimating the additional input parameters required.[3]

An example of such a model is the Merton (1976) jump-diffusion model.[4] The model assumes that the underlying asset follows a jump-diffusion process. However, the model requires two additional parameters to be estimated: the expected number of jumps per year λ and the percentage of the total volatility explained by the jumps γ.

$$c = \sum_{i=0}^{\infty} \frac{e^{-\lambda T}(\lambda T)^i}{i!} c_i(S, X, T, r, \sigma_i) \qquad (1.11)$$

$$p = \sum_{i=0}^{\infty} \frac{e^{-\lambda T}(\lambda T)^i}{i!} p_i(S, X, T, r, \sigma_i), \qquad (1.12)$$

where

$$\sigma_i = \sqrt{z^2 + \delta^2(i/T)}$$

$$\delta = \sqrt{\frac{\gamma \sigma^2}{\lambda}}, \qquad z = \sqrt{\sigma^2 - \lambda \delta^2}.$$

Computer algorithm

---

3. Recently, the introduction of implied tree models calibrated to the implied market distribution has received much attention by both academics and practitioners. This type of model will be described in detail in Chapter 3.

4. For more on option pricing under the assumptions of jump diffusion, see also Ball and Torous (1983), Ball and Torous (1985), Aase (1988), Bates (1991), and Amin (1993).

Function *JumpDiffusion(CallPutFlag* As String, *S* As Double, *X* As Double, _
    T As Double, *r* As Double, *v* As Double, *Lambda* As Double, _
    gamma As Double) As Double

    Dim *delta* As Double, *Sum* As Double, *z* As Double, *vi* As Double
    Dim *i* As Integer

    delta = *Sqr(gamma * v^2/Lambda)*
    z = *Sqr(v^2 − Lambda * delta^2)*
    Sum = 0
    For *i* = 0 To 10
        vi = *Sqr(z^2 + delta^2 * (i/T))*
        Sum = *Sum + Exp(−Lambda * T) * (Lambda * T)^i/* _
        *Application.Fact(i) * GBlackScholes(CallPutFlag, S, X, T, r, r, vi)*
    Next
    JumpDiffusion = *Sum*
End Function

where $CND(\cdot)$ is the cumulative normal distribution function, and the function *GBlackScholes*$(\cdot)$ is the generalized Black–Scholes function. Example: *JumpDiffusion*("c", 45, 55, 0.25, 0.10, 0.25, 3, 0.40) returns a call value of 0.2417.

T A B L E 1–1

Jump-Diffusion Call Values

$(S = 100, \sigma = 0.25, r = 0.08)$

		$\lambda = 1$ Time to Maturity			$\lambda = 5$ Time to Maturity			$\lambda = 10$ Time to Maturity		
γ	Strike	0.1	0.25	0.5	0.1	0.25	0.5	0.1	0.25	0.5
	80	20.67	21.74	23.63	20.65	21.70	23.61	20.64	21.70	23.28
	90	11.00	12.74	15.40	10.98	12.75	15.42	10.98	12.75	15.20
0.25	100	3.42	5.88	8.95	3.51	5.96	9.02	3.53	5.97	8.89
	110	0.55	2.11	4.67	0.56	2.16	4.73	0.56	2.17	4.66
	120	0.10	0.64	2.23	0.06	0.63	2.25	0.05	0.62	2.21
	80	20.72	21.83	23.71	20.66	21.73	23.63	20.65	21.71	23.28
	90	11.04	12.72	15.34	11.02	12.76	15.41	11.00	12.75	15.18
0.50	100	3.14	5.58	8.71	3.39	5.87	8.96	3.46	5.93	8.85
	110	0.53	1.93	4.42	0.58	2.11	4.67	0.57	2.14	4.62
	120	0.19	0.71	2.15	0.10	0.66	2.23	0.07	0.64	2.19
	80	20.79	21.96	23.86	20.68	21.78	23.67	20.66	21.74	23.30
	90	11.11	12.75	15.30	11.09	12.78	15.39	11.04	12.76	15.17
0.75	100	2.70	5.08	8.24	3.16	5.71	8.85	3.33	5.85	8.79
	110	0.54	1.69	3.99	0.62	2.05	4.57	0.60	2.11	4.56
	120	0.29	0.84	2.09	0.15	0.71	2.21	0.11	0.67	2.17

Table 1–1 shows values for the jump-diffusion call option model. Values are tabulated with different values for the option's Gamma γ, strike, number of jumps per year λ, and time to maturity.

1.2 THE PUT–CALL PARITY FOR EUROPEAN OPTIONS

If one knows the value of a call option, the put–call parity gives the value of a put option with the same strike price, and vice versa. If the put–call parity does not hold, an arbitrage opportunity exists.[5]

Stock Options

$$c = p + S - Xe^{-rT}, \quad p = c - S + Xe^{-rT} \tag{1.13}$$

Example

Consider a European call option on a nondividend-paying stock with a time to maturity of six months. The stock price is 100, the strike price is 105, the risk-free rate is 10% per annum, the call value is 8.5. What is the value of a put with the same parameters? $S = 100, X = 105, T = 0.5, r = 0.10, c = 8.5$.

$$p = 8.5 - 100 + 105e^{-0.10 \times 0.5} = 8.3791$$

Options on a Stock Paying Continuous Dividend Yield

$$c = p + Se^{-qT} - Xe^{-rT}, \quad p = c - Se^{-qT} + Xe^{-rT} \tag{1.14}$$

Futures Option

$$c = p + (F - X)e^{-rT}, \quad p = c - (F - X)e^{-rT} \tag{1.15}$$

Currency Option

$$c = p + Se^{-r_f T} - Xe^{-rT}, \quad p = c - Se^{-r_f T} + Xe^{-rT} \tag{1.16}$$

The Put–Call Parity for the Generalized Black–Scholes Formula

$$c = p + Se^{(b-r)T} - Xe^{-rT}, \quad p = c - Se^{(b-r)T} + Xe^{-rT}, \tag{1.17}$$

where b is the cost of carry of the underlying security.

$b = r =$ Cost of carry on a nondividend-paying stock.
$b = r - q =$ Cost of carry on a stock that pays a continuous dividend yield equal to q.
$b = 0 =$ Cost of carry on a future contract.
$b = r - r_f =$ Cost of carry on a currency position.

---

5. In practice, one would naturally need to take into account bid–ask spreads and other transaction costs.

1.3   OPTIONS SENSITIVITIES

The options sensitivities below are the partial derivatives of the generalized Black–Scholes formula introduced previously in this chapter. The partial derivatives give the sensitivity of the option price to a small movement in the underlying variables. For more details of how to derive the partial derivatives, see Appendix B.

1.3.1   Delta

Delta is the option's sensitivity to small movements in the underlying asset price.

Call

$$\Delta_{call} = \frac{\partial c}{\partial S} = e^{(b-r)T} N(d_1) > 0 \qquad (1.18)$$

Put

$$\Delta_{put} = \frac{\partial p}{\partial S} = e^{(b-r)T} [N(d_1) - 1] < 0 \qquad (1.19)$$

Example
Consider a futures option with six months to expiry. The futures price is 105, the strike price is 100, the risk-free interest rate is 10% per annum, and the volatility is 36% per annum. Thus $S = 105$, $X = 100$, $T = 0.5$, $r = 0.10$, $b = 0$, and $\sigma = 0.36$.

$$d_1 = \frac{\ln(105/100) + (0 + 0.36^2/2)0.5}{0.36\sqrt{0.5}} = 0.3189$$

$$N(d_1) = N(0.3189) = 0.6251$$

$$\Delta_{call} = e^{(0-0.10)0.5} N(d_1) = 0.5946$$

$$\Delta_{put} = e^{(0-0.10)0.5} [N(d_1) - 1] = -0.3566$$

Computer algorithm

Function *GDelta*(*CallPutFlag* As String, *S* As Double, *X* As Double, *T* As Double, _
        r As Double, *b* As Double, *v* As Double) As Double

    Dim *d*1 As Double

$d1 = (Log(S/X) + (b + v\hat{}2/2) * T)/(v * Sqr(T))$
If $CallPutFlag = "c"$ Then
    $GDelta = Exp((b - r) * T) * CND(d1)$
ElseIf $CallPutFlag = "p"$ Then
        $GDelta = Exp((b - r) * T) * (CND(d1) - 1)$
End If
End Function

1.3.2 Elasticity

The elasticity of an option is its sensitivity in percent to a percent movement in the underlying asset price.

Call

$$\Lambda_{call} = \Delta_{call} \frac{S}{call} = e^{(b-r)T} N(d_1) \frac{S}{call} > 1 \tag{1.20}$$

Put

$$\Lambda_{put} = \Delta_{put} \frac{S}{put} = e^{(b-r)T} [N(d_1) - 1] \frac{S}{put} < 0 \tag{1.21}$$

Example
What is the elasticity of a put option with the same parameters as under the delta example?

$$\Lambda_{put} = e^{(0-0.10)0.5} [N(d_1) - 1] \frac{105}{7.6767} = -4.8775$$

1.3.3 Gamma

Gamma is the delta's sensitivity to a small movement in the underlying asset price. Gamma is identical for put and call options.

$$\Gamma_{call,put} = \frac{\partial^2 c}{\partial S^2} = \frac{\partial^2 p}{\partial S^2} = \frac{n(d_1)e^{(b-r)T}}{S\sigma\sqrt{T}} > 0 \tag{1.22}$$

Example
Consider a stock option with nine months to expiry. The stock price is 55, the strike price is 60, the risk-free interest rate is 10% per annum, and the volatility is 30% per annum. $S = 55$, $X = 60$, $T = 0.75$, $r = 0.10$, $b = 0.10$, $\sigma = 0.30$.

$$d_1 = \frac{\ln(55/60) + (0.10 + 0.30^2/2)0.75}{0.30\sqrt{0.75}} = 0.0837$$

$$n(d_1) = n(0.0837) = \frac{1}{\sqrt{2\pi}} e^{-0.0837^2/2} = 0.3975$$

$$\Gamma_{call,put} = \frac{0.3975 e^{(0.10-0.10)0.75}}{55 \times 0.30\sqrt{0.75}} = 0.0278$$

1.3.4 Vega

Vega[6] is the option's sensitivity to a small movement in the volatility of the underlying asset. Vega is equal for put and call options.

$$Vega_{call,put} = \frac{\partial c}{\partial \sigma} = \frac{\partial p}{\partial \sigma} = Se^{(b-r)T}n(d_1)\sqrt{T} > 0 \qquad (1.23)$$

Example

What is the vega of an option with the same parameters as the gamma example?

$$Vega_{call,put} = 55e^{(0.10-0.10)0.75} \times 0.3975\sqrt{0.75} = 18.9358$$

1.3.5 Theta

Theta is the option's sensitivity to a small change in time to maturity. As time to maturity decreases, it is normal to express the theta as minus the partial derivative with respect to time.

Call

$$\Theta_{call} = -\frac{\partial c}{\partial T} = -\frac{Se^{(b-r)T}n(d_1)\sigma}{2\sqrt{T}} - (b-r)Se^{(b-r)T}N(d_1)$$

$$-rXe^{-rT}N(d_2) \lessgtr 0 \qquad (1.24)$$

Put

$$\Theta_{put} = -\frac{\partial p}{\partial T} = -\frac{Se^{(b-r)T}n(d_1)\sigma}{2\sqrt{T}} + (b-r)Se^{(b-r)T}N(-d_1)$$

$$+rXe^{-rT}N(-d_2) \lessgtr 0 \qquad (1.25)$$

---

6. While the names of the other options sensitivities have corresponding Greek letters, Vega is the name of a star.

Example

Consider a European put option on a stock index currently priced at 430. The strike price is 405, time to expiration is one month, the risk-free interest rate is 7% per annum, the dividend yield is 5% per annum, and the volatility is 20% per annum. $S = 430, X = 405, T = 0.0833, r = 0.07, b = 0.07 - 0.05 = 0.02, \sigma = 0.20$.

$$d_1 = \frac{\ln(430/405) + (0.02 + 0.20^2/2)0.0833}{0.20\sqrt{0.0833}} = 1.0952$$

$$d_2 = 1.0952 - 0.20\sqrt{0.0833} = 1.0375$$

$$n(d_1) = n(1.0952) = \frac{1}{\sqrt{2\pi}}e^{-1.0952^2/2} = 0.2190$$

$$N(-d_1) = N(-1.0952) = 0.1367, \qquad N(-d_2) = N(-1.0375) = 0.1498$$

$$\Theta_{put} = \frac{-430e^{(0.02-0.07)0.0833}n(d_1)0.20}{2\sqrt{0.0833}}$$
$$+(0.02 - 0.07)430e^{(0.02-0.07)0.0833}N(-d_1)$$
$$+0.07 \times 405e^{-0.07\times0.0833}N(-d_2) = -31.1924$$

Theta for a one day time decay is $-31.1924/365 = -0.0855$.

1.3.6   Rho

Rho is the option's sensitivity to a small change in the risk-free interest rate.

Call
when $b <> 0$

$$\rho_{call} = \frac{\partial c}{\partial r} = TXe^{-rT}N(d_2) > 0, \tag{1.26}$$

and when $b = 0$

$$\rho_{call} = \frac{\partial c}{\partial r} = -Tc < 0 \tag{1.27}$$

Put
when $b <> 0$

$$\rho_{put} = \frac{\partial p}{\partial r} = -TXe^{-rT}N(-d_2) < 0, \qquad (1.28)$$

and when $b = 0$

$$\rho_{put} = \frac{\partial c}{\partial r} = -Tp < 0 \qquad (1.29)$$

Example
Consider a European call option on a stock currently priced at 72. The strike price is 75, time to expiration is one year, the risk-free interest is 9% per annum, the volatility is 19% per annum. $S = 72$, $X = 75$, $T = 1$, $r = 0.09$, $b = 0.09$, $\sigma = 0.19$.

$$d_2 = \frac{\ln(72/75) + (0.09 - 0.19^2/2)1}{0.19\sqrt{1}} = 0.1638$$

$$N(d_2) = N(0.1638) = 0.5651$$

$$\rho_{call} = 1 \times 75e^{-0.09 \times 1}N(d_2) = 38.7325$$

If the risk-free interest rate goes from 9% to 10%, the call price will increase by approximately 0.3873.

1.3.7 Cost of Carry

This is the option's sensitivity to a marginal change in the cost of carry rate.

Cost of Carry Call

$$\frac{\partial c}{\partial b} = TSe^{(b-r)T}N(d_1) > 0 \qquad (1.30)$$

Cost of Carry Put

$$\frac{\partial p}{\partial b} = -TSe^{(b-r)T}N(-d_1) < 0 \qquad (1.31)$$

Example
What is the sensitivity to cost of carry on a put option with three months to expiry? Assume the stock index price is 500, the strike price is 490, the risk-free interest rate is 8% per annum, the dividend yield is 5% per annum,

and the volatility is 15% per annum. $S = 500$, $X = 490$, $T = 0.25$, $r = 0.08$, $b = 0.08 - 0.05 = 0.03$, $\sigma = 0.15$.

$$d_1 = \frac{\ln(500/490) + (0.03 + 0.15^2/2)0.25}{0.15\sqrt{0.25}} = 0.4069$$

$$N(-d_1) = N(-0.4069) = 0.3421$$

$$\frac{\partial p}{\partial b} = -0.25 \times 500 e^{(0.03-0.08)0.25} N(-d_1) = -42.2254$$

1.3.8   Net Weighted Vega Exposure

In the formula for net weighted vega, Haug (1993) takes into account the fact that the term structure of volatility does not shift in a parallel fashion. This can be useful when adding the vega risk of a portfolio of options on the same underlying security where the time to maturity of the options differs.

$$NWV = \sum_{T=1}^{m} \sum_{i=1}^{n} Q_{i,T} vega_{i,T} \frac{\Psi_T}{\Psi_R} \rho_{\sigma(T),\sigma(R)},$$

where

$m =$ Number of different maturities in the option portfolio.

$n =$ Number of different strikes with time to maturity T.

$vega_{i,T} =$ Vega value of an option with strike i and time to maturity T.

$Q_{i,T} =$ Number or quantity of options in the portfolio with $vega_{i,T}$.

$\Psi_T =$ Volatility of volatility with time to maturity T.

$\Psi_R =$ Volatility of reference volatility.

$\rho_{\sigma(T),\sigma(R)} =$ Correlation between the volatility with time to maturity T and the reference volatility.

Example

Let us assume that we own the portfolio shown in Table 1–2. How will the portfolio react to shifts in the term structure of volatility? To calculate *NWV*, we need estimates of future volatility of volatilities with different maturities, and correlation coefficients between different volatilities. We chose a reference volatility equal to the volatility of the option with the longest time to maturity, that is, 120-day volatility today, 119-day volatility tomorrow, and so on. Assume we have calculated the following historical volatilities of volatilities: 6.5 percentage points 30-day, 5.5 percentage points 60-day, 4.0 percentage points 120-day, and correlation coefficients of 0.65 between

TABLE 1–2

Option Portfolio

$(S = 100, \sigma = 0.25, r = 0.10, b = 0.10)$

Days to maturity	120	60	60	30
Strike	105.00	85.00	100.00	100.00
Call price	4.99	16.53	4.88	3.27
Vega	22.86	3.11	15.81	11.31
Number of contracts	450	100	−400	−300
Volatility of volatility	4.00%	5.50%	5.50%	6.50%
Correlation coefficients	1.00	0.85	0.85	0.65

Espen Gaarder Haug, "Opportunities and Perils of Using Option Sensitivities," *Journal of Financial Engineering*, vol. 2, no. 3, September 1993. Used by permission.

30-day volatility and the reference volatility (120-day), 0.85 for the 60-day volatility and, naturally, 1.0 between 120-day volatility and the reference volatility. It follows that $\Psi_1 = 6.5$, $\Psi_2 = 5.5$, $\Psi_3 = 4.0$, $\Psi_R = 4.0$, $\rho_{1,R} = 0.65$, $\rho_{2,R} = 0.85$, $\rho_{3,R} = 0.10$.

$$
\begin{aligned}
NWV &= \sum_{T=1}^{m} \sum_{i=1}^{n} Q_{i,T} \, vega_{i,T} \frac{\Psi_T}{\Psi_R} \rho_{\sigma(T),\sigma(R)} \\
&= -300 \times 11.31 \times \frac{6.5}{4.0} \times 0.65 - 400 \times 15.81 \times \frac{5.5}{4.0} \times 0.85 \\
&\quad + 100 \times 3.11 \times \frac{5.5}{4.0} \times 0.85 + 450 \times 22.86 \times \frac{4.0}{4.0} \times 1.0 \\
&= -324.55
\end{aligned}
$$

Hence, for each percentage point rise in the reference volatility (120-day), we will lose approximately \$325.

1.3.9 At-the-Money Forward Approximations

The at-the-money forward approximations published by Brenner and Subrahmanyam (1994) can be used for options that are at-the-money forward. To be at-the-money forward is defined as $S = Xe^{-bT}$ or $X = Se^{bT} = F$ (strike price equals the forward price of the underlying asset).

Approximation of the Black–Scholes Formula

$$
c \approx 0.4Se^{(b-r)T}\sigma\sqrt{T}, \quad p \approx 0.4Se^{(b-r)T}\sigma\sqrt{T} \tag{1.32}
$$

Example

Consider a put option with three months to expiry. The futures price is 70, the strike price is 70, the risk-free interest rate is 5% per annum, cost of carry is 0%, and the volatility is 28% per annum. $S = 70$, $X = 70$, $T = 0.25$, $r = 0.05$, $b = 0$, $\sigma = 0.28$.

$$p \approx 0.4 \times 70 e^{(0-0.05)T} 0.28 \sqrt{0.25} \approx 3.8713$$

For comparison, the exact Black-76 price is 3.8579.

Delta

$$\Delta_{call} \approx e^{(b-r)T}(1/2 + 0.2\sigma\sqrt{T}), \quad \Delta_{put} \approx e^{(b-r)T}(0.2\sigma\sqrt{T} - 1/2) \qquad (1.33)$$

Gamma

$$\Gamma_{call,put} \approx \frac{e^{(b-r)T}0.4}{S\sigma\sqrt{T}} \qquad (1.34)$$

Vega

$$Vega_{call,put} \approx Se^{(b-r)T}0.4\sqrt{T} \qquad (1.35)$$

Theta

$$\Theta_{call} \approx -\frac{Se^{(b-r)T}0.4\sigma}{2\sqrt{T}} - Se^{(b-r)T}[b(1/2 + 0.2\sigma\sqrt{T}) - 0.4r\sigma\sqrt{T}] \qquad (1.36)$$

$$\Theta_{put} \approx -\frac{Se^{(b-r)T}0.4\sigma}{2\sqrt{T}} + Se^{(b-r)T}[b(1/2 - 0.2\sigma\sqrt{T}) + 0.4r\sigma\sqrt{T}] \qquad (1.37)$$

Rho
when $b <> 0$

$$\rho_{call} \approx TXe^{-rT}(1/2 - 0.2\sigma\sqrt{T}) \qquad (1.38)$$

$$\rho_{put} \approx -TXe^{-rT}(1/2 + 0.2\sigma\sqrt{T}), \qquad (1.39)$$

when $b = 0$

$$\rho_{call} = -Tc \qquad (1.40)$$

$$\rho_{put} = -Tp \qquad (1.41)$$

Cost of Carry

$$\frac{\partial c}{\partial b} \approx TSe^{(b-r)T}(1/2 + 0.2\sigma\sqrt{T}) \qquad (1.42)$$

$$\frac{\partial p}{\partial b} \approx -TSe^{(b-r)T}(1/2 - 0.2\sigma\sqrt{T}) \qquad (1.43)$$

1.4 ANALYTICAL MODELS FOR AMERICAN OPTIONS

An American option can be exercised at any time up to its expiration date. This added freedom complicates the valuation of American options relative to their European counterparts. With a few exceptions, it is not possible to find an exact formula for the value of American options. Several researchers have, however, come up with excellent closed-form approximations. These approximations have become especially popular because they execute quickly on computers compared to numerical techniques.

1.4.1 American Calls on Stocks with Known Dividends

Roll (1977), Geske (1979a), and Whaley (1981) have developed a formula for the valuation of an American call option on a stock paying a single dividend of D, with time to dividend payout t.

$$
\begin{aligned}
C \;=\; & (S - De^{-rt})N(b_1) + (S - De^{-rt})M\left(a_1, -b_1;\, -\sqrt{\frac{t}{T}}\right) \\
& -Xe^{-rT}M\left(a_2, -b_2;\, -\sqrt{\frac{t}{T}}\right) - (X - D)e^{-rt}N(b_2),
\end{aligned}
\tag{1.44}
$$

where

$$
a_1 = \frac{\ln[(S - De^{-rt})/X] + (r + \sigma^2/2)T}{\sigma\sqrt{T}}
$$

$$
a_2 = a_1 - \sigma\sqrt{T}
$$

$$
b_1 = \frac{\ln[(S - De^{-rt})/I] + (r + \sigma^2/2)t}{\sigma\sqrt{t}}
$$

$$
b_2 = b_1 - \sigma\sqrt{t},
$$

where $N(x)$ is the cumulative normal distribution function, and $M(a,b;\, \rho)$ is the cumulative bivariate normal distribution function with upper integral limits a and b, and correlation coefficient ρ, as described in Appendix A. I is the critical ex-dividend stock price I that solves

$$
c(I, X, T - t) = I + D - X,
$$

where $c(I, X, T - t)$ is the value of a European call with stock price I and time to maturity $T - t$. If $D \leq X(1 - e^{-r(T-t)})$ or $I = \infty$, it will not be optimal to exercise the option before expiration, and the price of the American option can be found by using the European Black–Scholes formula where the stock price is replaced with the stock price minus the present value of the dividend payment $S - De^{-rt}$.

Example

Consider an American-style call option on a stock that will pay a dividend of 4 in exactly three months. The stock price is 80, the strike price is 82, time to maturity is four months, the risk-free interest rate is 6%, and the volatility is 30%. $S = 80, X = 82, t = 0.25, T = 0.3333, r = 0.06, D = 4, \sigma = 0.30$.

$$a_1 = \frac{\ln[(80 - 4e^{-0.06 \times 0.25})/82] + (0.06 + 0.30^2/2)0.3333}{0.30\sqrt{0.3333}} = -0.2321$$

$$a_2 = a_1 - 0.30\sqrt{0.3333} = -0.4053.$$

The critical stock price I must exdividend solve

$$c(I, 82, 0.3333 - 0.25) = I + 4 - 82$$

The solution, given by a numerical search algorithm, is $I = 80.1173$.

$$b_1 = \frac{\ln[(80 - 4e^{-0.06 \times 0.25})/80.1173] + (0.06 + 0.30^2/2)0.25}{0.30\sqrt{0.25}} = -0.1715$$

$$b_2 = b_1 - 0.30\sqrt{0.25} = -0.3215$$

$$M\left(a_1, -b_1; -\sqrt{\frac{0.25}{0.3333}}\right) = 0.0703, \quad M\left(a_2, -b_2; -\sqrt{\frac{0.25}{0.3333}}\right) = 0.0632$$

$$N(b_1) = N(-0.1715) = 0.4319, \qquad N(b_2) = N(-0.3215) = 0.3739$$

$$
\begin{aligned}
C \;=\; & (80 - 4e^{-0.06 \times 0.25})N(b_1) + (80 - 4e^{-0.06 \times 0.25})M\left(a_1, -b_1; -\sqrt{\frac{0.25}{0.3333}}\right) \\[4pt]
& -82e^{-0.06 \times 0.3333}M\left(a_2, -b_2; -\sqrt{\frac{0.25}{0.3333}}\right) \\[4pt]
& -(82 - 4)e^{-0.06 \times 0.25}N(b_2) = 4.3860
\end{aligned}
$$

The value of a similar European call is 3.5107.

Computer algorithm

```
Function RollGeskeWhaley(S As Double, X As Double, t1 As Double, T2 As Double, _
    r As Double, D As Double, v As Double) As Double

    Dim Sx As Double, I As Double
    Dim a1 As Double, a2 As Double, b1 As Double, b2 As Double
    Dim HighS As Double, LowS As Double, epsilon As Double
    Dim ci As Double, infinity As Double

    infinity = 100000000
    epsilon = 0.00001
    Sx = S - D * Exp(-r * t1)
    If D <= X * (1 - Exp(-r * (T2 - t1))) Then '// Not optimal to exercise
        RollGeskeWhaley = BlackScholes("c", Sx, X, T2, r, v)
        Exit Function
    End If
    ci = BlackScholes("c", S, X, T2 - t1, r, v)
    HighS = S
    While (ci - HighS - D + X) > 0 And HighS < infinity
            HighS = HighS * 2
            ci = BlackScholes("c", HighS, X, T2 - t1, r, v)
    Wend
    If HighS > infinity Then
        RollGeskeWhaley = BlackScholes("c", Sx, X, T2, r, v)
        Exit Function
    End If
    LowS = 0
    I = HighS * 0.5
    ci = BlackScholes("c", I, X, T2 - t1, r, v)
    '// Bisection search to find the critical stock price I
    While Abs(ci - I - D + X) > epsilon And HighS - LowS > epsilon
            If (ci - I - D + X) < 0 Then
                HighS = I
            Else
                LowS = I
            End If
            I = (HighS + LowS)/2
            ci = BlackScholes("c", I, X, T2 - t1, r, v)
    Wend
    a1 = (Log(Sx/X) + (r + v^2/2) * T2)/(v * Sqr(T2))
    a2 = a1 - v * Sqr(T2)
    b1 = (Log(Sx/I) + (r + v^2/2) * t1)/(v * Sqr(t1))
    b2 = b1 - v * Sqr(t1)
    RollGeskeWhaley = Sx * CND(b1) + Sx * CBND(a1, -b1, -Sqr(t1/T2)) - _
    X * Exp(-r * T2) * CBND(a2, -b2, -Sqr(t1/T2)) - _
    (X - D) * Exp(-r * t1) * CND(b2)
End Function
```

where $CND(\cdot)$ is the cumulative normal distribution function and $CBND(\cdot)$ is the cumulative bivariate normal distribution function described in Appendix A. Example: *RollGeskeWhaley*(80, 82, 0.25, 0.3333, 0.06, 4, 0.30) returns a call value of 4.3860 as in the numerical example above.

1.4.2   The Barone-Adesi and Whaley Approximation

The quadratic approximation method by Barone-Adesi and Whaley (1987) can be used to price American call and put options on an underlying asset with cost-of-carry rate b. When $b \geq r$, the American call value is equal to the European call value and can then be found by using the generalized Black–Scholes formula. The model is fast and accurate for most practical input values.

American Call

$$C(S,X,T) = \begin{cases} c_{GBS}(S,X,T) + A_2(S/S^*)^{q_2}, & \text{when} \quad S < S^* \\ S - X, & \text{when} \quad S \geq S^* \end{cases},$$

where $c_{GBS}(S,X,T)$ is the general Black–Scholes call formula, and

$$A_2 = \frac{S^*}{q_2}\{1 - e^{(b-r)T}N[d_1(S^*)]\}$$

$$d_1(S) = \frac{\ln(S/X) + (b + \sigma^2/2)T}{\sigma\sqrt{T}}$$

$$q_2 = \frac{-(N-1) + \sqrt{(N-1)^2 + 4M/K}}{2}$$

$$M = 2r/\sigma^2, \qquad N = 2b/\sigma^2, \qquad K = 1 - e^{-rT}$$

American Put

$$P(S,X,T) = \begin{cases} p_{GBS}(S,X,T) + A_1(S/S^{**})^{q_1}, & \text{when} \quad S > S^{**} \\ X - S, & \text{when} \quad S \leq S^{**} \end{cases},$$

where $p_{GBS}(S,X,T)$ is the general Black–Scholes put option formula, and

$$A_1 = -\frac{S^{**}}{q_1}\{1 - e^{(b-r)T}N[-d_1(S^{**})]\}$$

$$q_1 = \frac{-(N-1) - \sqrt{(N-1)^2 + 4M/K}}{2},$$

where S^* is the critical commodity price for the call option that satisfies

$$S^* - X = c(S^*,X,T) + \{1 - e^{(b-r)T}N[d_1(S^*)]\}S^*\frac{1}{q_2}$$

$$LHS(S_i) = S_i - X$$

$$RHS(S_i) = c(S_i, X, T) + \{1 - e^{(b-r)T} N[d_1(S_i)]\} S_i \frac{1}{q_2}.$$

This equation can be solved by using a Newton–Raphson algorithm. The slope of RHS at S_i is

$$\frac{\partial RHS}{\partial S_i} = b_i = e^{(b-r)T} N[d_1(S_i)](1 - 1/q_2) + \left\{1 - \frac{e^{(b-r)T} n[d_1(S_i)]}{\sigma\sqrt{T}}\right\} \frac{1}{q_2}$$

Given an initial value S_i, it follows directly from the Newton–Raphson method that the next and better estimate, S_{i+1}, is

$$S_{i+1} = \frac{[X + RHS(S_i) - b_i S_i]}{(1 - b_i)}$$

The iterative procedure should continue until the relative absolute error falls within an acceptable tolerance level. For instance,

$$|LHS(S_i) - RHS(S_i)| / X < 0.00001,$$

and S^{**} is the critical commodity price for the put option that satisfies

$$X - S^{**} = p(S^{**}, X, T) - \{1 - e^{(b-r)T} N[-d_1(S^{**})]\} S^{**} \frac{1}{q_1}$$

$$VS(S_j) = X - S_j$$

$$HS(S_j) = p(S_j, X, T) - \{1 - e^{(b-r)T} N[-d_1(S_j)]\} S_j \frac{1}{q_1}$$

$$\frac{\partial HS}{\partial S_j} = b_j = -e^{(b-r)T} N[-d_1(S_j)](1 - 1/q_1) - \left\{1 + \frac{e^{(b-r)T} n[-d_1(S_j)]}{\sigma\sqrt{T}}\right\} \frac{1}{q_1}$$

$$S_{j+1} = \frac{[X - HS(S_j) + b_j S_j]}{(1 + b_j)}.$$

As always with the use of the Newton–Raphson method, we need a seed value. Barone-Adesi and Whaley suggest using

$$S_1^* = X + [S^*(\infty) - X][1 - e^{h_2}], \qquad h_2 = -(bT + 2\sigma\sqrt{T})\left[\frac{X}{S^*(\infty) - X}\right]$$

$$S_1^{**} = S^{**}(\infty) + [X - S^{**}(\infty)]e^{h_1}, \qquad h_1 = (bT - 2\sigma\sqrt{T})\left[\frac{X}{X - S^{**}(\infty)}\right],$$

where $S(\infty)$ is the critical price when time to expiration is infinite:

$$S^*(\infty) = \frac{X}{1 - 2[-(N-1) + \sqrt{(N-1)^2 + 4M}]^{-1}}$$

$$S^{**}(\infty) = \frac{X}{1 - 2[-(N-1) - \sqrt{(N-1)^2 + 4M}]^{-1}}.$$

Table 1–3 compares option values given by the Barone-Adesi and Whaley Approximation (American style) and by the Black-76 formula (European style).

T A B L E 1–3

Comparison of the Barone-Adesi and Whaley American approximation and the Black–Scholes/Black-76 European Model

$(X = 100, r = 0.10, b = 0)$

Futures price:		90	100	110	90	100	110
Call Options			BAW			Black-76	
$T=0.1$	$\sigma=0.15$	0.0206	1.8771	10.0089	0.0205	1.8734	9.9413
	$\sigma=0.25$	0.3159	3.1280	10.3919	0.3150	3.1217	10.3556
	$\sigma=0.35$	0.9495	4.3777	11.1679	0.9474	4.3693	11.1381
$T=0.5$	$\sigma=0.15$	0.8208	4.0842	10.8087	0.8069	4.0232	10.5769
	$\sigma=0.25$	2.7437	6.8015	13.0170	2.7026	6.6997	12.7857
	$\sigma=0.35$	5.0063	9.5106	15.5689	4.9329	9.3679	15.308
Put Options			BAW			Black-76	
$T=0.1$	$\sigma=0.15$	10.0000	1.8770	0.0410	9.9210	1.8734	0.0408
	$\sigma=0.25$	10.2533	3.1277	0.4562	10.2155	3.1217	0.4551
	$\sigma=0.35$	10.8787	4.3777	1.2402	10.8479	4.3693	1.2376
$T=0.5$	$\sigma=0.15$	10.5595	4.0842	1.0822	10.3192	4.0232	1.0646
	$\sigma=0.25$	12.4419	6.8014	3.3226	12.2149	6.6997	3.2734
	$\sigma=0.35$	14.6945	9.5104	5.8823	14.4452	9.3679	5.7963

Computer algorithm

The *BAWAmericanCallApprox*(·) function can be used to calculate the value of an American call option using the Barone-Adesi and Whaley formula.

Function *BAWAmericanCallApprox*(S As Double, X As Double, _
         T As Double, r As Double, b As Double, v As Double) As Double

    Dim Sk As Double, N As Double, K As Double

Dim $d1$ As Double, $q2$ As Double, $a2$ As Double

If $b >= r$ Then
    $BAWAmericanCallApprox = GBlackScholes("c",S,X,T,r,b,v)$
Else
    $Sk = Kc(X,T,r,b,v)$
    $N = 2*b/v^2$
    $K = 2*r/(v^2*(1-Exp(-r*T)))$
    $d1 = (Log(Sk/X)+(b+v^2/2)*T)/(v*Sqr(T))$
    $q2 = (-(N-1)+Sqr((N-1)^2+4*K))/2$
    $a2 = (Sk/q2)*(1-Exp((b-r)*T)*CND(d1))$
    If $S < Sk$ Then
        $BAWAmericanCallApprox = GBlackScholes("c",S,X,T,r,b,v) +$ _
    $a2*(S/Sk)^q2$
    Else
        $BAWAmericanCallApprox = S - X$
    End If
    End If
End Function

The $Kc(\cdot)$ function below uses a Newton-Raphson algorithm to solve for the critical commodity price for a call option.

Function $Kc(X$ As Double, T As Double, r As Double, _
    b As Double, v As Double) As Double

    Dim N As Double, M As Double
    Dim Su As Double, Si As Double
    Dim $h2$ As Double, K As Double
    Dim $d1$ As Double, $q2$ As Double, $q2u$ As Double
    Dim LHS As Double, RHS As Double
    Dim bi As Double, E As Double

    '// Calculation of seed value, Si
    $N = 2*b/v^2$
    $M = 2*r/v^2$
    $q2u = (-(N-1)+Sqr((N-1)^2+4*M))/2$
    $Su = X/(1-1/q2u)$
    $h2 = -(b*T+2*v*Sqr(T))*X/(Su-X)$
    $Si = X+(Su-X)*(1-Exp(h2))$
    $K = 2*r/(v^2*(1-Exp(-r*T)))$
    $d1 = (Log(Si/X)+(b+v^2/2)*T)/(v*Sqr(T))$
    $q2 = (-(N-1)+Sqr((N-1)^2+4*K))/2$
    $LHS = Si - X$
    $RHS = GBlackScholes("c",Si,X,T,r,b,v) +$ _
    $(1-Exp((b-r)*T)*CND(d1))*Si/q2$
    $bi = Exp((b-r)*T)*CND(d1)*(1-1/q2) +$ _
    $(1-Exp((b-r)*T)*CND(d1)/(v*Sqr(T)))/q2$
    $E = 0.000001$
    '// Newton-Raphson algorithm for finding critical price Si
    While $Abs(LHS-RHS)/X > E$
        $Si = (X+RHS-bi*Si)/(1-bi)$

$d1 = (Log(Si/X) + (b + v\hat{}2/2) * T)/(v * Sqr(T))$
$LHS = Si - X$
$RHS = GBlackScholes("c", Si, X, T, r, b, v) + \_$
$(1 - Exp((b - r) * T) * CND(d1)) * Si/q2$
$bi = Exp((b - r) * T) * CND(d1) * (1 - 1/q2) + \_$
$(1 - Exp((b - r) * T) * ND(d1)/(v * Sqr(T)))/q2$

Wend
$Kc = Si$

End Function

1.4.3 The Bjerksund and Stensland Approximation

The Bjerksund and Stensland (1993b) approximation can be used to price American options on stocks, futures, and currencies. The method is analytical and extremely computer efficient. Bjerksund and Stensland's approximation is based on an exercise strategy corresponding to a flat boundary I (trigger price). Numerical investigation indicates that the Bjerksund and Stensland model is somewhat more accurate for long-term options than the Barone-Adesi and Whaley model presented earlier.

$$
\begin{aligned}
C \;=\; & \alpha S^{\beta} - \alpha\phi(S, T, \beta, I, I) \\
& + \phi(S, T, 1, I, I) - \phi(S, T, 1, X, I) \\
& - X\phi(S, T, 0, I, I) + X\phi(S, T, 0, X, I),
\end{aligned}
\qquad (1.45)
$$

where

$$
\alpha = (I - X)I^{-\beta}
$$

$$
\beta = \left(\frac{1}{2} - \frac{b}{\sigma^2}\right) + \sqrt{\left(\frac{b}{\sigma^2} - \frac{1}{2}\right)^2 + 2\frac{r}{\sigma^2}}.
$$

The function $\phi(S, T, \gamma, H, I)$ is given by

$$
\phi(S, T, \gamma, H, I) = e^{\lambda}S^{\gamma}\left[N(d) - \left(\frac{I}{S}\right)^{\kappa} N\left(d - \frac{2\ln(I/S)}{\sigma\sqrt{T}}\right)\right]
$$

$$
\lambda = [-r + \gamma b + \frac{1}{2}\gamma(\gamma - 1)\sigma^2]T
$$

$$
d = -\frac{\ln(S/H) + [b + (\gamma - \frac{1}{2})\sigma^2]T}{\sigma\sqrt{T}}.
$$

$$\kappa = \frac{2b}{\sigma^2} + (2\gamma - 1),$$

and the trigger price I is defined as

$$I = B_0 + (B_\infty - B_0)(1 - e^{h(T)})$$

$$h(T) = -(bT + 2\sigma\sqrt{T})\left(\frac{B_0}{B_\infty - B_0}\right)$$

$$B_\infty = \frac{\beta}{\beta - 1}X$$

$$B_0 = \max\left[X, \left(\frac{r}{r-b}\right)X\right].$$

If $S \geq I$, it is optimal to exercise the option immediately, and the value must be equal to the intrinsic value of $S - X$. On the other hand, if $b \geq r$, it will never be optimal to exercise the American call option before expiration, and the value can be found using the generalized version of the Black–Scholes formula. The value of the American put is given by the Bjerksund and Stensland put–call transformation

$$P(S,X,T,r,b,\sigma) = C(X,S,T,r-b,-b,\sigma),$$

where $C(\cdot)$ is the value of the American call with risk-free rate $r - b$ and drift $-b$. With use of this transformation, it is not necessary to develop a separate formula for an American put option.

Example

Consider an American-style call option with nine months to expiry. The stock price is 42, the strike price is 40, the risk-free rate is 4% per annum, the dividend yield is 8% per annum, the volatility is 35% per annum. $S = 42$, $X = 40$, $T = 0.75$, $r = 0.04$, $b = 0.04 - 0.08 = -0.04$, $\sigma = 0.35$.

$$\beta = \left(\frac{1}{2} - \frac{-0.04}{0.35^2}\right) + \sqrt{\left(\frac{-0.04}{0.35^2} - \frac{1}{2}\right)^2 + 2\frac{0.04}{0.35^2}} = 1.9825,$$

and the trigger price I is

$$B_\infty = \frac{\beta}{\beta - 1}40 = 80.7134$$

$$B_0 = \max\left[40, \left(\frac{0.04}{0.04 - (-0.04)}\right)40\right] = 40$$

$$h(T) = -(-0.04 \times 0.75 + 2 \times 0.35\sqrt{0.75})\left(\frac{B_0}{B_\infty - B_0}\right) = -0.5661$$

$$I = B_0 + (B_\infty - B_0)(1 - e^{h(T)}) = 57.5994$$

$$\alpha = (I - 40)I^{-\beta} = 0.005695,$$

and finally the American call value is

$$
\begin{aligned}
C \;=\; & \alpha 42^\beta - \alpha\phi(42, 0.75, \beta, I, I) \\
& + \phi(42, 0.75, 1, I, I) - \phi(42, 0.75, 1, 40, I) \\
& - 40\phi(42, 0.75, 0, I, I) + 40\phi(42, 0.75, 0, 40, I) = 5.2704.
\end{aligned}
$$

The value of a similar European call is 5.0975.

Computer algorithm

The computer code for the Bjerksund and Stensland American option approximation consists of three functions. The first one checks if the option is a call or put. If the option is a put, the function uses the American put–call transformation. The function then calls the main function $BSAmericanCallApprox(\cdot)$, which calculates the option value. The main function uses two other functions: the $phi(\cdot)$ function, which in the formula above is described as $\phi(S, T, \gamma, H, I)$, and the $GBlackScholes(\cdot)$ function, which is the general Black–Scholes formula described earlier in this chapter.

```
Function BSAmericanApprox(CallPutFlag As String, S As Double, X As Double, -
        T As Double, r As Double, b As Double, v As Double) As Double

    If CallPutFlag = "c" Then
        BSAmericanApprox = BSAmericanCallApprox(S,X,T,r,b,v)
    ElseIf CallPutFlag = "p" Then '// Use the put-call transformation
            BSAmericanApprox = BSAmericanCallApprox(X,S,T,r-b,-b,v)
    End If
End Function


Function BSAmericanCallApprox(S As Double, X As Double, T As Double, -
        r As Double, b As Double, v As Double) As Double

    Dim BInfinity As Double, B0 As Double
    Dim ht As Double, I As Double
```

Dim *Alfa* As Double, *Beta* As Double

If $b >= r$ Then '// Never optimal to exercise before maturity
   $BSAmericanCallApprox = GBlackScholes("c", S, X, T, r, b, v)$
Else
     $Beta = (1/2 - b/v^2) + Sqr((b/v^2 - 1/2)^2 + 2*r/v^2)$
     $BInfinity = Beta/(Beta - 1)*X$
     $B0 = Max(X, r/(r - b)*X)$
     $ht = -(b*T + 2*v*Sqr(T))*B0/(BInfinity - B0)$
     $I = B0 + (BInfinity - B0)*(1 - Exp(ht))$
     $Alfa = (I - X)*I^(-Beta)$
     If $S >= I$ Then
       $BSAmericanCallApprox = S - X$
     Else
       $BSAmericanCallApprox = Alfa*S^Beta - $ _
       $Alfa*phi(S, T, Beta, I, I, r, b, v) + $ _
       $phi(S, T, 1, I, I, r, b, v) - phi(S, T, 1, X, I, r, b, v) - $ _
       $X*phi(S, T, 0, I, I, r, b, v) + X*phi(S, T, 0, X, I, r, b, v)$
     End If
   End If
End Function

Function *phi*(*S* As Double, *T* As Double, *gamma* As Double, *H* As Double, *I* As Double, _
   r As Double, *b* As Double, *v* As Double) As Double

Dim *lambda* As Double, *kappa* As Double, *d* As Double

$lambda = (-r + gamma*b + 0.5*gamma*(gamma - 1)*v^2)*T$
$d = -(Log(S/H) + (b + (gamma - 0.5)*v^2)*T)/(v*Sqr(T))$
$kappa = 2*b/(v^2) + (2*gamma - 1)$
$phi = Exp(lambda)*S^gamma*(CND(d) - (I/S)^kappa*$ _
$CND(d - 2*Log(I/S)/(v*Sqr(T))))$
End Function

where $CND(\cdot)$ is the cumulative normal distribution function described in Appendix A. Example: *BSAmericanApprox*("c", 42, 40, 0.75, 0.04, −0.04, 0.35) returns an American call value of 5.2704 as in the numerical example above.

1.4.4 Put–Call Transformation American Options

The Bjerksund and Stensland (1993a) put–call transformation is very useful when calculating American option values. If you have a formula for an American call, the relationship below will give the value for the American put.

$$P(S, X, T, r, b, \sigma) = C(X, S, T, r - b, -b, \sigma)$$

1.5   RECENT DEVELOPMENTS IN COMMODITY OPTIONS

Miltersen and Schwartz (1997) have recently developed an interesting model
for pricing options on commodity futures. The model is a three-factor model
with stochastic futures prices, term structures of convenience yields,[7] and
interest rates.[8] The model is based on lognormal distributed commodity
prices and normal distributed (Gaussian) continuously compounded forward
interest rates and future convenience yields.

Investigations using this option pricing model show that the time lag
between the expiry on the option and the underlying futures will have a sig-
nificant effect on the option value. Even with three stochastic variables, Miltersen and Schwartz get a closed-form solution similar to a Black–Scholes
type formula. The model can be used to price European options on commodity futures[9]

$$c = P_t[F_T e^{-\sigma_{xz}} N(d_1) - X N(d_2)], \tag{1.46}$$

where t is the time to maturity of the option, F_T is a futures price with time
to expiration T $(T \geq t)$, and P_t is a zero-coupon bond that expires on the
option maturity.

$$d_1 = \frac{\ln(F_T/X) - \sigma_{xz} + \sigma_z^2/2}{\sigma_z}, \qquad d_2 = d_1 - \sigma_z,$$

and the variances and covariance can be calculated as[10]

$$\sigma_z^2 = \int_0^t \left\| \sigma_S(u) + \int_u^T [\sigma_f(u,s) - \sigma_\epsilon(u,s)] ds \right\|^2 du = \int_0^t \|\sigma_{F_T}(u)\|^2 du$$

$$\sigma_{xz} = \int_0^t \left[\int_u^t \sigma_f(u,s) ds \right] \cdot \left\{ \sigma_S(u) + \int_u^T [\sigma_f(u,s) - \sigma_\epsilon(u,s)] ds \right\} du$$

$$= -\int_0^t \sigma_{P_t}(u) \cdot \sigma_{F_T}(u) du,$$

---

7. The convenience yield can be seen as the benefits that accrue to the owner of the physical
commodity but not to the owner of a contract for delivery in the future.

8. The Miltersen and Schwartz (1997) model can be seen as a generalization of previous work
by Merton (1973), Gibson and Schwartz (1990), Amin and Jarrow (1992), Reismann (1992),
Cortazar and Schwartz (1994), Amin, Ng, and Pirrong (1995), and Schwartz (1997).

9. In the same paper, Miltersen and Schwartz (1997) also give a separate formula for options
on forwards, as well as developing a relationship between the forward and futures contract.

10. "·" denotes the standard Euclidean inner product of $\mathbb{R}^d$, and the corresponding norm is
defined as $\|x\|^2 = x \cdot x$ for any $x \in \mathbb{R}^d$.

where

$$\sigma_{P_T}(t) = -\int_t^T \sigma_f(t,s)ds$$

$$\sigma_{F_T}(t) = \sigma_S(t) + \int_t^T [\sigma_f(t,s) - \sigma_\epsilon(t,s)]ds.$$

This is an extremely flexible model where the variances and covariances can have several specifications. One possibility is to assume a three-factor Gaussian model, with three deterministic σ processes defined as follows:

$$\sigma_S(t) = \sigma_S \begin{pmatrix} 1 \\ 0 \\ 0 \end{pmatrix}$$

$$\sigma_\epsilon(t,s) = \sigma_\epsilon e^{-\kappa_\epsilon(s-t)} \begin{pmatrix} \rho_{S\epsilon} \\ \sqrt{1-\rho_{S\epsilon}^2} \\ 0 \end{pmatrix}$$

$$\sigma_f(t,s) = \sigma_f e^{-\kappa_f(s-t)} \begin{pmatrix} \rho_{Sf} \\ \frac{\rho_{\epsilon f}-\rho_{S\epsilon}\rho_{Sf}}{\sqrt{1-\rho_{S\epsilon}^2}} \\ \sqrt{1-\rho_{Sf}^2 - \frac{(\rho_{\epsilon f}-\rho_{S\epsilon}\rho_{Sf})^2}{\sqrt{1-\rho_{S\epsilon}^2}}} \end{pmatrix}$$

This leads to the following solution of σ_z and σ_{xz}:

$$\begin{aligned}
\sigma_z^2 &= \sigma_S^2 t + 2\sigma_S \left\{ \sigma_f \frac{\rho_{Sf}}{\kappa_f} \left[t - \frac{1}{\kappa_f}e^{-\kappa_f T}(e^{\kappa_f t}-1) \right] \right. \\
&\quad \left. -\sigma_\epsilon \frac{\rho_{S\epsilon}}{\kappa_\epsilon} \left[t - \frac{1}{\kappa_\epsilon}e^{-\kappa_\epsilon T}(e^{\kappa_\epsilon t}-1) \right] \right\} \\
&\quad +\frac{\sigma_\epsilon^2}{\kappa_\epsilon^2} \left[t + \frac{1}{2\kappa_\epsilon}e^{-2\kappa_\epsilon T}(e^{2\kappa_\epsilon t}-1) - \frac{2}{\kappa_\epsilon}e^{-\kappa_\epsilon T}(e^{\kappa_\epsilon t}-1) \right] \\
&\quad +\frac{\sigma_f^2}{\kappa_f^2} \left[t + \frac{1}{2\kappa_f}e^{-2\kappa_f T}(e^{2\kappa_f t}-1) - \frac{2}{\kappa_f}e^{-\kappa_f T}(e^{\kappa_f t}-1) \right] \\
&\quad -2\sigma_\epsilon \sigma_f \rho_{\epsilon f} \frac{1}{\kappa_\epsilon}\frac{1}{\kappa_f} \left[t - \frac{1}{\kappa_\epsilon}e^{-\kappa_\epsilon T}(e^{\kappa_\epsilon t}-1) - \frac{1}{\kappa_f}e^{-\kappa_f T}(e^{\kappa_f t}-1) \right. \\
&\quad \left. +\frac{1}{(\kappa_\epsilon+\kappa_f)}e^{-(\kappa_\epsilon+\kappa_f)T}(e^{(\kappa_\epsilon+\kappa_f)t}-1) \right]
\end{aligned}$$

$$\sigma_{xz} = \frac{\sigma_f}{\kappa_f}\left\{\sigma_S\rho_{Sf}\left[t - \frac{1}{\kappa_f}(1 - e^{-\kappa_f t})\right] + \frac{\sigma_f}{\kappa_f}\left[t - \frac{1}{\kappa_f}e^{-\kappa_f T}(e^{\kappa_f t} - 1)\right.\right.$$

$$\left. - \frac{1}{\kappa_f}(1 - e^{-\kappa_f t}) + \frac{1}{2\kappa_f}e^{-\kappa_f T}(e^{\kappa_f t} - e^{-\kappa_f t})\right]$$

$$- \sigma_\epsilon\frac{\rho_{\epsilon f}}{\kappa_\epsilon}\left[t - \frac{1}{\kappa_\epsilon}e^{-\kappa_\epsilon T}(e^{\kappa_\epsilon t} - 1) - \frac{1}{\kappa_f}(1 - e^{-\kappa_f t})\right.$$

$$\left.\left. + \frac{1}{(\kappa_\epsilon + \kappa_f)}e^{-\kappa_\epsilon T}(e^{\kappa_\epsilon t} - e^{-\kappa_f t})\right]\right\},$$

where

σ_S = Volatility of the spot commodity price.

σ_ϵ = Volatility of future convenience yield.

σ_f = Volatility of the forward interest rate.

κ_f = Speed of mean reversion of the forward interest rate.

κ_ϵ = Speed of mean reversion of the convenience yield.

ρ_{Sf} = Correlation between the spot commodity price and the forward interest rate.

$\rho_{S\epsilon}$ = Correlation between the spot commodity price and the convenience yield.

$\rho_{\epsilon f}$ = Correlation between the forward interest rate and the convenience yield.

Using these expressions of σ_z and σ_{xz} in the Miltersen and Schwartz model, we can easily calculate values for European call and put options on commodity futures with stochastic forward interest rates and convenience yields.[11] Table 1–4 compares the Black-76 model and the Miltersen and Schwartz model. The price difference between the two models will be strongly dependent on the input parameters.

---

11. This can be seen as a special case of the Miltersen and Schwartz option model where the underlying futures follows a stochastic process as described in the paper by Schwartz (1997).

T A B L E 1-4

Comparison of European Futures Option Prices Using the Miltersen and Schwartz Commodity Option Model and the Black-76 Modified Black–Scholes Model

$(F_T = 95,\ \sigma_S = 0.266,\ \sigma_\epsilon = 0.249,\ \sigma_f = 0.0096,\ \rho_{Sf} = 0.0964,$
$\rho_{S\epsilon} = 0.805,\ \rho_{\epsilon f} = 0.1243,\ \kappa_\epsilon = 1.045,\ \kappa_f = 0.2,\ P_t = e^{-0.05t})$

		X	Black-76	Miltersen–Schwartz
$t = 0.25$	$T = 0.25$	80	15.3430	15.1918
		95	4.9744	4.5669
		110	0.9159	0.6896
$t = 0.25$	$T = 0.3$	80	15.3430	15.1424
		95	4.9744	4.4170
		110	0.9159	0.6131
$t = 0.25$	$T = 0.5$	80	15.3430	15.0049
		95	4.9744	3.9251
		110	0.9159	0.3903
$t = 0.5$	$T = 1$	80	16.1917	15.0787
		95	6.9423	4.7245
		110	2.3311	0.7972

In this table, we follow the numerical examples used by Miltersen and Schwartz (1997) and are using the parameter estimates for the COMEX High Grade Copper Futures data presented in the Schwartz (1997) paper. In the Black-76 model, we set $\sigma = \sigma_S$.

2

⑥ EXOTIC OPTIONS

In this chapter, we present a large class of analytical formulas for so-called exotic options. The exotic option pricing formulas presented here are based on the Black–Scholes economy. The underlying asset is assumed to follow a geometric Brownian motion $dS = \mu S dt + \sigma S dz$, where μ is the expected instantaneous rate of return on the underlying asset, σ is the instantaneous variance of the rate of return, and dz is a Wiener process. The volatility and risk-free rate is assumed to be constant throughout the life of the option. Most of the formulas are written on a general form including a cost of carry term, which makes it possible to use the same formula to price options on a wide class of underlying assets: stocks, stock indexes paying a dividend yield, currencies, and futures. Since the formulas are closed-form solutions, they can in general only be used to price European-style options. For more on pricing American-style exotic options see Chapter 3 Numerical Methods in Options Pricing.

2.1 EXECUTIVE STOCK OPTIONS

The Jennergren and Naslund (1993) formula takes into account that an employee or executive often loses her options if she has to leave the company before option expiration:

$$c = e^{-\lambda T}[Se^{(b-r)T}N(d_1) - Xe^{-rT}N(d_2)] \tag{2.1}$$

$$p = e^{-\lambda T}[Xe^{-rT}N(-d_2) - Se^{(b-r)T}N(-d_1)], \tag{2.2}$$

where

$$d_1 = \frac{\ln(S/X) + (b + \sigma^2/2)T}{\sigma\sqrt{T}}, \quad d_2 = d_1 - \sigma\sqrt{T}.$$

(λ) is the jump rate per year. The value of the executive option equals the ordinary Black–Scholes option multiplied by the probability $e^{-\lambda T}$ that the executive will stay with the firm until the option expires.

Example

What is the value of an executive call option when the stock price is 60, the strike price is 64, time to maturity is two years, the risk-free rate is 7%, the dividend yield is 3%, the stock volatility is 38%, and the jump rate per year is 15%? $S = 60$, $X = 64$, $T = 2$, $r = 0.07$, $b = 0.07 - 0.03 = 0.04$, $\sigma = 0.38$, $\lambda = 0.15$.

$$d_1 = \frac{\ln(60/64) + (0.04 + 0.38^2/2)2}{0.38\sqrt{2}} = 0.2975$$

$$d_2 = d_1 - 0.38\sqrt{2} = -0.2399$$

$$N(d_1) = N(0.2975) = 0.6169, \quad N(d_2) = N(-0.2399) = 0.4052$$

$$c = e^{-0.15 \times 2}[60e^{(0.04 - 0.07)2}N(d_1) - 64e^{-0.07 \times 2}N(d_2)] = 9.1244$$

2.2 FORWARD START OPTIONS

A forward start option with time to maturity T starts at-the-money or proportionally in- or out-of-the-money after a known elapsed time t in the future. The strike is set equal to a positive constant α times the asset price S after the known time t. If α is less than unity, the call (put) will start $1 - \alpha$ percent in-the-money (out-of-the-money); if α is unity, the option will start at-the-money; and if α is larger than unity, the call (put) will start $\alpha - 1$ percentage out-of-the money (in-the-money). A forward start option can be priced using the Rubinstein (1990) formula:

$$c = Se^{(b-r)t}[e^{(b-r)(T-t)}N(d_1) - \alpha e^{-r(T-t)}N(d_2)] \tag{2.3}$$

$$p = Se^{(b-r)t}[\alpha e^{-r(T-t)}N(-d_2) - e^{(b-r)(T-t)}N(-d_1)], \tag{2.4}$$

where

$$d_1 = \frac{\ln(1/\alpha) + (b + \sigma^2/2)(T - t)}{\sigma\sqrt{T - t}}, \qquad d_2 = d_1 - \sigma\sqrt{T - t}.$$

Application

Employee options are often forward starting options. Ratchet options, also called cliquet options, consist of a series of forward starting options.

Example

Consider an employee who receives a call option with forward start three months from today. The options starts 10% out-of-the-money, time to maturity is one year from today, the stock price is 60, the risk-free interest rate is 8%, the continuous dividend yield is 4%, the expected volatility of the stock is 30%. $S = 60$, $\alpha = 1.1$, $t = 0.25$, $T = 1$, $r = 0.08$, $b = 0.08 - 0.04 = 0.04$, $\sigma = 0.30$.

$$d_1 = \frac{\ln(1/1.1) + (0.04 + 0.30^2/2)(1 - 0.25)}{0.30\sqrt{(1 - 0.25)}} = -0.1215$$

$$d_2 = d_1 - 0.30\sqrt{(1 - 0.25)} = -0.3813$$

$$N(d_1) = N(-0.1215) = 0.4517, \quad N(d_2) = N(-0.3813) = 0.3515$$

$$c = 60e^{(0.04-0.08)0.25}[e^{(0.04-0.08)(1-0.25)}N(d_1) - 1.1e^{-0.08(1-0.25)}N(d_2)] = 4.4064$$

2.3 RATCHET OPTIONS

A ratchet option (sometimes called a moving strike option or cliquet option) consists of a series of forward starting options where the strike price for the next exercise date is set equal to a positive constant times the asset price as of the previous exercise date. For instance, a one-year ratchet call option with quarterly payments will normally have four payments (exercise dates) equal to the difference between the asset price and the strike price fixed at the previous exercise date. The strike price of the first option is usually set equal to the asset price of today. A ratchet option can be priced as the sum of forward starting options.

$$c = \sum_{i=1}^{n} Se^{(b-r)t_i}[e^{(b-r)(T_i-t_i)}N(d_1) - \alpha e^{-r(T_i-t_i)}N(d_2)], \qquad (2.5)$$

where n is the number of settlements, t_i is the time to the forward start or strike fixing, and T_i is the time to maturity of the forward starting option. A ratchet put is similar to a sum of forward starting puts.

2.4 TIME-SWITCH OPTIONS

In a discrete time-switch call option, introduced by Pechtl (1995),[1] the investor receives an amount $A\Delta t$ at maturity T for each time interval Δt the

---

1. In the same paper, Pechtl (1995) shows how to value continuous time-switch options.

corresponding asset price $S_{i\Delta t}$ has exceeded the strike price X. The discrete time-switch put option gives a similar payoff $A\Delta t$ at maturity for each time interval the asset price $S_{i\Delta t}$ has been below the strike price X.

$$c = Ae^{-rT} \sum_{i=1}^{n} N\left(\frac{\ln(S/X) + (b - \sigma^2/2)i\Delta t}{\sigma\sqrt{i\Delta t}}\right)\Delta t \qquad (2.6)$$

$$p = Ae^{-rT} \sum_{i=1}^{n} N\left(\frac{-\ln(S/X) - (b - \sigma^2/2)i\Delta t}{\sigma\sqrt{i\Delta t}}\right)\Delta t, \qquad (2.7)$$

where $n = T/\Delta t$. If some of the option's total lifetime has already passed, it is necessary to add a fixed amount $\Delta t Ae^{-rT}m$ to the option-pricing formula, where m is the number of time units where the option already has fulfilled its condition.

Example

What is the price of a call time-switch option with one year to maturity, where the investor accumulates $5 \times 1/365$ for each day the stock price exceeds the strike price at 110? The stock price is currently 100, the risk-free rate is 6% and the volatility is 26%. $S = 100, A = 5, X = 110, T = 1, \Delta t = 1/365, r = b = 0.06, \sigma = 0.26, n = T/\Delta t = 365, m = 0.$

$$c = 5e^{-0.06 \times 1} \sum_{i=1}^{365} N\left(\frac{\ln(100/110) + (0.05 - 0.26^2/2)i \times 1/365}{0.26\sqrt{i \times 1/365}}\right)\frac{1}{365} = 1.3750$$

Computer algorithm

```
Function TimeSwitchOption(CallPutFlag As String, S As Double, X As Double, _
        A As Double, T As Double, m As Integer, dt As Double, r As Double, _
        b As Double, v As Double) As Double

    Dim Sum As Double, d As Double
    Dim i As Integer, n As Integer, z As Integer

    n = T/dt
    Sum = 0
    If CallPutFlag = "c" Then
        z = 1
    ElseIf CallPutFlag = "p" Then
        z = -1
    End If
    For i = 1 To n
        d = (Log(S/X) + (b - v^2/2) * i * dt)/(v * Sqr(i * dt))
        Sum = Sum + CND(z * d) * dt
    Next
    TimeSwitchOption = A * Exp(-r * T) * Sum + dt * A * Exp(-r * T) * m
End Function
```

Application

Discrete time-switch options have recently become quite popular in the interest-rate markets in the form of so-called accrual swaps. In a typical accrual swap, the fixed-rate receiver accumulates an amount equal to the notional of the swap times the fixed rate only for days when the floating rate, for example, LIBOR, is below or above a certain level. Accrual swaps can easily be priced as the sum of discrete time-switch options, under the assumptions of lognormally distributed forward rates with zero drift.

2.5 CHOOSER OPTIONS

2.5.1 Simple Chooser Options

A simple chooser option gives the holder the right to choose whether the option is to be a standard call or put after a time t_1, both with the same strike X and time to maturity T_2. The payoff from a simple chooser option at time t_1 $(t_1 < T_2)$ is

$$w(S,X,t_1,T_2) = \max[c_{GBS}(S,X,T_2), p_{GBS}(S,X,T_2)],$$

where $c_{GBS}(S,X,T_2)$ and $p_{GBS}(S,X,T_2)$ are the general Black–Scholes call and put formulas. A simple chooser option can be priced using the formula originally published by Rubinstein (1991c):

$$
\begin{aligned}
w &= Se^{(b-r)T_2}N(d) - Xe^{-rT_2}N(d - \sigma\sqrt{T_2}) - Se^{(b-r)T_2}N(-y) \\
&\quad + Xe^{-rT_2}N(-y + \sigma\sqrt{t_1}),
\end{aligned}
\tag{2.8}
$$

where

$$d = \frac{\ln(S/X) + (b + \sigma^2/2)T_2}{\sigma\sqrt{T_2}}, \qquad y = \frac{\ln(S/X) + bT_2 + \sigma^2 t_1/2}{\sigma\sqrt{t_1}}.$$

Example

Consider a simple chooser option with a time to expiration of six months and time to choose between a put or call equal to three months. The underlying stock price is 50, the strike price is 50, the risk-free interest rate is 8% per annum, and the volatility per annum is 25%. $S = 50$, $X = 50$, $T_2 = 0.5$, $t_1 = 0.25$, $r = 0.08$, $b = 0.08$, $\sigma = 0.25$.

$$d = \frac{\ln(50/50) + (0.08 + 0.25^2/2)0.5}{0.25\sqrt{0.5}} = 0.3147$$

$$y = \frac{\ln(50/50) + 0.08 \times 0.5 + 0.25^2 \times 0.25/2}{0.25\sqrt{0.25}} = 0.3825$$

$$N(d) = N(0.3147) = 0.6235$$

$$N(d - \sigma\sqrt{T_2}) = N(0.3147 - 0.25\sqrt{0.5}) = 0.5548$$

$$N(-y) = N(-0.3825) = 0.3510$$

$$N(-y + \sigma\sqrt{t_1}) = N(-0.3825 + 0.25\sqrt{0.25}) = 0.3984$$

$$
\begin{aligned}
w = \ & 50e^{(0.08-0.08)0.5}N(d) - 50e^{-0.08\times0.5}N(d - 0.25\sqrt{0.5}) \\
& - 50e^{(0.08-0.08)0.5}N(-y) + 50e^{-0.08\times0.5}N(-y + 0.25\sqrt{0.25}) = 6.1071
\end{aligned}
$$

2.5.2 Complex Chooser Options

A complex chooser option, introduced by Rubinstein (1991c),[2] gives the holder the right to choose whether the option is to be a standard call option after a time t, with time to expiration T_c and strike X_c, or a put option with time to maturity T_p and strike X_p. The payoff from a complex chooser option at time t $(T_p > t < T_c)$ is

$$w(S, X_c, X_p, t, T_c, T_p) = \max[c_{GBS}(S, X_c, T_c), p_{GBS}(S, X_p, T_p)],$$

where $c_{GBS}(S, X, T)$ and $p_{GBS}(S, X, T)$ are the generalized Black–Scholes call and put formulas, respectively.

$$
\begin{aligned}
w = \ & Se^{(b-r)T_c}M(d_1, y_1; \rho_1) \\
& - X_c e^{-rT_c}M(d_2, y_1 - \sigma\sqrt{T_c}; \rho_1) - Se^{(b-r)T_p}M(-d_1, -y_2; \rho_2) \\
& + X_p e^{-rT_p}M(-d_2, -y_2 + \sigma\sqrt{T_p}; \rho_2), \hspace{2cm} (2.9)
\end{aligned}
$$

where T_c is the time to maturity on the call, and T_p is the time to maturity on the put.

$$d_1 = \frac{\ln(S/I) + (b + \sigma^2/2)t}{\sigma\sqrt{t}}, \qquad d_2 = d_1 - \sigma\sqrt{t}$$

---

2. See also Nelken (1993).

$$y_1 = \frac{\ln(S/X_c) + (b + \sigma^2/2)T_c}{\sigma\sqrt{T_c}}, \qquad y_2 = \frac{\ln(S/X_p) + (b + \sigma^2/2)T_p}{\sigma\sqrt{T_p}}$$

$$\rho_1 = \sqrt{t/T_c}, \qquad \rho_2 = \sqrt{t/T_p},$$

and I is the solution to

$$Ie^{(b-r)(T_c-t)}N(z_1) - X_c e^{-r(T_c-t)}N(z_1 - \sigma\sqrt{T_c - t}) +$$
$$Ie^{(b-r)(T_p-t)}N(-z_2) - X_p e^{-r(T_p-t)}N(-z_2 + \sigma\sqrt{T_p - t}) = 0$$

$$z_1 = \frac{\ln(I/X_c) + (b + \sigma^2/2)(T_c - t)}{\sigma\sqrt{T_c - t}}, \qquad z_2 = \frac{\ln(I/X_p) + (b + \sigma^2/2)(T_p - t)}{\sigma\sqrt{T_p - t}}.$$

Example

Consider a complex chooser option that gives the holder the right to choose whether the option is to be a call with time to expiration six months and strike price 55, or a put with seven months to expiration and strike price 48. The time to choose between a put or call is three months, the underlying stock price is 50, the risk-free interest rate per annum is 10%, the dividend yield is 5% per annum, and the volatility per annum is 35%. $S = 50$, $X_c = 55$, $X_p = 48$, $T_c = 0.5$, $T_p = 0.5833$, $t = 0.25$, $r = 0.10$, $b = 0.10 - 0.05 = 0.05$, $\sigma = 0.35$.

$$d_1 = \frac{\ln(50/51.1158) + (0.05 + 0.35^2/2)0.25}{0.35\sqrt{0.25}} = 0.0328,$$

where a Newton-Raphson search gives the solution to the critical value $I = 51.1158$, and

$$d_2 = d_1 - 0.35\sqrt{0.25} = -0.1422$$

$$y_1 = \frac{\ln(50/55) + (0.05 + 0.35^2/2)0.5}{0.35\sqrt{0.5}} = -0.1604$$

$$y_2 = \frac{\ln(50/48) + (0.05 + 0.35^2/2)0.5833}{0.35\sqrt{0.5833}} = 0.3955$$

$$\rho_1 = \sqrt{0.25/0.5} = 0.7071, \qquad \rho_2 = \sqrt{0.25/0.5833} = 0.6547$$

$$M(d_1, y_1; \rho_1) = 0.3464, \quad M(d_2, y_1 - 0.35\sqrt{0.5}; \rho_1) = 0.2660$$

$$M(-d_1, -y_2; \rho_2) = 0.2725, \quad M(-d_2, -y_2 + 0.35\sqrt{0.5833}; \rho_2) = 0.3601$$

$$
\begin{aligned}
w \ = \ & 50e^{(0.05-0.10)0.5}M(d_1, y_1; \rho_1) \\
& - 55e^{-0.10\times0.5}M(d_2, y_1 - \sigma\sqrt{T_c}; \rho_1) \\
& - 50e^{(0.05-0.10)0.5833}M(-d_1, -y_2; \rho_2) \\
& + 48e^{-0.05\times0.5833}M(-d_2, -y_2 + \sigma\sqrt{T_p}; \rho_2) = 6.0508
\end{aligned}
$$

Computer algorithm

The computer code returns the value of a complex chooser option.

```
Function ComplexChooser(S As Double, Xc As Double, Xp As Double, T As Double, _
        Tc As Double, Tp As Double, r As Double, b As Double, v As Double) As Double

    Dim d1 As Double, d2 As Double, y1 As Double, y2 As Double
    Dim rho1 As Double, rho2 As Double, I As Double

    I = CriticalValueChooser(S,Xc,Xp,T,Tc,Tp,r,b,v)
    d1 = (Log(S/I) + (b + v^2/2)*T)/(v*Sqr(T))
    d2 = d1 - v*Sqr(T)
    y1 = (Log(S/Xc) + (b + v^2/2)*Tc)/(v*Sqr(Tc))
    y2 = (Log(S/Xp) + (b + v^2/2)*Tp)/(v*Sqr(Tp))
    rho1 = Sqr(T/Tc)
    rho2 = Sqr(T/Tp)
    ComplexChooser = S*Exp((b - r)*Tc)*CBND(d1,y1,rho1) - _
    Xc*Exp(-r*Tc)*CBND(d2,y1 - v*Sqr(Tc),rho1) - _
    S*Exp((b - r)*Tp)*CBND(-d1,-y2,rho2) + _
    Xp*Exp(-r*Tp)*CBND(-d2,-y2 + v*Sqr(Tp),rho2)
End Function
```

The critical stock value I is found by calling the function *CriticalValueChooser*($\cdot$) below, which basically is a Newton-Raphson algorithm.

```
Function CriticalValueChooser(S As Double, Xc As Double, Xp As Double, _
        T As Double, Tc As Double, Tp As Double, r As Double, _
        b As Double, v As Double) As Double

    Dim Sv As Double, ci As Double, pi As Double, epsilon As Double
    Dim dc As Double, dp As Double, yi As Double, di As Double

    Sv = S
    ci = GBlackScholes("c",Sv,Xc,Tc - T,r,b,v)
    pi = GBlackScholes("p",Sv,Xp,Tp - T,r,b,v)
    dc = GDelta("c",Sv,Xc,Tc - T,r,b,v)
    dp = GDelta("p",Sv,Xp,Tp - T,r,b,v)
    yi = ci - pi
    di = dc - dp
```

```
        epsilon = 0.000001
        While Abs(yi) > epsilon
                Sv = Sv − (yi)/di
                ci = GBlackScholes("c",Sv,Xc,T c − T,r,b,v)
                pi = GBlackScholes("p",Sv,X p,T p − T,r,b,v)
                dc = GDelta("c",Sv,Xc,T c − T,r,b,v)
                dp = GDelta("p",Sv,X p,T p − T,r,b,v)
                yi = ci − pi
                di = dc − dp
        Wend
        CriticalValueChooser = Sv
End Function
```

where $CND(\cdot)$ is the cumulative normal distribution function, and $CBND(\cdot)$ is the cumulative bivariate normal distribution function described in Appendix A. Example: *ComplexChooser*(50, 55, 48, 0.25, 0.5, 0.5833, 0.10, 0.05, 0.35) returns a chooser value of 6.0508 as in the numerical example above.

2.6   OPTIONS ON OPTIONS

A model for pricing options on options was first published by Geske (1977). It was later extended and discussed by Geske (1979b), Hodges and Selby (1987), and Rubinstein (1991a), and others.

Call on call

Payoff: $\max[c_{GBS}(S,X_1,T_2) - X_2; 0]$, where X_1 is the strike price of the underlying option, X_2 is the strike price of the option on the option, and $c_{GBS}(S,X_1,T_2)$ is the generalized Black–Scholes call option formula with strike X_1 and time to maturity T_2.

$$
\begin{aligned}
c_{call} &= Se^{(b-r)T_2}M(z_1,y_1;\ \rho) - X_1 e^{-rT_2}M(z_2,y_2;\ \rho) \\
&\quad - X_2 e^{-rt}N(y_2),
\end{aligned}
\tag{2.10}
$$

where

$$
y_1 = \frac{\ln(S/I) + (b + \sigma^2/2)t_1}{\sigma\sqrt{t_1}}, \qquad y_2 = y_1 - \sigma\sqrt{t_1}
$$

$$
z_1 = \frac{\ln(S/X_1) + (b + \sigma^2/2)T_2}{\sigma\sqrt{T_2}}, \qquad z_2 = z_1 - \sigma\sqrt{T_2}
$$

$$
\rho = \sqrt{t_1/T_2},
$$

where T_2 is the time to maturity on the underlying option, and t_1 is the time to maturity on the option on the option.

Put on call
Payoff: $\max[X_2 - c_{GBS}(S, X_1, T_2); 0]$

$$
\begin{aligned}
p_{call} \;=\; & X_1 e^{-rT_2} M(z_2, -y_2; -\rho) - S e^{(b-r)T_2} M(z_1, -y_1; -\rho) \\
& + X_2 e^{-rt} N(-y_2),
\end{aligned}
\tag{2.11}
$$

where the value of I is found by solving the equation

$$
c_{GBS}(I, X_1, T_2 - t_1) = X_2.
$$

Call on put
Payoff: $\max[p_{GBS}(S, X_1, T_2) - X_2; 0]$

$$
\begin{aligned}
c_{put} \;=\; & X_1 e^{-rT_2} M(-z_2, -y_2; \rho) - S e^{(b-r)T_2} M(-z_1, -y_1; \rho) \\
& - X_2 e^{-rt_1} N(-y_2)
\end{aligned}
\tag{2.12}
$$

Put on put
Payoff: $\max[X_2 - p_{GBS}(S, X_1, T_2); 0]$

$$
\begin{aligned}
p_{put} \;=\; & S e^{(b-r)T_2} M(-z_1, y_1; -\rho) - X_1 e^{-rT_2} M(-z_2, y_2; -\rho) \\
& + X_2 e^{-rt_1} N(y_2),
\end{aligned}
\tag{2.13}
$$

where the value of I is found by solving the equation

$$
p_{GBS}(I, X_1, T_2 - t_1) = X_2.
$$

Example
Consider a put-on-call option that gives the option holder the right to sell a call option for 50, three months from today. The strike on the underlying call option is 520, the time to maturity on the call is six months from today, the price on the underlying stock index is 500, the risk-free interest rate is 8%, and the stock index pays dividends at a rate of 3% annually and has a volatility of 35%. $S = 500$, $X_1 = 520$, $X_2 = 50$, $t_1 = 0.25$, $T_2 = 0.5$, $r = 0.08$, $b = 0.08 - 0.03 = 0.05$, $\sigma = 0.35$.

The critical value I is

$$
\begin{aligned}
c_{GBS}(I, X_1, T_2 - t_1) &= X_2 \\
c_{GBS}(I, 520, 0.5 - 0.25) &= 50 \\
I &= 538.3165
\end{aligned}
$$

$$y_1 = \frac{\ln(500/538.3165) + (0.05 + 0.35/2)0.25}{0.35\sqrt{0.25}} = -0.2630$$

$$y_2 = y_1 - 0.35\sqrt{0.25} = -0.4380$$

$$z_1 = \frac{\ln(500/520) + (0.05 + 0.35^2/2)0.5}{0.35\sqrt{0.5}} = 0.0663$$

$$z_2 = z_1 - 0.35\sqrt{0.5} = -0.1812$$

$$\rho = \sqrt{0.25/0.5} = 0.7071$$

$$M(z_2, -y_2; -\rho) = 0.1736, \qquad M(z_1, -y_1; -\rho) = 0.1996$$

$$N(-y_2) = 0.6693$$

$$
\begin{aligned}
p_{call} =\ & 520e^{-0.08 \times 0.5}M(z_2, -y_2; -\rho) \\
& -500e^{(0.05-0.08)0.5}M(z_1, -y_1; -\rho) \\
& +50e^{-0.08 \times 0.25}N(-y_2) = 21.1965
\end{aligned}
$$

Computer algorithm

The computer algorithm $OptionsOnOptions(\cdot)$ returns the value of an option on an option. Setting the $TypeFlag$ equal to "cc" gives a call on call, "cp" gives a call on a put, "pp" gives a put on a put, and "pc" gives a put on a call.

```
Function OptionsOnOptions(TypeFlag As String, S As Double, X1 As Double, _
        X2 As Double, t1 As Double, T2 As Double, r As Double, _
        b As Double, v As Double) As Double

    Dim y1 As Double, y2 As Double, z1 As Double, z2 As Double
    Dim I As Double, rho As Double

    I = CriticalValueOptionsOnOptions(TypeFlag, X1, X2, T2 - t1, r, b, v)
    rho = Sqr(t1 / T2)
    y1 = (Log(S / I) + (b + v^2/2) * t1) / (v * Sqr(t1))
    y2 = y1 - v * Sqr(t1)
    z1 = (Log(S / X1) + (b + v^2/2) * T2) / (v * Sqr(T2))
    z2 = z1 - v * Sqr(T2)
    If TypeFlag = "cc" Then
```

$$OptionsOnOptions = S * Exp((b-r)*T2)*CBND(z1,y1,rho) - \_$$
$$X1 * Exp(-r*T2)*CBND(z2,y2,rho) - X2 * Exp(-r*t1)*CND(y2)$$
ElseIf *TypeFlag* = "pc" Then
$$OptionsOnOptions = X1 * Exp(-r*T2)*CBND(z2,-y2,-rho) - \_$$
$$S * Exp((b-r)*T2)*CBND(z1,-y1,-rho) + X2 * \_$$
$$Exp(-r*t1)*CND(-y2)$$
ElseIf *TypeFlag* = "cp" Then
$$OptionsOnOptions = X1 * Exp(-r*T2)*CBND(-z2,-y2,rho) - \_$$
$$S * Exp((b-r)*T2)*CBND(-z1,-y1,rho) - X2 * \_$$
$$Exp(-r*t1)*CND(-y2)$$
ElseIf *TypeFlag* = "pp" Then
$$OptionsOnOptions = S * Exp((b-r)*T2)*CBND(-z1,y1,-rho) - \_$$
$$X1 * Exp(-r*T2)*CBND(-z2,y2,-rho) + \_$$
$$Exp(-r*t1)*X2*CND(y2)$$
End If
End Function

Function *CriticalValueOptionsOnOptions(CallPutFlag* As String, *X1* As Double, _
     X2 As Double, *T* As Double, *r* As Double, *b* As Double, _
     v As Double) As Double

     Dim *Si* As Double, *ci* As Double, *di* As Double, *epsilon* As Double

     If *CallPutFlag* = "cc" Or *CallPutFlag* = "pc" Then
       CallPutFlag = "c"
     Else
         CallPutFlag = "p"
     End If
     Si = *X1*
     ci = *GBlackScholes(CallPutFlag, Si, X1, T, r, b, v)*
     di = *GDelta(CallPutFlag, Si, X1, T, r, b, v)*
     epsilon = 0.000001
     While *Abs(ci − X2)* > *epsilon*
         Si = *Si − (ci − X2)/di*
         ci = *GBlackScholes(CallPutFlag, Si, X1, T, r, b, v)*
         di = *GDelta(CallPutFlag, Si, X1, T, r, b, v)*
     Wend
     CriticalValueOptionsOnOptions = *Si*
End Function

where $CND(\cdot)$ is the cumulative normal distribution function and $CBND(\cdot)$ is the cumulative bivariate normal distribution function described in Appendix A. Example: *OptionsOnOptions* ("pc", 500, 520, 50, 0.25, 0.5, 0.08, 0.05, 0.35) returns a put-on-call price of 21.1965, as in the numerical example above.

2.7 OPTIONS WITH EXTENDIBLE MATURITIES

Valuation of extendible options was introduced by Longstaff (1990). Extendible options can be found embedded in several financial contracts. For example, corporate warrants have frequently given the corporate issuer the right to extend the life of the warrants. Firms involved in leveraged buyouts from time to time issue extendible bonds where maturity can be extended at the firm's discretion. Another example is options on real estate where the holder can extend the expiration by paying an additional fee.

2.7.1 Options That Can Be Extended by the Holder

These are options that can be exercised at their maturity date t_1 but that also allow the holder at that time to extend the life of the option until T_2 by paying an additional premium A to the writer of the option. The strike price of the option can be adjusted from X_1 to X_2 at the time of the extension. The payoff from options that can be extended by the holder at time t_1 ($t_1 < T_2$) is

$$c(S,X_1,X_2,t_1,T_2) = \max[S - X_1; \; c_{GBS}(S,X_2,T_2 - t_1) - A; \; 0]$$

$$p(S,X_1,X_2,t_1,T_2) = \max[X_1 - S; \; p_{GBS}(S,X_2,T_2 - t_1) - A; \; 0],$$

where $c_{GBS}(S,X_2,T_2 - t_1)$ is the general Black–Scholes call formula, and $p_{GBS}(S,X_2,T_2 - t_1)$ is the general Black–Scholes put formula.

Extendible call

$$
\begin{aligned}
c \; = \; & c_{GBS}(S,X_1,t_1) + Se^{(b-r)T_2}M_2(y_1,y_2,-\infty,z_1; \; \rho) \\
& - X_2e^{-rT_2}M_2(y_1 - \sigma\sqrt{t_1},y_2 - \sigma\sqrt{t_1},-\infty,z_1 - \sigma\sqrt{T_2}; \; \rho) \\
& - Se^{(b-r)t_1}N_2(y_1,z_2) + X_1e^{-rt_1}N_2(y_1 - \sigma\sqrt{t_1},z_2 - \sigma\sqrt{t}) \\
& - Ae^{-rt_1}N_2(y_1 - \sigma\sqrt{t},y_2 - \sigma\sqrt{t_1}),
\end{aligned}
\tag{2.14}
$$

where

$$y_1 = \frac{\ln(S/I_2) + (b + \sigma^2/2)t_1}{\sigma\sqrt{t_1}}, \qquad y_2 = \frac{\ln(S/I_1) + (b + \sigma^2/2)t_1}{\sigma\sqrt{t_1}}$$

$$z_1 = \frac{\ln(S/X_2) + (b + \sigma^2/2)T_2}{\sigma\sqrt{T_2}}, \qquad z_2 = \frac{\ln(S/X_1) + (b + \sigma^2/2)t_1}{\sigma\sqrt{t_1}}$$

$$\rho = \sqrt{t_1/T_2},$$

where I_1 is the critical value of S at time t_1, below which the option is not extended. I_2 is the critical value of S at time t_1, where the option will be exercised rather than extended. The critical values I_1 and I_2 are the respective solutions to

$$c_{GBS}(I_1,X_2,T_2 - t_1) = A, \qquad c_{GBS}(I_2,X_2,T_2 - t_1) = I_2 - X_1 + A.$$

If $A = 0$, then $I_1 = 0$; and if $A < X_1 - X_2 e^{-r(T_2-t_1)}$, then $I_2 = \infty$. The call is extended only if $I_1 < S < I_2$. If $S < I_1$ at t_1, the option expires out-of-the-money, and if $S > I_2$ at t_1, it is optimal to exercise the option rather than extend it. The extendible call has several special cases:

- If $I_1 = 0$ and $I_2 = \infty$, the call will always be extended.
- If $I_1 > 0$ and $I_2 = \infty$, the value of the extendible call reduces to a standard call on a call with strike equal to A. The underlying call has strike X_2 and time to maturity $(T_2 - t_1)$.
- If $I_1 \geq X_1$, the extendible call will never be extended.

The probability $M_2(a,b,c,d;\ \rho)$ and $N_2(a,b)$ can be determined directly from the standard bivariate normal distribution and the standard normal distribution

$$M_2(a,b,c,d;\ \rho) = M(b,d;\ \rho) - M(a,d;\ \rho) - M(b,c;\ \rho) + M(a,c;\ \rho)$$

$$N_2(a,b) = N(b) - N(a)$$

Extendible put

$$
\begin{aligned}
p &= p_{GBS}(S,X_1,t_1) - Se^{(b-r)T_2}M_2(y_1,y_2,-\infty,-z_1;\ \rho) \\
&\quad + X_2 e^{-rT_2}M_2(y_1 - \sigma\sqrt{t_1}, y_2 - \sigma\sqrt{t_1}, -\infty, -z_1 + \sigma\sqrt{T_2};\ \rho) \\
&\quad + Se^{(b-r)t_1}N_2(z_2,y_2) - X_1 e^{-rt_1}N_2(z_2 - \sigma\sqrt{t_1}, y_2 - \sigma\sqrt{t_1}) \\
&\quad - Ae^{-rt_1}N_2(y_1 - \sigma\sqrt{t_1}, y_2 - \sigma\sqrt{t_1}),
\end{aligned}
\tag{2.15}
$$

where the variables I_1 and I_2 are solutions to

$$p_{GBS}(I_1, X_2, T_2 - t_1) = X_1 - I_1 + A, \qquad p_{GBS}(I_2, X_2, T_2 - t_1) = A.$$

If $A = 0$, then $I_2 = \infty$. The put is extended only if $I_1 < S < I_2$. The extendible put has several special cases:

- If $A = 0$ and $I_1 = 0$, the put will always be extended.
- If $A > 0$ and $I_1 = 0$, the value of the extendible put reduces to a standard call on a put with strike A. The underlying put has strike X_2 and time to maturity $(T_2 - t_1)$.
- If $I_2 < X_1$ or $I_1 = X_1$, the extendible put will never be extended.

Example

Consider an extendible call with initial time to maturity six months, extendible for an additional three months. The stock price is 100, the initial strike price is 100, the extended strike price is 105, the risk-free interest rate is 8% per annum, the volatility is 25% per annum, and the extension fee is 1. $S = 100, X_1 = 100, X_2 = 105, t_1 = 0.5, T_2 = 0.75, r = 0.08, b = 0.08, \sigma = 0.25, A = 1$.

$$y_1 = \frac{\ln(100/105.7138) + (0.08 + 0.25^2/2)0.5}{0.25\sqrt{0.5}} = 0.0003$$

The critical values I_1 and I_2 can easily be found by the Newton-Raphson algorithm. It gives $I_1 = 86.7406$ and $I_2 = 105.7138$.

$$y_2 = \frac{\ln(100/86.7406) + (0.08 + 0.25^2/2)0.5}{0.25\sqrt{0.5}} = 1.1193$$

$$z_1 = \frac{\ln(100/105) + (0.08 + 0.25^2/2)0.75}{0.25\sqrt{0.75}} = 0.1600$$

$$z_2 = \frac{\ln(100/100) + (0.08 + 0.25^2/2)0.5}{0.25\sqrt{0.5}} = 0.3147$$

$$\rho = \sqrt{0.5/0.75} = 0.8165$$

$$M_2(y_1, y_2, -10, z_1; \rho) = 0.1277$$

$$M_2(y_1 - 0.25\sqrt{0.5}, y_2 - 0.25\sqrt{0.5}, -10, z_1 - 0.25\sqrt{0.75}; \rho) = 0.1181$$

$$N_2(y_1, z_2) = 0.1234, \quad N_2(y_1 - 0.25\sqrt{0.5}, y_2 - 0.25\sqrt{0.5}) = 0.3971$$

$$N_2(y_1 - 0.25\sqrt{0.5}, z_2 - 0.25\sqrt{0.5}) = 0.1249$$

$$c_{GBS}(100, 100, 0.5) = 9.0412$$

$$\begin{aligned}
c = \ & 9.0412 + 100e^{(0.08-0.08)0.75}M_2(y_1, y_2, -\infty, z_1; \rho) \\
& - 105e^{-0.08 \times 0.75}M_2(y_1 - \sigma\sqrt{t_1}, y_2 - \sigma\sqrt{t_1}, -\infty, z_1 - \sigma\sqrt{T_2}; \rho) \\
& + 100e^{(0.08-0.08)0.5}N_2(y_1, z_2) + 100e^{-0.08 \times 0.5}N_2(y_1 - \sigma\sqrt{t_1}, z_2 - \sigma\sqrt{t}) \\
& - 1e^{-0.08 \times 0.5}N_2(y_1 - \sigma\sqrt{t}, y_2 - \sigma\sqrt{t_1}) = 9.4029
\end{aligned}$$

2.7.2   Writer-Extendible Options

These are options that can be exercised at their initial maturity date t_1 but are extended to T_2 if the option is out-of-the-money at t_1. The payoff from a writer-extendible call option at time t_1 $(t_1 < T_2)$ is

$$c(S,X_1,X_2,t_1,T_2) = (S-X_1) \quad \text{if} \quad S \geq X_1 \quad \text{else} \quad c_{GBS}(S,X_2,T_2-t_1),$$

and for a writer-extendible put is

$$p(S,X_1,X_2,t_1,T_2) = (X_1-S) \quad \text{if} \quad S < X_1 \quad \text{else} \quad p_{GBS}(S,X_2,T_2-t_1).$$

Writer-extendible call

$$
\begin{aligned}
c &= c_{GBS}(S,X_1,t_1) + Se^{(b-r)T_2}M(z_1,-z_2;\ -\rho) \\
  &\quad - X_2 e^{-rT_2}M(z_1 - \sigma\sqrt{T_2}, -z_2 + \sigma\sqrt{t_1};\ -\rho)
\end{aligned}
\tag{2.16}
$$

Writer-extendible put

$$
\begin{aligned}
p &= p_{GBS}(S,X_1,t_1) + X_2 e^{-rT_2}M(-z_1 + \sigma\sqrt{T_2}, z_2 - \sigma\sqrt{t_1};\ -\rho) \\
  &\quad - Se^{(b-r)T_2}M(-z_1,z_2;\ -\rho)
\end{aligned}
\tag{2.17}
$$

Example

Consider a writer-extendible call on a stock with original time to maturity six months, that will be extended three months if the option is out-of-the-money at t_1. The stock price is 80, and the initial strike price is 90. If the option is extended, the strike price is adjusted to 82. The risk-free interest rate is 10%, and the volatility is 30%. $S = 80$, $X_1 = 90$, $X_2 = 82$, $t_1 = 0.5$, $T_2 = 0.75$, $r = 0.10$, $b = 0.10$, $\sigma = 0.30$.

$$z_1 = \frac{\ln(80/82) + (0.10 + 0.30^2/2)0.75}{0.30\sqrt{0.75}} = 0.3235$$

$$z_2 = \frac{\ln(80/90) + (0.10 + 0.30^2/2)0.5}{0.30\sqrt{0.5}} = -0.2135$$

$$\rho = \sqrt{0.5/0.75} = 0.8165$$

$$M(z_1,-z_2;\ -\rho) = 0.2369, \quad M(z_1 - 0.30\sqrt{0.75}, -z_2 + 0.30\sqrt{0.5};\ -\rho) = 0.2192$$

$$c_{GBS}(80,90,0.5) = 4.5418$$

$$
\begin{aligned}
c &= 4.5418 + 80e^{(0.10-0.10)0.75}M(z_1, -z_2; -\rho) \\
&\quad - 82e^{-0.10\times0.75}M(z_1 - 0.30\sqrt{0.75}, -z_2 + 0.30\sqrt{0.5}; -\rho) = 6.8238
\end{aligned}
$$

2.8 OPTIONS ON TWO DIFFERENT ASSETS

2.8.1 Two-Asset Correlation Options

Payoff call: $\max(S_2 - X_2; 0)$ if $S_1 > X_1$ and 0 otherwise, and for a put: $\max(X_2 - S_2)$ if $S_1 < X_1$ and 0 otherwise. These options can be priced using the formulas of Zhang (1995b)

$$
\begin{aligned}
c &= S_2 e^{(b_2-r)T} M(y_2 + \sigma_2\sqrt{T}, y_1 + \rho\sigma_2\sqrt{T}; \rho) \\
&\quad - X_2 e^{-rT} M(y_2, y_1; \rho)
\end{aligned} \tag{2.18}
$$

$$
\begin{aligned}
p &= X_2 e^{-rT} M(-y_2, -y_1; \rho) \\
&\quad - S_2 e^{(b_2-r)T} M(-y_2 - \sigma_2\sqrt{T}, -y_1 - \rho\sigma_2\sqrt{T}; \rho),
\end{aligned} \tag{2.19}
$$

where ρ is the correlation coefficient between the returns on the two assets, and

$$
y_1 = \frac{\ln(S_1/X_1) + (b_1 - \sigma_1^2/2)T}{\sigma_1\sqrt{T}}, \qquad y_2 = \frac{\ln(S_2/X_2) + (b_2 - \sigma_2^2/2)T}{\sigma_2\sqrt{T}}.
$$

Example
Consider a call with six months to expiry. The price of stock A is 52, the price of stock B is 65, the strike price is 50, the payout level is 70, the volatility of stock A is 20%, the volatility of stock B is 30%, the risk-free interest rate is 10%, and the correlation between the two stocks is 0.75. $S_1 = 52$, $S_2 = 65$, $T = 0.5$, $X_1 = 50$, $X_2 = 70$, $\sigma_1 = 0.20$, $\sigma_2 = 0.30$, $r = 0.10$, $b_1 = b_2 = 0.10$, $\rho = 75$.

$$
y_1 = \frac{\ln(50/50) + (0.10 - 0.20^2/2)0.5}{0.20\sqrt{0.5}} = 0.5602
$$

$$
y_2 = \frac{\ln(65/70) + (0.10 - 0.30^2/2)0.5}{0.30\sqrt{0.5}} = -0.2197
$$

$$
M(y_2 + \sigma_2\sqrt{T}, y_1 + \rho\sigma_2\sqrt{T}; \rho) = 0.4753, \qquad M(y_2, y_1; \rho) = 0.3933
$$

$$
\begin{aligned}
c &= 65e^{(0.10-0.10)0.5}M(y_2 + \sigma_2\sqrt{T}, y_1 + \rho\sigma_2\sqrt{T}; \rho) \\
&\quad - 70e^{-0.10\times0.5}M(y_2, y_1; \rho) = 4.7073.
\end{aligned}
$$

2.8.2 Exchange-One-Asset-for-Another Options

An exchange-one-asset-for-another option, originally introduced by Margrabe (1978), gives the holder the right to exchange asset S_2 for S_1 at expiration. The payoff from an exchange-one-asset-for-another option is

$$c(S_1, S_2, T) = \max(Q_1 S_1 - Q_2 S_2; 0)$$

$$c = Q_1 S_1 e^{(b_1 - r)T} N(d_1) - Q_2 S_2 e^{(b_2 - r)T} N(d_2), \qquad (2.20)$$

where Q_1 is the quantity of asset S_1, and Q_2 is the quantity of asset S_2.

$$d_1 = \frac{\ln(Q_1 S_1 / Q_2 S_2) + (b_1 - b_2 + \hat{\sigma}^2 / 2)T}{\hat{\sigma}\sqrt{T}}$$

$$d_2 = d_1 - \hat{\sigma}\sqrt{T}$$

$$\hat{\sigma} = \sqrt{\sigma_1^2 + \sigma_2^2 - 2\rho\sigma_1\sigma_2},$$

where ρ is the correlation between the two assets. Table 2–1 shows values for European exchange options. Different values are given for time to maturity T, the volatility of the second asset σ_2, and the correlation between the two assets ρ.

T A B L E 2-1

Examples of European Exchange Options Values

($S_1 = 22$, $S_2 = 20$, $Q_1 = Q_2 = 1$, $r = 0.10$, $b_1 = 0.04$, $b_2 = 0.06$, $\sigma_1 = 0.20$)

σ_2	$T = 0.1$			$T = 0.50$		
	$\rho = -0.5$	$\rho = 0$	$\rho = 0.5$	$\rho = -0.5$	$\rho = 0$	$\rho = 0.5$
0.15	2.1251	2.0446	1.9736	2.7619	2.4793	2.1378
0.20	2.1986	2.0913	1.9891	2.9881	2.6496	2.2306
0.25	2.2827	2.1520	2.0189	3.2272	2.8472	2.3736

Application

Exchange options are embedded in several financial contracts. One example is when a corporation bids on another corporation by offering its own shares in exchange for the stocks in the takeover candidate. The stock owners of the takeover candidate get an option to exchange their stocks for the stocks in the acquiring corporation.

There are also exchange options that are embedded in short bond or note futures contracts. If you are short a bond future, you have to deliver a bond to the counterparty that is long the future at the expiry of the futures contract. However, the counterparty that is short the future can normally choose from a whole class of bonds to deliver. Such bonds can be valued as exchange options.

Example
Consider a European option to exchange bond B for bond A. Time to expiration is six months. Bond A is currently priced at 101, the coupon rate is 8%, and the volatility per annum is 18%. Bond B is currently priced at 104, the coupon rate is 6%, and the volatility per annum is 12%. The risk-free interest rate is 10%. The correlation between their rates of return is 0.80. $S_1 = 101$, $S_2 = 104$, $T = 0.5$, $r = 0.10$, $b_1 = 0.02$, $b_2 = 0.04$, $\sigma_1 = 0.18$, $\sigma_2 = 0.12$, $\rho = 0.80$.

$$\hat{\sigma} = \sqrt{0.18^2 + 0.12^2 - 2 \times 0.80 \times 0.18 \times 0.12} = 0.1106$$

$$d_1 = \frac{\ln(101/104) + (0.02 - 0.04 + 0.1106^2/2)0.5}{0.1106\sqrt{0.5}} = -0.4629$$

$$d_2 = d_1 - 0.1106\sqrt{0.5} = -0.5411$$

$$N(d_1) = N(-0.4629) = 0.3217, \qquad N(d_2) = N(-0.5411) = 0.2942$$

$$c = 101e^{(0.02-0.10)0.5}N(d_1) - 104e^{(0.04-0.10)0.5}N(d_2) = 1.5260$$

American Exchange-One-Asset-for-Another Option
Bjerksund and Stensland (1993b) have shown that an American option to exchange asset S_2 for asset S_1 can be simplified to the problem of pricing a standard American call[3] with underlying asset S_1 with risk-adjusted drift equal to $b_1 - b_2$, strike price S_2, time to maturity T, risk-free rate equal to $r - b_2$, and the volatility replaced by $\hat{\sigma}$.

$$C = C_{\text{plain vanilla}}(Q_1 S_1, Q_2 S_2, T, r - b_2, b_1 - b_2, \hat{\sigma}),$$

where $C_{\text{plain vanilla}}(S, X, T, r, b, \sigma)$ is the value of a plain vanilla American call option, for example, the Bjerksund and Stensland (1993a) closed-form approximation. $\hat{\sigma}$ is defined as in the case of the European exchange option.

---

3. An alternative would be to price the American exchange options in a binomial tree using the technique described by Rubinstein (1991b).

Table 2–2 gives values of an American exchange option using different input parameters. The input parameters are as in Table 2–1, and illustrates that the American-style Exchange option is more valuable than its European counterpart.

T A B L E 2-2

Examples of American Exchange Options Values

$(S_1 = 22, S_2 = 20, Q_1 = Q_2 = 1, r = 0.10, b_1 = 0.04, b_2 = 0.06, \sigma_1 = 0.20)$

	$T = 0.1$			$T = 0.50$		
σ_2	$\rho = -0.5$	$\rho = 0$	$\rho = 0.5$	$\rho = -0.5$	$\rho = 0$	$\rho = 0.5$
0.15	2.1357	2.0592	2.0001	2.8051	2.5282	2.2053
0.20	2.2074	2.1032	2.0110	3.0288	2.6945	2.2906
0.25	2.2902	2.1618	2.0359	3.2664	2.8893	2.4261

2.8.3 Exchange Options on Exchange Options

Exchange options on exchange options can be found embedded in many sequential exchange opportunities. An example described by Carr (1988) is a bond holder converting into a stock, later exchanging the shares received for stocks of an acquiring firm. Carr also introduces formulas for pricing this type of rather complex option.

The value of the option to exchange the option to exchange a fixed quantity Q of asset S_2 for the option to exchange asset S_2 for S_1 is

$$
\begin{aligned}
c \;=\; & S_1 e^{(b_1-r)T_2} M(d_1, y_1; \sqrt{t_1/T_2}) - S_2 e^{(b_2-r)T_2} M(d_2, y_2; \sqrt{t_1/T_2}) \\
& - Q S_2 e^{(b_2-r)t_1} N(d_2)
\end{aligned} \tag{2.21}
$$

The value of the option to exchange asset S_2 for S_1 in return for a fixed quantity Q of asset S_2 is

$$
\begin{aligned}
c \;=\; & S_2 e^{(b_2-r)T_2} M(d_3, y_2; -\sqrt{t_1/T_2}) - S_1 e^{(b_1-r)T_2} M(d_4, y_1; -\sqrt{t_1/T_2}) \\
& + Q S_2 e^{(b_2-r)t_1} N(d_3),
\end{aligned} \tag{2.22}
$$

where

$$
d_1 = \frac{\ln(S_1/IS_2) + (b_1 - b_2 + \sigma^2/2)t_1}{\sigma\sqrt{t_1}}, \quad d_2 = d_1 - \sigma\sqrt{t_1}
$$

$$
d_3 = \frac{\ln(IS_2/S_1) + (b_2 - b_1 + \sigma^2/2)t_1}{\sigma\sqrt{t_1}}, \quad d_4 = d_3 - \sigma\sqrt{t_1}
$$

$$y_1 = \frac{\ln(S_1/S_2) + (b_1 - b_2 + \sigma^2/2)T_2}{\sigma\sqrt{T_2}}, \quad y_2 = y_1 - \sigma\sqrt{T_2}$$

$$y_3 = \frac{\ln(S_2/S_1) + (b_2 - b_1 + \sigma^2/2)T_2}{\sigma\sqrt{T_2}}, \quad y_4 = y_3 - \sigma\sqrt{T_2}$$

$$\sigma = \sqrt{\sigma_1^2 + \sigma_2^2 - 2\rho\sigma_1\sigma_2}$$

I is the unique critical price ratio $I_1 = \frac{S_1 e^{(b_1-r)(T_2-t_1)}}{S_2 e^{(b_2-r)(T_2-t_1)}}$ solving

$$I_1 N(z_1) - N(z_2) = Q$$

$$z_1 = \frac{\ln(I_1) + (T_2 - t_1)\sigma^2/2}{\sigma\sqrt{T_2 - t_1}}, \quad z_2 = z_1 - \sigma\sqrt{T_2 - t_1}$$

where

$S_1 = $ Asset 1.
$S_2 = $ Asset 2.
$t_1 = $ Time to expiration of the "original" option.
$T_2 = $ Time to expiration of the underlying option $(T_2 > t_1)$.
$b_1 = $ Cost of carry rate, asset S_1.
$b_2 = $ Cost of carry rate, asset S_2.
$\sigma_1 = $ Volatility of asset S_1.
$\sigma_2 = $ Volatility of asset S_2.
$\rho = $ Correlation between asset S_1 and S_2.
$Q = $ Quantity of asset delivered if option is exercised.

The value of the option to exchange a fixed quantity Q of asset S_2 for the option to exchange asset S_1 for S_2 is

$$c = S_2 e^{(b_2-r)T_2} M(d_3, y_3; \sqrt{t_1/T_2}) - S_1 e^{(b_1-r)T_2} M(d_4, y_4; \sqrt{t_1/T_2})$$
$$- Q S_2 e^{(b_2-r)t_1} N(d_3) \tag{2.23}$$

The value of the option to exchange the option to exchange asset S_1 for S_2 in return for a fixed quantity Q of asset S_2 is

$$c = S_1 e^{(b_1-r)T_2} M(d_1, y_4; -\sqrt{t_1/T_2}) - S_2 e^{(b_2-r)T_2} M(d_2, y_3; -\sqrt{t_1/T_2})$$
$$+ Q S_2 e^{(b_2-r)t_1} N(d_2), \tag{2.24}$$

where *I* is now the unique critical price ratio $I_2 = \frac{S_2 e^{(b_2-r)(T_2-t_1)}}{S_1 e^{(b_1-r)(T_2-t_1)}}$ solving

$$N(z_1) - I_2 N(z_2) = Q$$

$$z_1 = \frac{\ln(I_2) + (T_2 - t_1)\sigma^2/2}{\sigma\sqrt{T_2 - t_1}}, \quad z_2 = z_1 - \sigma\sqrt{T_2 - t_1}.$$

Table 2–3 shows values of an Exchange option on an Exchange option. Values are given for a range of volatilities, correlations, and asset prices.

T A B L E 2–3

Exchange Options on Exchange Options Values

$(S_2 = 100, t_1 = 0.75, T_2 = 1, r = 0.10, b_1 = 0.10, b_2 = 0.10, Q = 0.10)$

		$\rho = -0.5$		$\rho = 0$		$\rho = 0.5$	
σ_1	σ_2	$S_1 = 100$	$S_1 = 105$	$S_1 = 100$	$S_1 = 105$	$S_1 = 100$	$S_1 = 105$
Option to exchange QS_2 for the option to exchange S_2 for S_1							
0.20	0.20	8.5403	10.9076	6.2333	8.4333	3.3923	5.2802
0.20	0.25	10.1756	12.6391	7.5787	9.8819	4.3605	6.3758
0.25	0.20	10.1756	12.6391	7.5787	9.8819	4.3605	6.3758
Option to exchange the option to exchange S_2 for S_1 in return for QS_2							
0.20	0.20	4.7893	4.1747	4.9870	4.2359	5.4267	4.3746
0.20	0.25	4.6948	4.1492	4.8607	4.1961	5.2395	4.3166
0.25	0.20	4.6948	4.1492	4.8607	4.1961	5.2395	4.3166
Option to exchange QS_2 for the option to exchange S_1 for S_2							
0.20	0.20	7.3679	5.9428	5.3005	3.9927	2.7895	1.7663
0.20	0.25	8.8426	7.3670	6.5040	5.1199	3.6392	2.4929
0.25	0.20	8.8426	7.3670	6.5040	5.1199	3.6392	2.4929
Option to exchange the option to exchange S_1 for S_2 in return for QS_2							
0.20	0.20	3.6169	4.2099	4.0542	4.7954	4.8239	5.8607
0.20	0.25	3.3619	3.8771	3.7859	4.4341	4.5182	5.4337
0.25	0.20	3.3619	3.8771	3.7859	4.4341	4.5182	5.4337

2.8.4 Options on the Maximum or the Minimum of Two Risky Assets

Formulas for pricing options on the minimum or maximum of two risky assets were originally introduced by Stulz (1982) and have later been extended and discussed by Johnson (1987), Boyle, Evnine, and Gibbs (1989), Boyle and Tse (1990), Rubinstein (1991d), Rich and Chance (1993), and others.

Call on the minimum of two assets
Payoff: $\max[\min(S_1, S_2) - X, 0]$

$$
\begin{aligned}
c_{min}(S_1,S_2,X,T) \;=\;& S_1 e^{(b_1-r)T} M(y_1,-d;\,-\rho_1) \\
&+ S_2 e^{(b_2-r)T} M(y_2,d-\sigma\sqrt{T};\,-\rho_2) \\
&- X e^{-rT} M(y_1-\sigma_1\sqrt{T}, y_2-\sigma_2\sqrt{T};\,\rho),
\end{aligned}
\qquad (2.25)
$$

where

$$
d = \frac{\ln(S_1/S_2) + (b_1 - b_2 + \sigma^2/2)T}{\sigma\sqrt{T}}
$$

$$
y_1 = \frac{\ln(S_1/X) + (b_1 + \sigma_1^2/2)T}{\sigma_1\sqrt{T}}, \qquad
y_2 = \frac{\ln(S_2/X) + (b_2 + \sigma_2^2/2)T}{\sigma_2\sqrt{T}}
$$

$$
\sigma = \sqrt{\sigma_1^2 + \sigma_2^2 - 2\rho\sigma_1\sigma_2}, \qquad
\rho_1 = \frac{\sigma_1 - \rho\sigma_2}{\sigma}, \qquad
\rho_2 = \frac{\sigma_2 - \rho\sigma_1}{\sigma}
$$

Call on the maximum of two assets
Payoff: $\max[\max(S_1,S_2) - X, 0]$

$$
\begin{aligned}
c_{max}(S_1,S_2,X,T) \;=\;& S_1 e^{(b_1-r)T} M(y_1,d;\,\rho_1) \\
&+ S_2 e^{(b_2-r)T} M(y_2,-d+\sigma\sqrt{T};\,\rho_2) - X e^{-rT} \\
&\times [1 - M(-y_1+\sigma_1\sqrt{T}, -y_2+\sigma_2\sqrt{T};\,\rho)]
\end{aligned}
\qquad (2.26)
$$

Put on the minimum of two assets
Payoff: $\max[X - \min(S_1,S_2), 0]$

$$
p_{min}(S_1,S_2,X,T) = X e^{-rT} - c_{min}(S_1,S_2,0,T) + c_{min}(S_1,S_2,X,T),
\qquad (2.27)
$$

where

$$
\begin{aligned}
c_{min}(S_1,S_2,0,T) \;=\;& S_1 e^{(b_1-r)T} \\
&- S_1 e^{(b_1-r)T} N(d) + S_2 e^{(b_2-r)T} N(d-\sigma\sqrt{T})
\end{aligned}
$$

Put on the maximum of two assets
Payoff: $\max[X - \max(S_1,S_2), 0]$

$$
p_{max}(S_1,S_2,X,T) = X e^{-rT} - c_{max}(S_1,S_2,0,T) + c_{max}(S_1,S_2,X,T),
\qquad (2.28)
$$

where

$$c_{max}(S_1,S_2,0,T) = S_2 e^{(b_2-r)T}$$
$$+ S_1 e^{(b_1-r)T} N(d) - S_2 e^{(b_2-r)T} N(d - \sigma\sqrt{T}).$$

Example

Consider a put option that gives the holder the right to sell the maximum of stock index A and stock index B at a strike price of 98. Time to maturity is six months, stock index A pays a dividend yield of 6%, stock index B pays a dividend yield of 9%, the price of index A is currently 100, the price of index B is 105, the volatility of index A is 11%, the volatility of index B is 16%, the risk-free interest rate is 5%, and the correlation between the return on the two stock indexes is 0.63. $S_1 = 100$, $S_2 = 105$, $X = 98$, $T = 0.5$, $r = 0.05$, $b_1 = 0.05 - 0.06 = -0.01$, $b_2 = 0.05 - 0.09 = -0.04$, $\sigma_1 = 0.11$, $\sigma_2 = 0.16$, $\rho = 0.63$.

$$\sigma = \sqrt{0.11^2 + 0.16^2 - 2 \times 0.63 \times 0.11 \times 0.16} = 0.1246$$

$$\rho_1 = \frac{0.11 - 0.63 \times 0.16}{0.1246} = 0.0738, \qquad \rho_2 = \frac{0.16 - 0.63 \times 0.11}{0.1246} = 0.7280$$

$$d = \frac{\ln(100/105) + (-0.01 + 0.04 + 0.1246^2/2)0.5}{0.1246\sqrt{0.5}} = -0.3395$$

$$y_1 = \frac{\ln(100/98) + (-0.01 + 0.11^2/2)0.5}{0.11\sqrt{0.5}} = 0.2343$$

$$y_2 = \frac{\ln(105/98) + (-0.04 + 0.16^2/2)0.5}{0.16\sqrt{0.5}} = 0.4896$$

$$c_{max}(S_1,S_2,0,T) = 105e^{(-0.04-0.05)0.5} + 100e^{(-0.01-0.05)0.5}N(d)$$
$$- 105e^{(-0.04-0.05)0.5}N(d - 0.1246\sqrt{0.5}) = 102.4324$$

$$c_{max}(S_1,S_2,X,T) = 100e^{(-0.01-0.05)0.5}M(y_1,d; \rho_1)$$
$$+ 105e^{(-0.04-0.05)0.5}M(y_2,-d + 0.1246\sqrt{0.5}; \rho_2)$$
$$- 98e^{-0.05\times0.5}[1$$
$$- M(-y_1 + 0.11\sqrt{0.5}, -y_2 + 0.16\sqrt{0.5}; \rho)] = 8.0700$$

$$p_{max}(S_1,S_2,X,T) = 98e^{-0.05\times0.5} - 102.4324 + 8.0701 = 1.2181$$

2.8.5 Spread-Option Approximation

The payoff from a European call spread option on two futures contracts is $\max(F_1 - F_2 - X, 0)$. The payoff from a put option is similarly $\max(X - F_1 + F_2, 0)$. A European spread option on forward or futures contracts can be valued using the standard Black (1976) model by performing the following transformation, as originally shown by Kirk (1995):[4]

$$c = \max(F_1 - F_2 - X, 0) = \max\left(\frac{F_1}{(F_2 + X)} - 1, 0\right) \times (F_2 + X)$$

$$p = \max(X - F_1 + F_2, 0) = \max\left(1 - \frac{F_1}{(F_2 + X)}, 0\right) \times (F_2 + X)$$

The value of a call or put is:

$$c = (F_2 + X)\{e^{-rT}[FN(d_1) - N(d_2)]\} \tag{2.29}$$

$$p = (F_2 + X)\{e^{-rT}[N(-d_2) - FN(-d_1)]\}, \tag{2.30}$$

where

$$d_1 = \frac{\ln(F) + (\sigma^2/2)T}{\sigma\sqrt{T}}, \quad d_2 = d_1 - \sigma\sqrt{T}$$

$$F = \frac{F_1}{F_2 + X},$$

and the volatility of $\frac{F_1}{F_2 + X}$ can be approximated by

$$\sigma = \sqrt{\sigma_1^2 + \left[\sigma_2 \frac{F_2}{(F_2 + X)}\right]^2 - 2\rho\sigma_1\sigma_2 \frac{F_2}{(F_2 + X)}}$$

where

---

4. For valuation of spread options see also Boyle (1988), Wilcox (1991), Bjerksund and Stensland (1994), Rubinstein (1994b), Shimko (1994), and Pearson (1995).

F_1 = Price on futures contract 1.
F_2 = Price on futures contract 2.
X = Strike price.
T = Time to expiration of the option in years.
r = Risk-free interest rate.
σ_1 = Volatility of futures 1.
σ_2 = Volatility of futures 2.
ρ = Correlation between the two futures contracts.

Table 2–4 illustrates how call spread option values vary with changes in correlation ρ, volatilities σ_1 and σ_2, and time to maturity T.

T A B L E 2–4

Examples of Call Spread Options on Futures Values
($F_1 = 122, F_2 = 120, X = 3, r = 0.10$)

		$T = 0.1$			$T = 0.50$		
σ_1	σ_2	$\rho = -0.5$	$\rho = 0$	$\rho = 0.5$	$\rho = -0.5$	$\rho = 0$	$\rho = 0.5$
0.20	0.20	4.7530	3.7970	2.5537	10.7517	8.7020	6.0257
0.25	0.20	5.4275	4.3712	3.0086	12.1941	9.9340	7.0067
0.20	0.25	5.4061	4.3451	2.9723	12.1483	9.8780	6.9284

Example

Consider a call option with three months to expiry on the spread between two futures contracts. The price of futures contract 1 is 28, the price of futures contract 2 is 20, the strike is 7, the risk-free interest rate is 5% per annum, the volatility of futures 1 is 29% per annum, the volatility of futures 2 is 36%, and the correlation between the instantaneous returns on the two futures is 0.42. $F_1 = 28$, $F_2 = 20$, $X = 7$, $T = 0.25$, $r = 0.05$, $\sigma_1 = 0.29$, $\sigma_2 = 0.36$, $\rho = 0.42$.

$$F = \frac{28}{20+7} = 1.0370$$

$$\sigma = \sqrt{0.29^2 + \left[0.36\frac{20}{(20+7)}\right]^2 - 2 \times 0.42 \times 0.29 \times 0.36 \times \frac{20}{(20+7)}} = 0.3004$$

$$d_1 = \frac{\ln(1.0370) + (0.3004^2/2)0.25}{0.3004\sqrt{0.25}} = 0.3172$$

$$d_2 = d_1 - 0.3004\sqrt{0.25} = 0.1670$$

$$N(d_1) = N(0.3172) = 0.6245, \quad N(d_2) = N(0.1670) = 0.5663$$

$$c = (20+7)\{e^{-0.05 \times 0.25}[1.0370N(d_1) - N(d_2)]\} = 2.1670$$

2.9 LOOKBACK OPTIONS

2.9.1 Floating Strike Lookback Options

A floating strike lookback call gives the holder of the option the right to buy the underlying security at the lowest price observed, S_{min}, in the life of the option. Similarly, a floating strike lookback put gives the option holder the right to sell the underlying security at the highest price observed, S_{max}, in the option's lifetime. The payoff from a standard floating strike lookback call option is

$$c(S, S_{min}, T) = \max(S - S_{min}; 0) = S - S_{min},$$

and for a put it is

$$p(S, S_{max}, T) = \max(S_{max} - S; 0) = S_{max} - S.$$

Floating strike lookback options were originally introduced by Goldman, Sosin, and Gatto (1979).[5]

Floating strike lookback call

$$
\begin{aligned}
c &= Se^{(b-r)T}N(a_1) - S_{min}e^{-rT}N(a_2) \\
&\quad + Se^{-rT}\frac{\sigma^2}{2b}\left[\left(\frac{S}{S_{min}}\right)^{-\frac{2b}{\sigma^2}}N\left(-a_1 + \frac{2b}{\sigma}\sqrt{T}\right) - e^{bT}N(-a_1)\right],
\end{aligned}
\quad (2.31)
$$

where

$$a_1 = \frac{\ln(S/S_{min}) + (b + \sigma^2/2)T}{\sigma\sqrt{T}}$$

$$a_2 = a_1 - \sigma\sqrt{T}$$

---

5. See also Garman (1989).

Floating strike lookback put

$$p = S_{max}e^{-rT}N(-b_2) - Se^{(b-r)T}N(-b_1)$$

$$+ Se^{-rT}\frac{\sigma^2}{2b}\left[-\left(\frac{S}{S_{max}}\right)^{-\frac{2b}{\sigma^2}}N\left(b_1 - \frac{2b}{\sigma}\sqrt{T}\right) + e^{bT}N(b_1)\right], \quad (2.32)$$

where

$$b_1 = \frac{\ln(S/S_{max}) + (b + \sigma^2/2)T}{\sigma\sqrt{T}}$$

$$b_2 = b_1 - \sigma\sqrt{T}.$$

Example
Consider a lookback call option with six months left to expiry. Assume it gives the right to buy the underlying stock index at the lowest price recorded during the life of the option and that the minimum stock index price observed so far is 100, the stock price is 120, the risk-free interest rate is 10%, the dividend yield is 6%, and the volatility is 30%. $S = 120$, $S_{min} = 100$, $T = 0.5$, $r = 0.10$, $b = 0.10 - 0.06 = 0.04$, $\sigma = 0.30$.

$$a_1 = \frac{\ln(120/100) + (0.04 + 0.30^2/2)0.5}{0.30\sqrt{0.5}} = 1.0598$$

$$a_2 = a_1 - 0.30\sqrt{0.5} = 0.8472$$

$$N(a_1) = N(1.0598) = 0.8554, \quad N(-a_1) = N(-1.0598) = 0.1446$$

$$N(a_2) = N(0.8472) = 0.8017, \quad N\left(-a_1 + \frac{2 \times 0.04}{0.30}\sqrt{0.5}\right) = 0.1918$$

$$c = 120e^{(0.04-0.10)0.5}N(a_1) - 100e^{-0.10\times0.5}N(a_2) + 120e^{-0.10\times0.5}\frac{0.30^2}{2 \times 0.04}$$

$$\times \left[\left(\frac{120}{100}\right)^{-\frac{2\times0.04}{0.30^2}}N\left(-a_1 + \frac{2 \times 0.04}{0.30}\sqrt{0.5}\right) - e^{0.04\times0.5}N(-a_1)\right] = 25.3533$$

Application
Floating strike lookback options can be used to construct what is sometimes marketed as a range, or hi–lo, option. A range option guarantees a payout equal to the observed range of the underlying asset, through the life of the option. This is actually just a lookback straddle: a long lookback call plus a long lookback put with the same time to maturity.

2.9.2 Fixed Strike Lookback Options

In a fixed strike lookback call, the strike is fixed in advance, and at expiry the option pays out the maximum of the difference between the highest observed price, S_{max}, in the option lifetime and the strike X, and 0. Similarly, a put at expiry pays out the maximum of the difference between the fixed strike X and the minimum observed price, S_{min}, and 0. Fixed strike lookback options can be priced using the Conze and Viswanathan (1991) formula.

Fixed strike lookback call

$$c = Se^{(b-r)T}N(d_1) - Xe^{-rT}N(d_2)$$

$$+ Se^{-rT}\frac{\sigma^2}{2b}\left[-\left(\frac{S}{X}\right)^{-\frac{2b}{\sigma^2}}N\left(d_1 - \frac{2b}{\sigma}\sqrt{T}\right) + e^{bT}N(d_1)\right], \quad (2.33)$$

where

$$d_1 = \frac{\ln(S/X) + (b + \sigma^2/2)T}{\sigma\sqrt{T}}, \qquad d_2 = d_1 - \sigma\sqrt{T},$$

and when $X \le S_{max}$

$$c = e^{-rT}(S_{max} - X) + Se^{(b-r)T}N(e_1) - S_{max}e^{-rT}N(e_2)$$

$$+ Se^{-rT}\frac{\sigma^2}{2b}\left[-\left(\frac{S}{S_{max}}\right)^{-\frac{2b}{\sigma^2}}N\left(e_1 - \frac{2b}{\sigma}\sqrt{T}\right) + e^{bT}N(e_1)\right],$$

where

$$e_1 = \frac{\ln(S/S_{max}) + (b + \sigma^2/2)T}{\sigma\sqrt{T}}, \qquad e_2 = e_1 - \sigma\sqrt{T}$$

Fixed strike lookback put

$$p = Xe^{-rT}N(-d_2) - Se^{(b-r)T}N(-d_1)$$

$$+ Se^{-rT}\frac{\sigma^2}{2b}\left[\left(\frac{S}{X}\right)^{-\frac{2b}{\sigma^2}}N\left(-d_1 + \frac{2b}{\sigma}\sqrt{T}\right) - e^{bT}N(-d_1)\right], \quad (2.34)$$

and when $X \ge S_{min}$

$$p = e^{-rT}(X - S_{min}) - Se^{(b-r)T}N(-f_1) + S_{min}e^{-rT}N(-f_2)$$

$$+ Se^{-rT}\frac{\sigma^2}{2b}\left[\left(\frac{S}{S_{min}}\right)^{-\frac{2b}{\sigma^2}}N\left(-f_1 + \frac{2b}{\sigma}\sqrt{T}\right) - e^{bT}N(-f_1)\right],$$

where

$$f_1 = \frac{\ln(S/S_{min}) + (b + \sigma^2/2)T}{\sigma\sqrt{T}}, \qquad f_2 = f_1 - \sigma\sqrt{T}.$$

Table 2–5 gives values for fixed strike lookback call and put options, for different values of time to maturity T, strike price X, and volatility σ.

T A B L E 2–5

Fixed Strike Lookback Option Values

$(S = S_{min} = S_{max} = 100, r = 0.10, b = 0.10)$

		Call			Put	
X	$\sigma = 0.10$	$\sigma = 0.20$	$\sigma = 0.30$	$\sigma = 0.10$	$\sigma = 0.20$	$\sigma = 0.30$
95	13.2687	18.9263	24.9857	0.6899	4.4448	8.9213
$T = 0.5$ 100	8.5126	14.1702	20.2296	3.3917	8.3177	13.1579
105	4.3908	9.8905	15.8512	8.1478	13.0739	17.9140
95	18.3241	26.0731	34.7116	1.0534	6.2813	12.2376
$T = 1$ 100	13.8000	21.5489	30.1874	3.8079	10.1294	16.3889
105	9.5445	17.2965	25.9002	8.3321	14.6536	20.9130

2.9.3 Partial-Time Floating Strike Lookback Options

In the partial-time floating strike lookback options, the lookback period is at the beginning of the option's lifetime. Time to expiry is T_2, and time to the end of the lookback period is t_1 $(t_1 \leq T_2)$. Except for the partial lookback period, the partial-time floating strike lookback option is similar to a standard floating strike lookback option. However, a partial lookback option must naturally be cheaper than a similar standard floating strike lookback option. Heynen and Kat (1994c) have developed formulas for pricing partial-time floating strike lookback options.

Partial-time floating strike lookback call

$$
\begin{aligned}
c = {} & Se^{(b-r)T_2}N(d_1 - g_1) - \lambda S_{min}e^{-rT_2}N(d_2 - g_1) \\
& + \lambda Se^{-rT_2}\frac{\sigma^2}{2b}\left[\left(\frac{S}{S_{min}}\right)^{-\frac{2b}{\sigma^2}} M\left(-f_1 + \frac{2b\sqrt{t_1}}{\sigma},\right.\right. \\
& \left.\left. -d_1 + \frac{2b\sqrt{T_2}}{\sigma} - g_1; \sqrt{t_1/T_2}\right)\right. \\
& \left. - e^{bT_2}\lambda^{\frac{2b}{\sigma^2}}M(-d_1 - g_1, e_1 + g_2; -\sqrt{1 - t_1/T_2})\right]
\end{aligned}
$$

$$+Se^{(b-r)T_2}M(-d_1+g_1,e_1-g_2; -\sqrt{1-t_1/T_2})$$

$$+\lambda S_{min}e^{-rT_2}M(-f_2,d_2-g_1; -\sqrt{t_1/T_2})$$

$$-e^{-b(T_2-t_1)}\left(1+\frac{\sigma^2}{2b}\right)\lambda Se^{(b-r)T_2}N(e_2-g_2)N(-f_1) \qquad (2.35)$$

The λ factor enables the creation of so-called "fractional" lookback options where the strike is fixed at some percentage above or below the actual extremum, $\lambda \geq 1$ for calls and $0 < \lambda \leq 1$ for puts.

$$d_1 = \frac{\ln(S/M_0)+(b+\sigma^2/2)T_2}{\sigma\sqrt{T_2}}, \qquad d_2 = d_1 - \sigma\sqrt{T_2}$$

$$e_1 = \frac{(b+\sigma^2/2)(T_2-t_1)}{\sigma\sqrt{T_2-t_1}}, \qquad e_2 = e_1 - \sigma\sqrt{T_2-t_1}$$

$$f_1 = \frac{\ln(S/M_0)+(b+\sigma^2/2)t_1}{\sigma\sqrt{t_1}}, \qquad f_2 = f_1 - \sigma\sqrt{t_1}$$

$$g_1 = \frac{\ln(\lambda)}{\sigma\sqrt{T_2}}, \qquad g_2 = \frac{\ln(\lambda)}{\sigma\sqrt{T_2-t_1}}$$

where

$$M_0 = \begin{cases} S_{min} & \text{if call,} \\ S_{max} & \text{if put} \end{cases}$$

Partial-time floating strike lookback put

$$p = \lambda S_{max}e^{-rT_2}N(-d_2+g_1) - Se^{(b-r)T_2}N(-d_1+g_1)$$

$$+ \lambda Se^{-rT_2}\frac{\sigma^2}{2b}\left[-\left(\frac{S}{S_{max}}\right)^{-\frac{2b}{\sigma^2}}M\left(f_1-\frac{2b\sqrt{t_1}}{\sigma},\right.\right.$$

$$d_1 - \frac{2b\sqrt{T_2}}{\sigma}+g_1; \sqrt{t_1/T_2}\bigg)$$

$$+ e^{bT_2}\lambda^{\frac{2b}{\sigma^2}}M(d_1+g_1,-e_1-g_2; -\sqrt{1-t_1/T_2})\bigg]$$

$$- Se^{(b-r)T_2}M(d_1-g_1,-e_1+g_2; -\sqrt{1-t_1/T_2})$$

$$- \lambda S_{max}e^{-rT_2}M(f_2,-d_2+g_1; -\sqrt{t_1/T_2})$$

$$+ e^{-b(T_2-t_1)}\left(1+\frac{\sigma^2}{2b}\right)\lambda Se^{(b-r)T_2}N(-e_2+g_2)N(f_1) \qquad (2.36)$$

Table 2–6 shows values for partial-time floating strike lookback call and put options. Different input parameters are used for the volatility σ, the asset price S, and the time to the end of the lookback period t_1.

TABLE 2–6

Partial-Time Floating Strike Lookback Option Values

$(T_2 = 1, r = 0.06, b = 0.06, \lambda = 1)$

	$S = S_{min} = S_{max} = 90$			$S = S_{min} = S_{max} = 110$		
	$t_1 = 0.25$	$t_1 = 0.5$	$t_1 = 0.75$	$t_1 = 0.25$	$t_1 = 0.5$	$t_1 = 0.75$
call $\sigma = 0.10$	8.6524	9.2128	9.5567	10.5751	11.2601	11.6804
call $\sigma = 0.20$	13.3402	14.5121	15.3140	16.3047	17.7370	18.7171
call $\sigma = 0.30$	17.9831	19.6618	20.8493	21.9793	24.0311	25.4825
put $\sigma = 0.10$	2.7189	3.4639	4.1912	3.3231	4.2336	5.1226
put $\sigma = 0.20$	7.9153	9.5825	11.0362	9.6743	11.7119	13.4887
put $\sigma = 0.30$	13.4719	16.1495	18.4071	16.4657	19.7383	22.4976

2.9.4 Partial-Time Fixed Strike Lookback Options

In the partial-time fixed strike lookback option described here, the lookback period starts at a predetermined date t_1 after the initialization date of the option. The partial-time fixed strike lookback call gives a payoff equal to maximum of the highest observed price of the underlying asset, S_{max}, in the lookback period minus the strike price X, and 0. The put gives a payoff equal to the maximum of the fixed strike price X minus the minimum observed asset price, S_{min}, in the lookback period $(T_2 - t_1)$, and 0. The partial-time fixed strike lookback option is naturally cheaper than a similar standard fixed strike lookback option. Heynen and Kat (1994c) have published closed-form solutions for these types of options.

Partial-time fixed strike lookback call

$$
\begin{aligned}
c = {} & Se^{(b-r)T_2}N(d_1) - Xe^{-rT_2}N(d_2) \\
& + Se^{-rT_2}\frac{\sigma^2}{2b}\left[-\left(\frac{S}{X}\right)^{-\frac{2b}{\sigma^2}} M \right. \\
& \times (d_1 - \frac{2b\sqrt{T_2}}{\sigma}, -f_1 + \frac{2b\sqrt{t_1}}{\sigma}; -\sqrt{t_1/T_2}) \\
& \left. + e^{bT_2}M(e_1, d_1; \sqrt{1 - t_1/T_2})\right]
\end{aligned}
$$

$$-Se^{(b-r)T_2}M(-e_1,d_1; -\sqrt{1-t_1/T_2})$$
$$-Xe^{-rT_2}M(f_2,-d_2; -\sqrt{t_1/T_2})$$
$$+e^{-b(T_2-t_1)}(1-\frac{\sigma^2}{2b})Se^{(b-r)T_2}N(f_1)N(-e_2), \qquad (2.37)$$

where d_1, e_1, f_1 are defined under the floating strike lookback options.

Partial-time fixed strike lookback put

$$p = Xe^{-rT_2}N(-d_2) - Se^{(b-r)T_2}N(-d_1) + Se^{-rT_2}\frac{\sigma^2}{2b}$$

$$\times \left[\left(\frac{S}{X}\right)^{-\frac{2b}{\sigma^2}} M(-d_1+\frac{2b\sqrt{T_2}}{\sigma}, f_1-\frac{2b\sqrt{t_1}}{\sigma}; -\sqrt{t_1/T_2}) \right.$$

$$\left. - e^{bT_2}M(-e_1,-d_1; \sqrt{1-t_1/T_2}) \right]$$

$$+ Se^{(b-r)T_2}M(e_1,-d_1; -\sqrt{1-t_1/T_2})$$

$$+ Xe^{-rT_2}M(-f_2,d_2; -\sqrt{t_1/T_2})$$

$$- e^{-b(T_2-t_1)}(1-\frac{\sigma^2}{2b})Se^{(b-r)T_2}N(-f_1)N(e_2) \qquad (2.38)$$

Table 2–7 shows examples of partial-time fixed strike lookback call and put option values. The input parameters are varied as in Table 2–6.

T A B L E   2–7

Partial-Time Fixed Strike Lookback Option Values

($S=100$, $T_2=1$, $r=0.06$, $b=0.06$)

	X = 90			X = 110		
	$t_1=0.25$	$t_1=0.5$	$t_1=0.75$	$t_1=0.25$	$t_1=0.5$	$t_1=0.75$
call $\sigma=0.10$	20.2845	19.6239	18.6244	4.0432	3.9580	3.7015
call $\sigma=0.20$	27.5385	25.8126	23.4957	11.4895	10.8995	9.8244
call $\sigma=0.30$	35.4578	32.7172	29.1473	19.7250	18.4025	16.2976
put $\sigma=0.10$	0.4973	0.4632	0.3863	12.6978	10.9492	9.1555
put $\sigma=0.20$	4.5863	4.1925	3.5831	19.0255	16.9433	14.6505
put $\sigma=0.30$	9.9348	9.1111	7.9267	25.2112	22.8217	20.0566

2.9.5   Extreme Spread Options

The time to maturity of an extreme spread option is divided into two periods: one period starting today and ending at time t_1, and another period starting at t_1 and ending at the maturity of the option T_2. A payoff at maturity of an extreme spread call (put) option equals the positive part of the difference between the maximum (minimum) value of the underlying asset, S_{max}, of the second (first) period and the maximum (minimum) value of the underlying asset of the first (second) period. Likewise, the payoff at maturity of a reverse extreme spread call (put) equals the positive part of the difference between the minimum (maximum) of the underlying asset, S_{min}, of the second (first) period and the minimum (maximum) value of the underlying asset of the second (first) period. Formulas for valuation of these types of options were introduced by Bermin (1996b).

Extreme spread option values

$$
\begin{aligned}
w = {} & \eta \left[S e^{(b-r)T_2} \left(1 + \frac{\sigma^2}{2b} \right) N_\eta \left(\frac{-m + \mu_2 T_2}{\sigma \sqrt{T_2}} \right) - e^{-b(T_2 - t_1)} S e^{(b-r)T_2} \right. \\
& \times \left(1 + \frac{\sigma^2}{2b} \right) N_\eta \left(\frac{-m + \mu_2 t_1}{\sigma \sqrt{t_1}} \right) + e^{-rT_2} M_0 N_\eta \left(\frac{m - \mu_1 T_2}{\sigma \sqrt{T_2}} \right) \\
& - e^{-rT_2} M_0 \frac{\sigma^2}{2b} e^{\frac{2\mu m}{\sigma^2}} N_\eta \left(\frac{-m - \mu_1 T_2}{\sigma \sqrt{T_2}} \right) - e^{-rT_2} M_0 N_\eta \left(\frac{m - \mu_1 t_1}{\sigma \sqrt{t_1}} \right) \\
& \left. + e^{-rT_2} M_0 \frac{\sigma^2}{2b} e^{\frac{2\mu m}{\sigma^2}} N_\eta \left(\frac{-m - \mu_1 t_1}{\sigma \sqrt{t_1}} \right) \right],
\end{aligned}
\tag{2.39}
$$

where $N_\eta(x) = N(\eta x)$, and

$$
m = \ln(M_0/S), \qquad \mu_1 = b - \sigma^2/2, \qquad \mu_2 = b + \sigma^2/2
$$

$$
\eta = \begin{cases} 1 & \text{if call} \\ -1 & \text{if put} \end{cases}, \qquad
\phi = \begin{cases} 1 & \text{if extreme spread} \\ -1 & \text{if reverse extreme spread} \end{cases}
$$

$$
M_0 = \begin{cases} S_{max} & \text{if} \quad \phi\eta = 1 \\ S_{min} & \text{if} \quad \phi\eta = -1 \end{cases},
$$

where S_{min} is the observed minimum, and S_{max} is the observed maximum.

Reverse extreme spread option values

$$
\begin{aligned}
w = {} & -\eta \left[S e^{(b-r)T_2} \left(1 + \frac{\sigma^2}{2b} \right) N_\eta \left(\frac{m - \mu_2 T_2}{\sigma \sqrt{T_2}} \right) \right. \\
& + e^{-rT_2} M_0 N_\eta \left(\frac{-m + \mu_1 T_2}{\sigma \sqrt{T_2}} \right) \\
& - e^{-rT_2} M_0 \frac{\sigma^2}{2b} e^{\frac{2\mu m}{\sigma^2}} N_\eta \left(\frac{m + \mu_1 T_2}{\sigma \sqrt{T_2}} \right)
\end{aligned}
$$

$$-Se^{(b-r)T_2}\left(1+\frac{\sigma^2}{2b}\right)N_\eta\left(\frac{-\mu_2(T_2-t_1)}{\sigma\sqrt{T_2-t_1}}\right)$$

$$-e^{-b(T_2-t_1)}Se^{(b-r)T_2}\left(1-\frac{\sigma^2}{2b}\right)N_\eta\left(\frac{\mu_1(T_2-t_1)}{\sigma\sqrt{T_2-t_1}}\right)\Bigg] \quad (2.40)$$

Table 2–8 shows values for extreme and reverse extreme call options for a range of input parameter values.

T A B L E 2–8

Extreme and Reverse Extreme Call Option Values

$(S = 100, T_2 = 1, r = b = 0.10)$

		Intitial time period t_1			
		0.00	0.25	0.5	0.75
	S_{max}	Extreme Spread Values			
	100	17.5212	10.6618	6.7967	3.3218
$\sigma = 0.15$	110	9.6924	8.4878	5.8519	2.9676
	120	4.6135	4.5235	3.6613	2.0566
	100	30.1874	17.4998	10.9444	5.2735
$\sigma = 0.30$	110	22.0828	16.3674	10.4668	5.0942
	120	15.7847	13.5892	9.2051	4.6071
	S_{min}	Reverse Extreme Spread Values			
	100	0.0000	2.7046	5.7250	9.3347
$\sigma = 0.15$	90	3.6267	6.3314	9.3517	12.9615
	80	11.3474	14.0521	17.0724	20.6821
	100	0.0000	3.6120	7.8702	13.3404
$\sigma = 0.30$	90	1.4769	5.0890	9.3471	14.8173
	80	5.7133	9.3253	13.5835	19.0537

2.10 BARRIER OPTIONS

Barrier options on stocks are known to have been traded in the OTC market since 1967. Barrier options have become extremely popular and are certainly the most popular class of exotic options. The Chicago Board Option Exchange and the American Option Exchange now have lists of up-and-out call options and down-and-out put options on stock indexes. Several barrier options are traded actively in the OTC market: currency, interest-rate, and commodity options.

2.10.1 Standard Barrier Options

Merton (1973) and Reiner and Rubinstein (1991a)[6] have developed formulas for pricing standard barrier options:

$$A = \phi S e^{(b-r)T} N(\phi x_1) - \phi X e^{-rT} N(\phi x_1 - \phi \sigma \sqrt{T})$$

$$B = \phi S e^{(b-r)T} N(\phi x_2) - \phi X e^{-rT} N(\phi x_2 - \phi \sigma \sqrt{T})$$

$$C = \phi S e^{(b-r)T} (H/S)^{2(\mu+1)} N(\eta y_1) - \phi X e^{-rT} (H/S)^{2\mu} N(\eta y_1 - \eta \sigma \sqrt{T})$$

$$D = \phi S e^{(b-r)T} (H/S)^{2(\mu+1)} N(\eta y_2) - \phi X e^{-rT} (H/S)^{2\mu} N(\eta y_2 - \eta \sigma \sqrt{T})$$

$$E = K e^{-rT} [N(\eta x_2 - \eta \sigma \sqrt{T}) - (H/S)^{2\mu} N(\eta y_2 - \eta \sigma \sqrt{T})]$$

$$F = K[(H/S)^{\mu+\lambda} N(\eta z) + (H/S)^{\mu-\lambda} N(\eta z - 2\eta \lambda \sigma \sqrt{T})],$$

where

$$x_1 = \frac{\ln(S/X)}{\sigma \sqrt{T}} + (1+\mu)\sigma \sqrt{T}, \qquad x_2 = \frac{\ln(S/H)}{\sigma \sqrt{T}} + (1+\mu)\sigma \sqrt{T}$$

$$y_1 = \frac{\ln(H^2/SX)}{\sigma \sqrt{T}} + (1+\mu)\sigma \sqrt{T}, \qquad y_2 = \frac{\ln(H/S)}{\sigma \sqrt{T}} + (1+\mu)\sigma \sqrt{T}$$

$$z = \frac{\ln(H/S)}{\sigma \sqrt{T}} + \lambda \sigma \sqrt{T}, \qquad \mu = \frac{b - \sigma^2/2}{\sigma^2}, \qquad \lambda = \sqrt{\mu^2 + \frac{2r}{\sigma^2}}.$$

"In" Barriers

In options are paid for today but first come into existence if the asset price S hits the barrier H before expiration. It is possible to include a prespecified cash rebate K, which is paid out at option expiration if the option has not been knocked in during its lifetime.

Down-and-in call $S > H$

Payoff: $\max(S - X; 0)$ if $S \leq H$ before T else R at expiry.

$$c_{di(X>H)} = C + E \qquad\qquad \eta = 1,\ \phi = 1$$
$$c_{di(X<H)} = A - B + D + E \qquad\qquad \eta = 1,\ \phi = 1$$

---

6. See also Rich (1994).

Up-and-in call $S < H$
Payoff: $\max(S - X; 0)$ if $S \geq H$ before T else R at expiry.

$c_{ui(X>H)} = A + E$ $\qquad\qquad$ $\eta = -1, \phi = 1$

$c_{ui(X<H)} = B - C + D + E$ $\qquad\qquad$ $\eta = -1, \phi = 1$

Down-and-in put $S > H$
Payoff: $\max(X - S; 0)$ if $S \leq H$ before T else R at expiry.

$p_{di(X>H)} = B - C + D + E$ $\qquad\qquad$ $\eta = 1, \phi = -1$

$p_{di(X<H)} = A + E$ $\qquad\qquad$ $\eta = 1, \phi = -1$

Up-and-in put $S < H$
Payoff: $\max(X - S; 0)$ if $S \geq H$ before T else R at expiry.

$p_{ui(X>H)} = A - B + D + E$ $\qquad\qquad$ $\eta = -1, \phi = -1$

$p_{ui(X<H)} = C + E$ $\qquad\qquad$ $\eta = -1, \phi = -1$

"Out" Barriers

Out options are similar to standard options except that the option is knocked out or becomes worthless if the asset price S hits the barrier before expiration. It is possible to include a prespecified cash rebate K, which is paid out if the option is knocked out before expiration.

Down-and-out call $S > H$
Payoff: $\max(S - X; 0)$ if $S > H$ before T else R at hit

$c_{do(X>H)} = A - C + F$ $\qquad\qquad$ $\eta = 1, \phi = 1$

$c_{do(X<H)} = B - D + F$ $\qquad\qquad$ $\eta = 1, \phi = 1$

Up-and-out call $S < H$
Payoff: $\max(S - X; 0)$ if $S < H$ before T else R at hit

$c_{uo(X>H)} = F$ $\qquad\qquad$ $\eta = -1, \phi = 1$

$c_{uo(X<H)} = A - B + C - D + F$ $\qquad\qquad$ $\eta = -1, \phi = 1$

Down-and-out put $S > H$
Payoff: $\max(X - S; 0)$ if $S > H$ before T else R at hit

$p_{do(X>H)} = A - B + C - D + F$ $\qquad\qquad$ $\eta = 1, \phi = -1$

$p_{do(X<H)} = F$ $\qquad\qquad$ $\eta = 1, \phi = -1$

Up-and-out put $S < H$
Payoff: $\max(X - S; 0)$ if $S < H$ before T else R

$p_{uo(X>H)} = B - D + F$ $\qquad\qquad$ $\eta = -1, \phi = -1$

$p_{uo(X<H)} = A - C + F$ $\qquad\qquad$ $\eta = -1, \phi = -1$

Table 2–9 shows values for standard barrier options. Values are tabulated with different values for the strike price X, barrier H, and volatility σ.

TABLE 2-9

Value of Standard Barrier Options

$(S = 100, K = 3, T = 0.5, r = 0.08, b = 0.04)$

Type	X	H	$\sigma = 0.25$	$\sigma = 0.30$	Type	X	H	$\sigma = 0.25$	$\sigma = 0.30$
c_{do}	90	95	9.0246	8.8334	p_{do}	90	95	2.2798	2.4170
c_{do}	100	95	6.7924	7.0285	p_{do}	100	95	2.2947	2.4258
c_{do}	110	95	4.8759	5.4137	p_{do}	110	95	2.6252	2.6246
c_{do}	90	100	3.0000	3.0000	p_{do}	90	100	3.0000	3.0000
c_{do}	100	100	3.0000	3.0000	p_{do}	100	100	3.0000	3.0000
c_{do}	110	100	3.0000	3.0000	p_{do}	110	100	3.0000	3.0000
c_{uo}	90	105	2.6789	2.6341	p_{uo}	90	105	3.7760	4.2293
c_{uo}	100	105	2.3580	2.4389	p_{uo}	100	105	5.4932	5.8032
c_{uo}	110	105	2.3453	2.4315	p_{uo}	110	105	7.5187	7.5649
c_{di}	90	95	7.7627	9.0093	p_{di}	90	95	2.9586	3.8769
c_{di}	100	95	4.0109	5.1370	p_{di}	100	95	6.5677	7.7989
c_{di}	110	95	2.0576	2.8517	p_{di}	110	95	11.9752	13.3078
c_{di}	90	100	13.8333	14.8816	p_{di}	90	100	2.2845	3.3328
c_{di}	100	100	7.8494	9.2045	p_{di}	100	100	5.9085	7.2636
c_{di}	110	100	3.9795	5.3043	p_{di}	110	100	11.6465	12.9713
c_{ui}	90	105	14.1112	15.2098	p_{ui}	90	105	1.4653	2.0658
c_{ui}	100	105	8.4482	9.7278	p_{ui}	100	105	3.3721	4.4226
c_{ui}	110	105	4.5910	5.8350	p_{ui}	110	105	7.0846	8.3686

2.10.2   Double Barrier Options

A double barrier option is knocked in or out if the underlying price touches a lower boundary L or upper boundary U prior to expiration. The formulas below pertain only to double knock-out options. The price of a double knock-in call is equal to the portfolio of a long standard call and a short double knock-out call, with the same strike and time to expiration. Similarly, a double knock-in put is equal to a long standard put and a short double knock-out put. Double barrier options can be priced using the Ikeda and Kunitomo (1992) formula.[7]

Call-up-and-out-down-and-out

Payoff: $c(S, U, L, T) = \max(S - X; 0)$ if $L < S < U$ before T else 0.

---

7. For the valuation of double barrier options, see also Bhagavatula and Carr (1995) and Geman and Yor (1996).

$$
\begin{aligned}
c \;=\; & Se^{(b-r)T} \sum_{n=-\infty}^{\infty} \left\{ \left(\frac{U^n}{L^n}\right)^{\mu_1} \left(\frac{L}{S}\right)^{\mu_2} [N(d_1) - N(d_2)] \right. \\
& \left. - \left(\frac{L^{n+1}}{U^n S}\right)^{\mu_3} [N(d_3) - N(d_4)] \right\} \\
& - X e^{-rT} \sum_{n=-\infty}^{\infty} \left\{ \left(\frac{U^n}{L^n}\right)^{\mu_1-2} \left(\frac{L}{S}\right)^{\mu_2} \right. \\
& \times [N(d_1 - \sigma\sqrt{T}) - N(d_2 - \sigma\sqrt{T})] \\
& \left. - \left(\frac{L^{n+1}}{U^n S}\right)^{\mu_3-2} [N(d_3 - \sigma\sqrt{T}) - N(d_4 - \sigma\sqrt{T})] \right\},
\end{aligned}
\qquad (2.41)
$$

where

$$
d_1 = \frac{\ln(SU^{2n}/XL^{2n}) + (b+\sigma^2/2)T}{\sigma\sqrt{T}}
$$

$$
d_2 = \frac{\ln(SU^{2n}/FL^{2n}) + (b+\sigma^2/2)T}{\sigma\sqrt{T}}
$$

$$
d_3 = \frac{\ln(L^{2n+2}/XSU^{2n}) + (b+\sigma^2/2)T}{\sigma\sqrt{T}}
$$

$$
d_4 = \frac{\ln(L^{2n+2}/FSU^{2n}) + (b+\sigma^2/2)T}{\sigma\sqrt{T}}
$$

$$
\mu_1 = \frac{2[b - \delta_2 - n(\delta_1 - \delta_2)]}{\sigma^2} + 1, \quad \mu_2 = 2n\frac{(\delta_1 - \delta_2)}{\sigma^2}
$$

$$
\mu_3 = \frac{2[b - \delta_2 + n(\delta_1 - \delta_2)]}{\sigma^2} + 1, \quad F = U e^{\delta_1 T},
$$

where δ_1 and δ_2 determine the curvature of the lower L and upper U absorbing boundaries. The case of

1. $\delta_1 = \delta_2 = 0$ corresponds to two flat boundaries.
2. $\delta_1 < 0 < \delta_2$ corresponds to a lower boundary exponentially growing as time elapses, while the upper boundary will be exponentially decaying.
3. $\delta_1 > 0 > \delta_2$ corresponds to a convex downward lower boundary and a convex upward upper boundary.

Put-up-and-out-down-and-out
Payoff: $p(S,U,L,T) = \max(X - S; 0)$ if $L < S < U$ before T else 0.

$$
\begin{aligned}
p \;=\; & +Xe^{-rT} \sum_{n=-\infty}^{\infty} \left\{ \left(\frac{U^n}{L^n}\right)^{\mu_1-2} \left(\frac{L}{S}\right)^{\mu_2} \right. \\
& \times \left[N(y_1 - \sigma\sqrt{T}) - N(y_2 - \sigma\sqrt{T})\right] \\
& \left. - \left(\frac{L^{n+1}}{U^n S}\right)^{\mu_3-2} \left[N(y_3 - \sigma\sqrt{T}) - N(y_4 - \sigma\sqrt{T})\right] \right\} \\
& - Se^{(b-r)T} \sum_{n=-\infty}^{\infty} \left\{ \left(\frac{U^n}{L^n}\right)^{\mu_1} \left(\frac{L}{S}\right)^{\mu_2} [N(y_1) - N(y_2)] \right. \\
& \left. - \left(\frac{L^{n+1}}{U^n S}\right)^{\mu_3} [N(y_3) - N(y_4)] \right\},
\end{aligned}
\tag{2.42}
$$

where

$$
y_1 = \frac{\ln(SU^{2n}/EL^{2n}) + (b + \sigma^2/2)T}{\sigma\sqrt{T}}
$$

$$
y_2 = \frac{\ln(SU^{2n}/XL^{2n}) + (b + \sigma^2/2)T}{\sigma\sqrt{T}}
$$

$$
y_3 = \frac{\ln(L^{2n+2}/ESU^{2n}) + (b + \sigma^2/2)T}{\sigma\sqrt{T}}
$$

$$
y_4 = \frac{\ln(L^{2n+2}/XSU^{2n}) + (b + \sigma^2/2)T}{\sigma\sqrt{T}}
$$

$$
E = Le^{\delta_2 T}
$$

The double barrier options are expressed as infinite series of weighted normal distribution functions. However, numerical studies show that the convergence of the formula is quite rapid. The numerical studies done by Ikeda and Kunitomo (1992) suggest that it suffices to calculate the leading two or three terms in most cases.

Table 2–10 gives examples of call-up-and-out-down-and-out option values for different choices of lower L and upper U barrier, barrier curvatures δ_1 and δ_1, volatility σ, and time to maturity T.

Computer algorithm
The *DoubleBarrier*(·) function can be used to value four types of double barrier options.

T A B L E 2–10

Examples of Call-Up-and-Out-Down-and-Out Values

$(S = 100, X = 100, r = 0.10, b = 0.10)$

| | | | | T = 0.25 | | | T = 0.50 | | |
L	U	δ_1	δ_2	$\sigma = 0.15$	$\sigma = 0.25$	$\sigma = 0.35$	$\sigma = 0.15$	$\sigma = 0.25$	$\sigma = 0.35$
50	150	0	0	4.3515	6.1644	7.0373	6.9853	7.9336	6.5088
60	140	0	0	4.3505	5.8500	5.7726	6.8082	6.3383	4.3841
70	130	0	0	4.3139	4.8293	3.7765	5.9697	4.0004	2.2563
80	120	0	0	3.7516	2.6387	1.4903	3.5805	1.5098	0.5635
90	110	0	0	1.2055	0.3098	0.0477	0.5537	0.0441	0.0011
50	150	−0.1	0.1	4.3514	6.0997	6.6987	6.8974	6.9821	5.2107
60	140	−0.1	0.1	4.3478	5.6351	5.2463	6.4094	5.0199	3.1503
70	130	−0.1	0.1	4.2558	4.3291	3.1540	4.8182	2.6259	1.3424
80	120	−0.1	0.1	3.2953	1.9868	1.0351	1.9245	0.6455	0.1817
90	110	−0.1	0.1	0.5887	0.1016	0.0085	0.0398	0.0002	0.0000
50	150	0.1	−0.1	4.3515	6.2040	7.3151	7.0086	8.6080	7.7218
60	140	0.1	−0.1	4.3512	5.9998	6.2395	6.9572	7.4267	5.6620
70	130	0.1	−0.1	4.3382	5.2358	4.3859	6.6058	5.3761	3.3446
80	120	0.1	−0.1	4.0428	3.2872	2.0048	5.0718	2.6591	1.1871
90	110	0.1	−0.1	1.9229	0.6451	0.1441	1.7079	0.3038	0.0255

1. *TypeFlag* set equal to "*co*" gives the value of an up-and-out-down-and-out call.

2. *TypeFlag* set equal to "*ci*" gives the value of an up-and-in-down-and-in call.

3. *TypeFlag* set equal to "*po*" gives the value of an up-and-out-down-and-out put.

4. *TypeFlag* set equal to "*pi*" gives the value of an up-and-in-down-and-in put.

```
Function DoubleBarrier(TypeFlag As String, S As Double, X As Double, _
        L As Double, U As Double, T As Double, r As Double, b As Double, _
        v As Double, delta1 As Double, delta2 As Double) As Double

    Dim E As Double, F As Double
    Dim Sum1 As Double, Sum2 As Double
    Dim d1 As Double, d2 As Double
    Dim d3 As Double, d4 As Double
    Dim mu1 As Double, mu2 As Double, mu3 As Double
    Dim OutValue As Double, n As Integer

    F = U * Exp(delta1 * T)
    E = L * Exp(delta2 * T)
    Sum1 = 0
    Sum2 = 0
    If TypeFlag = "co" Or TypeFlag = "ci" Then
        For n = -5 To 5
            d1 = (Log(S * U^(2 * n) / (X * L^(2 * n))) + (b + v^2/2) * T) / (v * Sqr(T))
            d2 = (Log(S * U^(2 * n) / (F * L^(2 * n))) + (b + v^2/2) * T) / (v * Sqr(T))
            d3 = (Log(L^(2 * n + 2) / (X * S * U^(2 * n))) + (b + v^2/2) * T) / (v * Sqr(T))
            d4 = (Log(L^(2 * n + 2) / (F * S * U^(2 * n))) + (b + v^2/2) * T) / (v * Sqr(T))
            mu1 = 2 * (b - delta2 - n * (delta1 - delta2)) / v^2 + 1
            mu2 = 2 * n * (delta1 - delta2) / v^2
```

$mu3 = 2*(b - delta2 + n*(delta1 - delta2))/v\hat{\ }2 + 1$
$Sum1 = Sum1 + (U\hat{\ }n/L\hat{\ }n)\hat{\ }mu1*(L/S)\hat{\ }mu2*$
$(CND(d1) - CND(d2)) -$ _
$(L\hat{\ }(n+1)/(U\hat{\ }n*S))\hat{\ }mu3*(CND(d3) - CND(d4))$
$Sum2 = Sum2 + (U\hat{\ }n/L\hat{\ }n)\hat{\ }(mu1 - 2)*(L/S)\hat{\ }(CND(d1 - v*Sqr(T)) -$ _
$CND(d2 - v*Sqr(T))) - (L\hat{\ }(n+1)/(U\hat{\ }n*S))\hat{\ }(mu3 - 2)*$ _
$(CND(d3 - v*Sqr(T)) - CND(d4 - v*Sqr(T)))$

    Next

$OutValue = S*Exp((b - r)*T)*Sum1 - X*Exp(-r*T)*Sum2$

ElseIf *TypeFlag* = "po" Or *TypeFlag* = "pi" Then

    For $n = -5$ To 5

$d1 = (Log(S*U\hat{\ }(2*n)/(E*L\hat{\ }(2*n))) + (b + v\hat{\ }2/2)*T)/(v*Sqr(T))$
$d2 = (Log(S*U\hat{\ }(2*n)/(X*L\hat{\ }(2*n))) + (b + v\hat{\ }2/2)*T)/(v*Sqr(T))$
$d3 = (Log(L\hat{\ }(2*n+2)/(E*S*U\hat{\ }(2*n))) + (b + v\hat{\ }2/2)*T)/(v*Sqr(T))$
$d4 = (Log(L\hat{\ }(2*n+2)/(X*S*U\hat{\ }(2*n))) + (b + v\hat{\ }2/2)*T)/(v*Sqr(T))$
$mu1 = 2*(b - delta2 - n*(delta1 - delta2))/v\hat{\ }2 + 1$
$mu2 = 2*n*(delta1 - delta2)/v\hat{\ }2$
$mu3 = 2*(b - delta2 + n*(delta1 - delta2))/v\hat{\ }2 + 1$
$Sum1 = Sum1 + (U\hat{\ }n/L\hat{\ }n)\hat{\ }mu1*(L/S)\hat{\ }mu2*(CND(d1) - CND(d2)) -$ _
$(L\hat{\ }(n+1)/(U\hat{\ }n*S))\hat{\ }mu3*(CND(d3) - CND(d4))$
$Sum2 = Sum2 + (U\hat{\ }n/L\hat{\ }n)\hat{\ }(mu1 - 2)*(L/S)\hat{\ }mu2*$ _
$(CND(d1 - v*Sqr(T)) - CND(d2 - v*Sqr(T))) - (L\hat{\ }(n+1)/$ _
$(U\hat{\ }n*S))\hat{\ }(mu3 - 2)*(CND(d3 - v*Sqr(T)) - CND(d4 - v*Sqr(T)))$

    Next

$OutValue = X*Exp(-r*T)*Sum2 - S*Exp((b - r)*T)*Sum1$

End If

If *TypeFlag* = "co" Or *TypeFlag* = "po" Then

    DoubleBarrier = *OutValue*

ElseIf *TypeFlag* = "ci" Then

    DoubleBarrier = *GBlackScholes*("c", S, X, T, r, b, v) - *OutValue*

ElseIf *TypeFlag* = "pi" Then

    DoubleBarrier = *GBlackScholes*("p", S, X, T, r, b, v) - *OutValue*

End If

End Function

The computer code calculates the value of a double-out barrier option. If the option is a double-in option, the computer code uses the barrier parity. An up-and-in-down-and-in call can, for instance, be constructed by going long a standard call option and going short an up-and-out-down-and-out call. The *GBlackScholes*($\cdot$) function at the end of the *DoubleBarrier*($\cdot$) function calls the generalized Black–Scholes function from Chapter 1.

2.10.3 Partial-Time Single-Asset Barrier Options

In single asset partial-time-barrier options, the period during which the underlying price is monitored for hits of the barrier is restricted to only a fraction of the option's lifetime. Partial-time-start-barrier options, which we call type A options, will have the location of the monitoring period starting at the option's starting date and ending at an arbitrary date t_1 before expiration. Partial-time-end-barrier options will have the location of the monitoring period starting at an arbitrary date t_1 before expiration, and ending at expiration T_2. Formulas for pricing this type of options were originally published by Heynen and Kat (1994b).

Partial-time-start-out-options

$$c_A = Se^{(b-r)T_2}\left[M(d_1,\eta e_1; \eta\rho) - \left(\frac{H}{S}\right)^{2(\mu+1)} M(f_1,\eta e_3; \eta\rho)\right]$$

$$- Xe^{-rT_2}\left[M(d_2,\eta e_2; \eta\rho) - \left(\frac{H}{S}\right)^{2\mu} M(f_2,\eta e_4; \eta\rho)\right], \quad (2.43)$$

where $\eta = -1$ for an up-and-out call (c_{uoA}) and $\eta = 1$ for a down-and-out call (c_{doA}), and

$$d_1 = \frac{\ln(S/X) + (b+\sigma^2/2)T_2}{\sigma\sqrt{T_2}}, \quad d_2 = d_1 - \sigma\sqrt{T_2}$$

$$f_1 = \frac{\ln(S/X) + 2\ln(H/S) + (b+\sigma^2/2)T_2}{\sigma\sqrt{T_2}}, \quad f_2 = f_1 - \sigma\sqrt{T_2}$$

$$e_1 = \frac{\ln(S/H) + (b+\sigma^2/2)t_1}{\sigma\sqrt{t_1}}, \quad e_2 = e_1 - \sigma\sqrt{t_1}$$

$$e_3 = e_1 + \frac{2\ln(H/S)}{\sigma\sqrt{t_1}}, \quad e_4 = e_3 - \sigma\sqrt{t_1}$$

$$\mu = \frac{b-\sigma^2/2}{\sigma^2}, \quad \rho = \sqrt{t_1/T_2}.$$

Partial-time-start-in-options
The price of "in" options of type A can be found using "out" options in combination with plain vanilla call options.

Up-and-in call

$$c_{uiA} = call - c_{uoA}$$

Down-and-in call

$$c_{diA} = call - c_{doA}$$

Partial-time-end-out-calls
There are two types of partial-time end barrier options. Type B1 is defined such that only a barrier hit or crossed causes the option to be knocked out. We do not distinguish between the asset price hitting the barrier from above

or below. In this case, there is no difference between up and down options.

When $X > H$ the knock-out call value is given by

$$
c_{oB1} = Se^{(b-r)T_2} \left[M(d_1, e_1; \rho) - \left(\frac{H}{S} \right)^{2(\mu+1)} M(f_1, -e_3; -\rho) \right]
$$

$$
- Xe^{-rT_2} \left[M(d_2, e_2; \rho) - \left(\frac{H}{S} \right)^{2\mu} M(f_2, -e_4; -\rho) \right], \qquad (2.44)
$$

and when $X < H$ the knock-out call value is given by

$$
c_{oB1} = Se^{(b-r)T_2} \left[M(-g_1, -e_1; \rho) - \left(\frac{H}{S} \right)^{2(\mu+1)} M(-g_3, e_3; -\rho) \right]
$$

$$
- Xe^{-rT_2} \left[M(-g_2, -e_2; \rho) - \left(\frac{H}{S} \right)^{2\mu} M(-g_4, e_4; -\rho) \right]
$$

$$
- Se^{(b-r)T_2} \left[M(-d_1, -e_1; \rho) - \left(\frac{H}{S} \right)^{2(\mu+1)} M(-f_1, e_3; -\rho) \right]
$$

$$
+ Xe^{-rT_2} \left[M(-d_2, -e_2; \rho) - \left(\frac{H}{S} \right)^{2\mu} M(-f_2, e_4; -\rho) \right]
$$

$$
+ Se^{(b-r)T_2} \left[M(g_1, e_1; \rho) - \left(\frac{H}{S} \right)^{2(\mu+1)} M(g_3, -e_3; -\rho) \right]
$$

$$
- Xe^{-rT_2} \left[M(g_2, e_2; \rho) - \left(\frac{H}{S} \right)^{2\mu} M(g_4, -e_4; -\rho) \right], \qquad (2.45)
$$

where

$$
g_1 = \frac{\ln(S/H) + (b + \sigma^2/2)T_2}{\sigma\sqrt{T_2}}, \qquad g_2 = g_1 - \sigma\sqrt{T_2}
$$

$$
g_3 = g_1 + \frac{2\ln(H/S)}{\sigma\sqrt{T_2}}, \qquad g_4 = g_3 - \sigma\sqrt{T_2}.
$$

Table 2–11 shows values for partial-time-end-barrier call options for a range of input parameters.

Type B2 partial-end barrier options are defined such that a down-and-out call is knocked out as soon as the underlying price is below the barrier. Similarly, an up-and-out call is knocked out as soon as the underlying price

T A B L E 2–11

Partial-Time-End-Barrier Call Type B1 Option Values

$(H = 100, r = b = 0.20, \sigma = 0.25, T_2 = 1)$

		Barrier Monitoring Time t_1				
S	X	0.00	0.25	0.5	0.75	1.00
95	90	0.0393	6.2747	10.3345	13.4342	17.1612
95	110	0.0000	3.7352	5.8712	7.1270	7.5763
105	90	9.8751	15.6324	19.2896	22.0753	25.4213
105	110	6.2303	9.6812	11.6055	12.7342	13.1376

is above the barrier.

Down-and-out call $X < H$

$$c_{doB2} = Se^{(b-r)T_2}\left[M(g_1, e_1; \rho) - \left(\frac{H}{S}\right)^{2(\mu+1)} M(g_3, -e_3; -\rho)\right]$$

$$- Xe^{-rT_2}\left[M(g_2, e_2; \rho) - \left(\frac{H}{S}\right)^{2\mu} M(g_4, -e_4; -\rho)\right] \quad (2.46)$$

Up-and-out call $X < H$

$$c_{uoB2} = Se^{(b-r)T_2}\left[M(-g_1, -e_1; \rho) - \left(\frac{H}{S}\right)^{2(\mu+1)} M(-g_3, -e_3; -\rho)\right]$$

$$- Xe^{-rT2}\left[M(-g_2, e_2; \rho) - \left(\frac{H}{S}\right)^{2\mu} M(-g_4, e_4; -\rho)\right]$$

$$- Se^{(b-r)T_2}\left[M(-d_1, -e_1; \rho) - \left(\frac{H}{S}\right)^{2(\mu+1)} M(e_3, -f_1; -\rho)\right]$$

$$+ Xe^{-rT_2}\left[M(-d_2, -e_2; \rho) - \left(\frac{H}{S}\right)^{2\mu} M(e_4, -f_2; -\rho)\right] \quad (2.47)$$

2.10.4 Two-Asset Barrier Options

In a two-asset barrier option, one of the underlying assets, S_1, determines how much the option is in or out-of-the-money, and the other asset, S_2, is linked to barrier hits. Heynen and Kat (1994a) have developed the following pricing formula:

$$w = \eta S_1 e^{(b_1-r)T_2} \left\{ M(\eta d_1, \phi e_1; -\eta \phi \rho) \right.$$

$$\left. - \exp\left[\frac{2(\mu_2 + \rho \sigma_1 \sigma_2) \ln(H/S_2)}{\sigma_2^2}\right] M(\eta d_3, \phi e_3; -\eta \phi \rho) \right\}$$

$$- \eta X e^{-rT} \left\{ M(\eta d_2, \phi e_2; -\eta \phi \rho) \right.$$

$$\left. - \exp\left[\frac{2\mu_2 \ln(H/S_2)}{\sigma_2^2}\right] M(\eta d_4, \phi e_4; -\eta \phi \rho) \right\}, \quad (2.48)$$

where

$$d_1 = \frac{\ln(S_1/X) + (\mu_1 + \sigma_1^2)T}{\sigma_1 \sqrt{T}}, \qquad d_2 = d_1 - \sigma_1 \sqrt{T}$$

$$d_3 = d_1 + \frac{2\rho \ln(H/S_2)}{\sigma_2 \sqrt{T}}, \qquad d_4 = d_2 + \frac{2\rho \ln(H/S_2)}{\sigma_2 \sqrt{T}}$$

$$e_1 = \frac{\ln(H/S_2) - (\mu_2 + \rho \sigma_1 \sigma_2)T}{\sigma_2 \sqrt{T}}, \qquad e_2 = e_1 + \rho \sigma_1 \sqrt{T}$$

$$e_3 = e_1 - \frac{2 \ln(H/S_2)}{\sigma_2 \sqrt{T}} \qquad e_4 = e_2 - \frac{2 \ln(H/S_2)}{\sigma_2 \sqrt{T}}$$

$$\mu_1 = b_1 - \sigma_1^2/2, \qquad \mu_2 = b_2 - \sigma_2^2/2.$$

Two-asset "Out" barriers

Down-and-out call (c_{do}) $\eta = 1, \quad \phi = -1$
Payoff: $\max(S_1 - X; 0)$ if $S_2 > H$ before T else 0 at hit

Up-and-out call (c_{uo}) $\eta = 1, \quad \phi = 1$
Payoff: $\max(S_1 - X; 0)$ if $S_2 < H$ before T else 0 at hit

Down-and-out put (p_{do}) $\eta = -1, \quad \phi = -1$
Payoff: $\max(X - S_1; 0)$ if $S_2 > H$ before T else 0 at hit

Up-and-out put (p_{uo}) $\eta = -1, \quad \phi = 1$
Payoff: $\max(X - S_1; 0)$ if $S_2 < H$ before T else 0

Two-asset "In" barriers

Down-and-in call $\qquad\qquad\qquad\qquad c_{di} = call - c_{do}$
Payoff: $\max(S_1 - X; 0)$ if $S_2 > H$ before T else 0 at expiry.

Up-and-in call $\qquad\qquad\qquad\qquad c_{ui} = call - c_{uo}$
Payoff: $\max(S_1 - X; 0)$ if $S_2 < H$ before T else 0 at expiry.

Down-and-in put $\qquad\qquad\qquad\qquad p_{di} = put - p_{do}$
Payoff: $\max(X - S_2; 0)$ if $S_2 > H$ before T else 0 at expiry.

Up-and-in put $\qquad\qquad\qquad\qquad p_{ui} = put - p_{uo}$
Payoff: $\max(X - S_2; 0)$ if $S_2 < H$ before T else 0 at expiry.

Table 2–12 shows values for two-asset barrier call and put options for different choices of strike price X, barrier H, and the correlation between the two assets ρ.

T A B L E 2–12

Two-Asset Barrier Option Values

$(S_1 = S_2 = 100, T = 0.5, \sigma_1 = \sigma_2 = 0.20, r = 0.08, b_1 = b_2 = 0.08)$

Type	X	H	$\rho = -0.5$	$\rho = 0$	$\rho = 0.5$
c_{do}	90	95	3.2941	4.9485	6.6592
c_{do}	100	95	1.4173	2.6150	3.8906
c_{do}	110	95	0.4737	1.1482	1.8949
c_{uo}	90	105	4.6670	3.1827	1.8356
c_{uo}	100	105	2.8198	1.6819	0.7367
c_{uo}	110	105	1.4285	0.7385	0.2263
p_{do}	90	95	0.6184	0.3498	0.1141
p_{do}	100	95	2.0075	1.2821	0.6114
p_{do}	110	95	4.3298	3.0813	1.8816
p_{uo}	90	105	0.0509	0.2250	0.4795
p_{uo}	100	105	0.3042	0.8246	1.4811
p_{uo}	110	105	1.0134	1.9818	3.0712

Application

To illustrate the use of two-asset barrier options, consider a Norwegian oil producer. As oil is typically sold for USD per barrel, the producer's income in Norwegian currency (NOK) depends on both the oil price and the currency price NOK per USD. The oil producer may wish to hedge his currency risk with the use of a currency option. However, if the oil price (dollar per barrel) should increase, the oil producer can afford to have a lower currency price. An ideal option would therefore be a currency option that is knocked out if the oil price increases to a particular level. This two-asset barrier option will naturally be cheaper than a similar standard currency option.

2.10.5   Partial-Time Two-Asset Barrier Options

A partial-time two-asset barrier option is similar to a standard two-asset barrier option, except that the barrier hits are monitored only for a fraction of the option's lifetime. The option is knocked "in" or "out" if asset S_2 hits the barrier H during the monitoring period, while the payoff depends on asset S_1 and the strike price X. The formula of Bermin (1996c) can be used to price European partial-time two-asset barrier options, where the barrier monitoring is set to cover the first part t_1 of the full time to expiration T_2:

$$
\begin{aligned}
w \;=\; & \eta S_1 e^{(b_1 - r)T_2} \left\{ M(\eta d_1, \phi e_1; -\eta\phi\rho\sqrt{t_1/T_2}) \right. \\
& - \exp\left[\frac{2(\mu_2 + \rho\sigma_1\sigma_2)\ln(H/S_2)}{\sigma_2^2} \right] M(\eta d_3, \phi e_3; -\eta\phi\rho\sqrt{t_1/T_2}) \Bigg\} \\
& - \eta X e^{-rT} \left\{ M(\eta d_2, \phi e_2; -\eta\phi\rho\sqrt{t_1/T_2}) \right. \\
& - \exp\left[\frac{2\mu_2\ln(H/S_2)}{\sigma_2^2} \right] M(\eta d_4, \phi e_4; -\eta\phi\rho\sqrt{t_1/T_2}) \Bigg\}, \qquad (2.49)
\end{aligned}
$$

where

$$
d_1 = \frac{\ln(S_1/X) + (\mu_1 + \sigma_1^2)T_2}{\sigma_1\sqrt{T_2}}, \qquad d_2 = d_1 - \sigma_1\sqrt{T_2}
$$

$$
d_3 = d_1 + \frac{2\rho\ln(H/S_2)}{\sigma_2\sqrt{T_2}}, \qquad d_4 = d_2 + \frac{2\rho\ln(H/S_2)}{\sigma_2\sqrt{T_2}}
$$

$$
e_1 = \frac{\ln(H/S_2) - (\mu_2 + \rho\sigma_1\sigma_2)t_1}{\sigma_2\sqrt{t_1}}, \qquad e_2 = e_1 + \rho\sigma_1\sqrt{t_1}
$$

$$
e_3 = e_1 - \frac{2\ln(H/S_2)}{\sigma_2\sqrt{t_1}}, \qquad e_4 = e_2 - \frac{2\ln(H/S_2)}{\sigma_2\sqrt{t_1}}
$$

$$
\mu_1 = b_1 - \sigma_1^2/2, \qquad \mu_2 = b_2 - \sigma_2^2/2
$$

η is set equal to 1 for a call option and -1 for a put option. ϕ is set equal to 1 if the option is an up-and-out and equal to -1 if the option is a down-and-out.

Table 2–13 gives examples of partial-time two-asset barrier option values. The values are given for a range of input parameters.

2.10.6   Look-Barrier Options

Look-barrier options, introduced by Bermin (1996a), can be regarded as a combination of a partial time barrier option and a forward starting fixed

TABLE 2–13

Partial-Time Two-Asset Barrier Option Values

($S_1 = S_2 = X = 100$, $H = 85$, $T_2 = 1$, $r = b_1 = b_2 = 0.10$, $\sigma_1 = 0.25$, $\sigma_2 = 0.30$)

		Barrier Monitoring Time t_1				
Type	ρ	0.00	0.25	0.5	0.75	1.00
c_{do}	0.5	14.9758	12.3793	10.9409	10.2337	9.8185
p_{do}	0.5	5.4595	3.5109	2.3609	1.7502	1.3607
c_{do}	0.0	14.9758	11.2067	8.9828	7.8016	7.0480
p_{do}	0.0	5.4595	4.0855	3.2747	2.8441	2.5694
c_{do}	−0.5	14.9758	9.8818	6.8660	5.2576	4.2271
p_{do}	−0.5	5.4595	4.5801	4.1043	3.8778	3.7497

c_{do} and p_{do} indicate a down-and-out call and put, respectively.

strike lookback option. The look-barrier option's barrier monitoring period starts at the option's starting date and ends at an arbitrary date t_1 before expiration. If the barrier is not hit during the monitoring period, the fixed strike lookback option will be initiated at the same time the barrier ceases to exist. By introducing a knock-out barrier in the first part of the option's lifetime, the option will be cheaper than a standard partial-time fixed strike lookback option.

$$
\begin{aligned}
w = \;& \eta\Bigg\{ Se^{(b-r)T_2}\left(1+\frac{\sigma^2}{2b}\right)\Bigg[M_\eta\left(\frac{m-\mu_2 t_1}{\sigma\sqrt{t_1}}, \frac{-k+\mu_2 T_2}{\sigma\sqrt{T_2}}; -\rho\right) \\
& -e^{2\mu_2 h/\sigma^2} M_\eta\left(\frac{m-2h-\mu_2 t_1}{\sigma\sqrt{t_1}}, \frac{2h-k+\mu_2 T_2}{\sigma\sqrt{T_2}}; -\rho\right)\Bigg] \\
& - e^{-rT_2} X\Bigg[M_\eta\left(\frac{m-\mu_1 t_1}{\sigma\sqrt{t_1}}, \frac{-k+\mu_1 T_2}{\sigma\sqrt{T_2}}; -\rho\right) \\
& -e^{2\mu h/\sigma^2} M_\eta\left(\frac{m-2h-\mu_1 t_1}{\sigma\sqrt{t_1}}, \frac{2h-k+\mu_1 T_2}{\sigma\sqrt{T_2}}; -\rho\right)\Bigg] \\
& - e^{-rT_2}\left(\frac{\sigma^2}{2b}\right)\Bigg[S\left(\frac{S}{X}\right)^{-\frac{2b}{\sigma^2}} M_\eta\left(\frac{m+\mu_1 t_1}{\sigma\sqrt{t_1}}, \frac{-k-\mu_1 T_2}{\sigma\sqrt{T_2}}; -\rho\right) \\
& -H\left(\frac{H}{X}\right)^{-\frac{2b}{\sigma^2}} M_\eta\left(\frac{m-2h+\mu_1 t_1}{\sigma\sqrt{t_1}}, \frac{2h-k-\mu_1 T_2}{\sigma\sqrt{T_2}}; -\rho\right)\Bigg] \\
& + Se^{(b-r)T_2}\Bigg[\left(1+\frac{\sigma^2}{2b}\right) N_\eta\left(\frac{\mu_2(T_2-t_1)}{\sigma\sqrt{T_2-t_1}}\right) + e^{-b(T_2-t_1)}\left(1-\frac{\sigma^2}{2b}\right) \\
& \times N_\eta\left(\frac{-\mu_1(T_2-t_1)}{\sigma\sqrt{T_2-t_1}}\right)\Bigg] g_1 - e^{-rT_2} X g_2 \Bigg\}, \qquad (2.50)
\end{aligned}
$$

where $N_\eta(x) = N(\eta x)$, and $M_\eta(a,b;\,\rho) = M(\eta a, \eta b;\,\rho)$,

$$\eta = \begin{cases} 1 & \text{if up-and-out call} \\ -1 & \text{if down-and-out put} \end{cases}$$

$$m = \begin{cases} \min(h,k) & \text{when} \quad \eta = 1 \\ \max(h,k) & \text{when} \quad \eta = -1 \end{cases}$$

$$h = \ln(H/S), \qquad k = \ln(X/S)$$

$$\mu_1 = b - \sigma^2/2, \qquad \mu_2 = b + \sigma^2/2, \qquad \rho = \sqrt{\frac{t_1}{T_2}}$$

$$g_1 = \left\{ \left[N_\eta \left(\frac{h - \mu_2 t_1}{\sigma \sqrt{t_1}} \right) - e^{2\mu_2 h/\sigma^2} N_\eta \left(\frac{-h - \mu_2 t_1}{\sigma \sqrt{t_1}} \right) \right] \right.$$
$$\left. - \left[N_\eta \left(\frac{m - \mu_2 t_1}{\sigma \sqrt{t_1}} \right) - e^{2\mu_2 h/\sigma^2} N_\eta \left(\frac{m - 2h - \mu_2 t_1}{\sigma \sqrt{t_1}} \right) \right] \right\}$$

$$g_2 = \left\{ \left[N_\eta \left(\frac{h - \mu_1 t_1}{\sigma \sqrt{t_1}} \right) - e^{2\mu_1 h/\sigma^2} N_\eta \left(\frac{-h - \mu_1 t_1}{\sigma \sqrt{t_1}} \right) \right] \right.$$
$$\left. - \left[N_\eta \left(\frac{m - \mu_1 t_1}{\sigma \sqrt{t_1}} \right) - e^{2\mu_1 h/\sigma^2} N_\eta \left(\frac{m - 2h - \mu_1 t_1}{\sigma \sqrt{t_1}} \right) \right] \right\}$$

Table 2–14 shows examples of look-barrier up-and-out call option values. It reports values for different choices of barrier H, barrier monitoring time t_1, and volatility σ.

T A B L E 2–14

Look-Barrier Up-and-Out Call Values

$(S = X = 100, T_2 = 1, r = b = 0.10)$

	H	\multicolumn{5}{c}{Barrier Monitoring Time t_1}
		0.00	0.25	0.5	0.75	1.00
	110	17.5212	9.6529	4.2419	1.7112	0.2388
$\sigma = 0.15$	120	17.5212	16.0504	11.0593	6.4404	2.1866
	130	17.5212	17.0597	14.9975	11.1547	5.5255
	110	30.1874	7.4146	2.7025	0.8896	0.0357
$\sigma = 0.30$	120	30.1874	16.4987	7.5509	3.1682	0.4259
	130	30.1874	23.1605	13.1118	6.6034	1.5180

2.10.7 Discrete-Barrier Options

All the barrier options pricing formulas presented so far assume continuous monitoring of the barrier. In practice, the barrier is normally monitored only at discrete points in time. An exception is the currency options market, where the barrier is frequently monitored almost continuously. For equity, commodity, and interest-rate options, the barrier is typically monitored against an official daily closing price. Discrete monitoring will naturally lower the probability of barrier hits compared with continuous barrier monitoring. Broadie, Glasserman, and Kou (1995) have developed an approximation for a continuity correction for discrete barrier options pricing formulas. The correction shifts the barrier (or the barriers) away from the underlying asset. Thus, the probability of barrier hits is reduced in the model. To price any discrete barrier option, it is only necessary to replace the continuously monitored barrier H in continuous barrier options formulas with a discrete barrier level H_D equal to

$$H_D = He^{\beta \sigma \sqrt{\Delta t}}$$

if the barrier is above the underlying security, and to

$$H_D = He^{-\beta \sigma \sqrt{\Delta t}}$$

if the barrier is below the underlying security. Δt is the time between monitoring instants, and $\beta = -\zeta \left(\frac{1}{2}\right)/\sqrt{2\pi} \approx 0.5826$, where ζ is the Riemann zeta function. Broadie, Glasserman, and Kou (1995) show both theoretically and experimentally that discrete barrier options can be priced with remarkable accuracy using this simple correction. Other methods for pricing discrete barrier options have been published by Kat and Verdonk (1995), Reimer and Sandemann (1995), and Heynen and Kat (1996b).

2.10.8 Soft-Barrier Options

A soft-barrier option is similar to a standard barrier option, except that the barrier is no longer a single level. Rather, it's a soft range between an upper level U and a lower level L. Soft-barrier options are knocked in or out proportionally. For instance, consider a soft down-and-out call with current asset price 100, with a soft-barrier range from $U = 90$ to $L = 80$. If the lowest asset price during the lifetime is 86, then 40% of the call will be knocked out. The valuation formula originally introduced by Hart and Ross (1994) can be used to price soft-down-and-in-call and soft-up-and-in-put options:

$$
w = \frac{1}{U-L} \left\{ \eta Se^{(b-r)T} S^{-2\mu} \frac{(SX)^{\mu+0.5}}{2(\mu+0.5)} \left[\left(\frac{U^2}{SX} \right)^{\mu+0.5} \right. \right.
$$

$$
\left. N(\eta d_1) - \lambda_1 N(\eta d_2) - \left(\frac{L^2}{SX} \right)^{\mu+0.5} N(\eta e_1) + \lambda_1 N(\eta e_2) \right]
$$

$$
- \eta X e^{-rT} S^{-2(\mu-1)} \frac{(SX)^{\mu-0.5}}{2(\mu-0.5)} \left[\left(\frac{U^2}{SX} \right)^{\mu-0.5} N(\eta d_3) \right.
$$

$$
\left. \left. - \lambda_2 N(\eta d_4) - \left(\frac{L^2}{SX} \right)^{\mu-0.5} N(\eta e_3) + \lambda_2 N(\eta e_4) \right] \right\}, \tag{2.51}
$$

where η is set to 1 for a call and -1 for a put, and

$$
d_1 = \frac{\ln(U^2/SX)}{\sigma\sqrt{T}} + \mu\sigma\sqrt{T}, \qquad d_2 = d_1 - (\mu+0.5)\sigma\sqrt{T}
$$

$$
d_3 = \frac{\ln(U^2/SX)}{\sigma\sqrt{T}} + (\mu-1)\sigma\sqrt{T}, \qquad d_4 = d_3 - (\mu-0.5)\sigma\sqrt{T}
$$

$$
e_1 = \frac{\ln(L^2/SX)}{\sigma\sqrt{T}} + \mu\sigma\sqrt{T}, \qquad e_2 = e_1 - (\mu+0.5)\sigma\sqrt{T}
$$

$$
e_3 = \frac{\ln(L^2/SX)}{\sigma\sqrt{T}} + (\mu-1)\sigma\sqrt{T}, \qquad e_4 = e_3 - (\mu-0.5)\sigma\sqrt{T}
$$

$$
\lambda_1 = e^{-0.5[\sigma^2 T(\mu+0.5)(\mu-0.5)]}, \qquad \lambda_2 = e^{-0.5[\sigma^2 T(\mu-0.5)(\mu-1.5)]}
$$

$$
\mu = \frac{b+\sigma^2/2}{\sigma^2}
$$

The value of a soft-down-and-out call is equal to the value of a standard call minus the value of a soft-down-and-in call. Similarly, the value of a soft-up-and-out put is equal to the value of a standard put minus a soft-up-and-in put.

Application
Standard-type barrier options are hard to delta hedge when the asset price is close to the barrier. The barrier option will then have a high gamma risk. Soft-barrier options will typically have a significantly lower gamma risk and will for that reason also be easier to hedge.

TABLE 2–15

Soft-Barrier Down-and-Out Call Values

$(S = 100, X = 100, U = 95, r = 0.10, b = 0.05)$

	T = 0.5			T = 1		
L	$\sigma = 0.10$	$\sigma = 0.20$	$\sigma = 0.30$	$\sigma = 0.10$	$\sigma = 0.20$	$\sigma = 0.30$
95	3.8075	4.5263	4.7297	5.4187	5.3614	5.2300
90	4.0175	5.5615	6.2595	6.0758	6.9776	7.2046
85	4.0529	6.0394	7.2496	6.2641	7.9662	8.7092
80	4.0648	6.2594	7.8567	6.3336	8.5432	9.8118
75	4.0708	6.3740	8.2253	6.3685	8.8822	10.5964
70	4.0744	6.4429	8.4578	6.3894	9.0931	11.1476
65	4.0768	6.4889	8.6142	6.4034	9.2343	11.5384
60	4.0785	6.5217	8.7260	6.4133	9.3353	11.8228
55	4.0798	6.5463	8.8099	6.4208	9.4110	12.0369
50	4.0808	6.5654	8.8751	6.4266	9.4698	12.2036

Table 2–15 shows values for soft-barrier down-and-out call options. Different choices for time to maturity T, lower barrier level L, and volatility σ are reported.

2.11 BINARY OPTIONS

Binary options, also known as digital options, are popular in the OTC markets for hedging and speculation. They are also important to financial engineers as building blocks for constructing more complex options products.

2.11.1 Gap Options

The payoff from a call is 0 if $S \leq X_1$ and $S - X_2$ if $S > X_1$. Similarly, the payoff from a put is 0 if $S \geq X_1$ and $X_2 - S$ if $S < X_1$. The Reiner and Rubinstein (1991b) formula can be used to price these options:

$$c = Se^{(b-r)T}N(d_1) - X_2 e^{-rT}N(d_2) \qquad (2.52)$$

$$p = X_2 e^{-rT}N(-d_2) - Se^{(b-r)T}N(-d_1), \qquad (2.53)$$

where

$$d_1 = \frac{\ln(S/X_1) + (b + \sigma^2/2)T}{\sigma\sqrt{T}}, \quad d_2 = d_1 - \sigma\sqrt{T}$$

Notice that this option actually can take negative values, depending on the settings of X_1 and X_2. When the difference between X_1 and X_2 is such that the value of the option is zero, the option is often referred to as a pay-later option.

Example

Consider a gap call option with six months to expiry. The stock price is 50, the first strike is 50, the payoff strike is 57, the risk-free interest rate is 9% per annum, and the volatility is 20% per annum. $S = 50$, $X_1 = 50$, $X_2 = 57$, $T = 0.5$, $r = b = 0.09$, $\sigma = 0.20$.

$$d_1 = \frac{\ln(50/50) + (0.09 + 0.20^2/2)0.5}{0.20\sqrt{0.5}} = 0.3889, \quad d_2 = d_1 - 0.20\sqrt{0.5} = 0.2475$$

$$N(d_1) = 0.6513, \quad N(d_2) = 0.5977$$

$$c = 50e^{(0.09-0.09)0.5}N(d_1) - 57e^{-0.09\times0.5}N(d_2) = -0.0053$$

2.11.2 Cash-or-Nothing Options

The cash-or-nothing option pays out a cash amount K at expiry if the option is in-the-money. The payoff from a call is 0 if $S \le X$ and K if $S > X$. The payoff from a put option is 0 if $S \ge X$ and K if $S < X$. Valuation of cash-or-nothing options can be made using the formula described by Reiner and Rubinstein (1991b):

$$c = Ke^{-rT}N(d)$$

$$p = Ke^{-rT}N(-d)$$

This is nothing but the last part of the Black–Scholes formula, where

$$d = \frac{\ln(S/X) + (b - \sigma^2/2)T}{\sigma\sqrt{T}}.$$

Example

What is the value of a cash-or-nothing put option with nine months to expiry? The futures price is 100, the strike price is 80, the cash payout is 10, the risk-free interest rate is 6% per annum, and the volatility is 35% per annum. $S = 100$, $X = 80$, $K = 10$, $T = 0.75$, $r = 0.06$, $b = 0$, $\sigma = 0.35$.

$$d = \frac{\ln(100/80) + (0 - 0.35^2/2)0.75}{0.35\sqrt{0.75}} = 0.5846$$

$$N(-d) = N(-0.5846) = 0.2794$$

$$p = 10e^{-0.06\times0.75}N(-d) = 2.6710$$

2.11.3 Two-Asset Cash-or-Nothing Options

Four types of two-asset cash-or-nothing options exist:

1. A two-asset cash-or-nothing call pays out a fixed cash amount K if asset one, S_1, is above the strike X_1 and asset two, S_2, is above strike X_2 at expiration.

2. A two-asset cash-or-nothing put pays out a fixed cash amount if asset one, S_1, is below the strike X_1 and asset two, S_2, is below strike X_2 at expiration.

3. A two-asset cash-or-nothing up-down pays out a fixed cash amount if asset one, S_1, is above the strike X_1 and asset two, S_2, is below strike X_2 at expiration.

4. A two-asset cash-or-nothing down-up pays out a fixed cash amount if asset one, S_1, is below the strike X_1 and asset two, S_2, is above strike X_2 at expiration.

The formulas published by Heynen and Kat (1996a) can be used to price these binary options:

$$[1] = Ke^{-rT}M(d_{1,1}, d_{2,2}; \rho) \tag{2.54}$$

$$[2] = Ke^{-rT}M(-d_{1,1}, -d_{2,2}; \rho) \tag{2.55}$$

$$[3] = Ke^{-rT}M(d_{1,1}, -d_{2,2}; -\rho) \tag{2.56}$$

$$[4] = Ke^{-rT}M(-d_{1,1}, d_{2,2}; -\rho), \tag{2.57}$$

where

$$d_{i,j} = \frac{\ln(S_i/X_j) + (b_i - \sigma_i^2/2)T}{\sigma_i\sqrt{T}}.$$

Table 2–16 reports values for two-asset cash-or-nothing options of types 1, 2, 3, and 4, for different choices of time to maturity T and correlation ρ.

Application

Two-asset cash-or-nothing options can be useful building blocks for constructing more complex exotic option products. One example is a C-Brick option, which pays out a prespecified cash amount K if asset S_1 is between X_1 and X_2 and asset S_2 is between X_3 and X_4. This option can be engineered by using four type [1] two-asset cash-or-nothing call options with different strikes:

T A B L E   2–16

Two-Asset Cash-or-Nothing Options

($S_1 = S_2 = 100$, $X_1 = 110$, $X_2 = 90$, $K = 10$, $r = 0.10$, $b_1 = 0.05$, $b_2 = 0.06$, $\sigma_1 = 0.20$, $\sigma_2 = 0.25$)

Type	$T = 0.5$			$T = 1$		
	$\rho = -0.5$	$\rho = 0$	$\rho = 0.5$	$\rho = -0.5$	$\rho = 0$	$\rho = 0.5$
1	1.45845	2.03611	2.49875	1.73130	2.37027	2.94710
2	1.11639	1.69406	2.15669	1.04202	1.68099	2.25782
3	1.25311	0.67545	0.21281	1.63473	0.99576	0.41893
4	5.68434	5.10667	4.64404	4.64032	4.00136	3.42452

$$\text{C-Brick} = Ke^{-rT}[M(d_{1,1}, d_{2,3}; \rho) - M(d_{1,2}, d_{2,3}; \rho)$$
$$- M(d_{1,1}, d_{2,4}; \rho) + M(d_{1,2}, d_{2,4}; \rho)]$$

In a similar way, Heynen and Kat (1996a) show how to value four types of bivariate asset-or-nothing options.

2.11.4   Asset-or-Nothing Options

At expiry, the asset-or-nothing call option pays 0 if $S \leq X$ and S if $S > X$. Similarly, a put option pays 0 if $S \geq X$ and S if $S < X$. The option can be valued using the Cox and Rubinstein (1985) formula:[8]

$$c = Se^{(b-r)T}N(d)$$

$$p = Se^{(b-r)T}N(-d),$$

where

$$d = \frac{\ln(S/X) + (b + \sigma^2/2)T}{\sigma\sqrt{T}}.$$

Example

Consider an asset-or-nothing put option with six months to expiry. The stock price is 70, the strike price is 65, the dividend yield is 5% per annum, the risk-free interest rate is 7% per annum, and the volatility is 27% per annum. $S = 70$, $X = 65$, $T = 0.5$, $r = 0.07$, $b = 0.07 - 0.05 = 0.02$, $\sigma = 0.27$.

$$d = \frac{\ln(70/65) + (0.02 + 0.27^2/2)0.5}{0.27\sqrt{0.5}} = 0.5360$$

---

8. See also Reiner and Rubinstein (1991b).

$$N(-d) = N(-0.5360) = 0.2960$$

$$p = 70e^{(0.02-0.07)0.5}N(-d) = 20.2069$$

2.11.5 Supershare Options

A supershare option, originally introduced by Hakansson (1976), entitles its holder to a payoff of S/X_L if $X_L \le S < X_H$ and 0 otherwise.

$$w = (Se^{(b-r)T}/X_L)[N(d_1) - N(d_2)], \tag{2.58}$$

where

$$d_1 = \frac{\ln(S/X_L) + (b+\sigma^2/2)T}{\sigma\sqrt{T}}, \qquad d_2 = \frac{\ln(S/X_H) + (b+\sigma^2/2)T}{\sigma\sqrt{T}}.$$

Application
A portfolio of supershare options can be used to construct what is known as a superfund—traded at the American Stock Exchange under the name SuperUnits and at the Chicago Board Options Exchange as SuperShares.[9]

Example
Consider a supershare option with three months to expiry. The futures price is 100, the lower boundary X_L is 90, the upper boundary X_H is 110, the risk-free interest rate is 10% per annum, and the volatility is 20% per annum. $S = 100, X_L = 90, X_H = 110, T = 0.25, r = 0.10, b = 0, \sigma = 0.20$.

$$d_1 = \frac{\ln(100/90) + (0+0.20^2/2)0.25}{0.20\sqrt{0.25}} = 1.1036$$

$$d_2 = \frac{\ln(100/110) + (0+0.20^2/2)0.25}{0.20\sqrt{0.25}} = -0.9031$$

$$N(d_1) = N(1.1036) = 0.8651, \quad N(d_2) = N(-0.9031) = 0.1832$$

$$w = (100e^{(0-0.10)0.25}/90)[N(d_1) - N(d_2)] = 0.7389$$

---

9. For more on supershares, see the articles by Cox and Rubinstein (1985), Hakansson (1991), and Rubinstein (1995b).

2.11.6 Binary Barrier Options

Reiner and Rubinstein (1991b) present a set of formulas that can be used to price 28 different types of so-called binary barrier options. The binary barrier options presented here can be divided into two main categories:

1. Cash-or-nothing barrier options. These either pay out a prespecified cash amount or nothing, depending on whether the asset price has hit the barrier or not.

2. Asset-or-nothing barrier options, which pay out the value of the asset or nothing, depending on whether the asset price has hit the barrier or not.

We start by introducing nine formulas:

$$A_1 = Se^{(b-r)T}N(\phi x_1)$$

$$B_1 = Ke^{-rT}N(\phi x_1 - \phi\sigma\sqrt{T})$$

$$A_2 = Se^{(b-r)T}N(\phi x_2)$$

$$B_2 = Ke^{-rT}N(\phi x_2 - \phi\sigma\sqrt{T})$$

$$A_3 = Se^{(b-r)T}(H/S)^{2(\mu+1)}N(\eta y_1)$$

$$B_3 = Ke^{-rT}(H/S)^{2\mu}N(\eta y_1 - \eta\sigma\sqrt{T})$$

$$A_4 = Se^{(b-r)T}(H/S)^{2(\mu+1)}N(\eta y_2)$$

$$B_4 = Ke^{-rT}(H/S)^{2\mu}N(\eta y_2 - \eta\sigma\sqrt{T})$$

$$A_5 = K[(H/S)^{\mu+\lambda}N(\eta z) + (H/S)^{\mu-\lambda}N(\eta z - 2\eta\lambda\sigma\sqrt{T}),$$

where K is a prespecified cash amount. The binary variables η and ϕ each take the value 1 or -1. Further,

$$x_1 = \frac{\ln(S/X)}{\sigma\sqrt{T}} + (\mu+1)\sigma\sqrt{T}, \qquad x_2 = \frac{\ln(S/H)}{\sigma\sqrt{T}} + (\mu+1)\sigma\sqrt{T}$$

$$y_1 = \frac{\ln(H^2/SX)}{\sigma\sqrt{T}} + (\mu+1)\sigma\sqrt{T}, \qquad y_2 = \frac{\ln(H/S)}{\sigma\sqrt{T}} + (\mu+1)\sigma\sqrt{T}$$

$$z = \frac{\ln(H/S)}{\sigma\sqrt{T}} + \lambda\sigma\sqrt{T}, \qquad \mu = \frac{b-\sigma^2/2}{\sigma^2}, \qquad \lambda = \sqrt{\mu^2 + \frac{2r}{\sigma^2}}$$

By using these nine formulas, A_1 to A_5 and B_1 to B_4, in different combinations, one can price the 28 binary barrier options described below:

1. Down-and-in cash-(at-hit)-or-nothing $(S > H)$:

Value: A_5 $\eta = 1$

2. Up-and-in cash-(at-hit)-or-nothing $(S < H)$:
Value: A_5 $\eta = -1$

3. Down-and-in asset-(at-hit)-or-nothing $(S > H)$:
Value: $(K = H)$: A_5 $\eta = 1$

4. Up-and-in asset-(at-hit)-or-nothing $(S < H)$:
Value: $(K = H)$: A_5 $\eta = -1$

5. Down-and-in cash-(at-expiry)-or-nothing $(S > H)$:
Value: $B_2 + B_4$ $\eta = 1,$ $\phi = -1$

6. Up-and-in cash-(at-expiry)-or-nothing $(S < H)$:
Value: $B_2 + B_4$ $\eta = -1,$ $\phi = 1$

7. Down-and-in asset-(at-expiry)-or-nothing $(S > H)$:
Value: $A_2 + A_4$ $\eta = 1,$ $\phi = -1$

8. Up-and-in asset-(at-expiry)-or-nothing $(S < H)$:
Value: $A_2 + A_4$ $\eta = -1,$ $\phi = 1$

9. Down-and-out cash-or-nothing $(S > H)$:
Value: $B_2 - B_4$ $\eta = 1,$ $\phi = 1$

10. Up-and-out cash-or-nothing $(S < H)$:
Value: $B_2 - B_4$ $\eta = -1,$ $\phi = -1$

11. Down-and-out asset-or-nothing $(S > H)$:
Value: $A_2 - A_4$ $\eta = 1,$ $\phi = 1$

12. Up-and-out asset-or-nothing $(S < H)$:
Value: $A_2 - A_4$ $\eta = -1,$ $\phi = -1$

13. Down-and-in cash-or-nothing call $(S > H)$:
Value: $(X > H)$: B_3 $\eta = 1$
Value: $(X < H)$: $B_1 - B_2 + B_4$ $\eta = 1,$ $\phi = 1$

14. Up-and-in cash-or-nothing call $(S < H)$:
Value: $(X > H)$: B_1 $\phi = 1$
Value: $(X < H)$: $B_2 - B_3 + B_4$ $\eta = -1,$ $\phi = 1$

15. Down-and-in asset-or-nothing call $(S > H)$:
Value: $(X > H)$: A_3 $\eta = 1$

Value:　　$(X < H)$:　　$A_1 - A_2 + A_4$　　　　$\eta = 1$,　　$\phi = 1$

16. Up-and-in asset-or-nothing call $(S < H)$:
　　Value:　　$(X > H)$:　　A_1　　　　　　　$\phi = 1$
　　Value:　　$(X < H)$:　　$A_2 - A_3 + A_4$　　$\eta = -1$,　　$\phi = 1$

17. Down-and-in cash-or-nothing put $(S > H)$:
　　Value:　　$(X > H)$:　　$B_2 - B_3 + B_4$　　$\eta = 1$,　　$\phi = -1$
　　Value:　　$(X < H)$:　　B_1　　　　　　　$\phi = -1$

18. Up-and-in cash-or-nothing put $(S < H)$:
　　Value:　　$(X > H)$:　　$B_1 - B_2 + B_4$　　$\eta = -1$,　　$\phi = -1$
　　Value:　　$(X < H)$:　　B_3　　　　　　　$\phi = -1$

19. Down-and-in asset-or-nothing put $(S > H)$:
　　Value:　　$(X > H)$:　　$A_2 - A_3 + A_4$　　$\eta = 1$,　　$\phi = -1$
　　Value:　　$(X < H)$:　　A_1　　　　　　　$\phi = -1$

20. Up-and-in asset-or-nothing put $(S < H)$:
　　Value:　　$(X > H)$:　　$A_1 - A_2 + A_3$　　$\eta = -1$,　　$\phi = -1$
　　Value:　　$(X < H)$:　　A_3　　　　　　　$\phi = -1$

21. Down-and-out cash-or-nothing call $(S > H)$:
　　Value:　　$(X > H)$:　　$B_1 - B_3$　　　　$\eta = 1$,　　$\phi = 1$
　　Value:　　$(X < H)$:　　$B_2 - B_4$　　　　$\eta = 1$,　　$\phi = 1$

22. Up-and-out cash-or-nothing call $(S < H)$:
　　Value:　　$(X > H)$:　　0
　　Value:　　$(X < H)$:　　$B_1 - B_2 + B_3 - B_4$　　$\eta = -1$,　　$\phi = 1$

23. Down-and-out asset-or-nothing call $(S > H)$:
　　Value:　　$(X > H)$:　　$A_1 - A_3$　　　　$\eta = 1$,　　$\phi = 1$
　　Value:　　$(X < H)$:　　$A_2 - A_4$　　　　$\eta = 1$,　　$\phi = 1$

24. Up-and-out asset-or-nothing call $(S < H)$:
　　Value:　　$(X > H)$:　　0
　　Value:　　$(X < H)$:　　$A_1 - A_2 + A_3 - A_4$　　$\eta = -1$,　　$\phi = 1$

25. Down-and-out cash-or-nothing put $(S > H)$:
　　Value:　　$(X > H)$:　　$B_1 - B_2 + B_3 - B_4$　　$\eta = 1$,　　$\phi = -1$
　　Value:　　$(X < H)$:　　0

26. Up-and-out cash-or-nothing put $(S < H)$:
　　Value:　　$(X > H)$:　　$B_2 - B_4$　　　　$\eta = -1$,　　$\phi = -1$
　　Value:　　$(X < H)$:　　$B_1 - B_3$　　　　$\eta = -1$,　　$\phi = -1$

27. Down-and-out asset-or-nothing put $(S > H)$:
    Value: $(X > H)$: $A_1 - A_2 + A_3 - A_4$ $\eta = 1,$ $\phi = -1$
    Value: $(X < H)$: 0

28. Up-and-out asset-or-nothing put $(S < H)$:
    Value: $(X > H)$: $A_2 - A_4$ $\eta = -1,$ $\phi = -1$
    Value: $(X < H)$: $A_1 - A_3$ $\eta = -1,$ $\phi = -1$

Table 2–18 gives examples of values for 28 different types of binary barrier options.

T A B L E 2–18

Binary Barrier Option Values

$(H = 100, T = 0.5, r = 0.10, b = 0.10, \sigma = 0.20)$
$K = 15$, except for option numbers (3) and (4) where $K = H$

Option #	S	X = 102	X = 98	Option #	S	X = 102	X = 98
(1)	105	9.7264	9.7264	(15)	105	37.2782	45.8530
(2)	95	11.6553	11.6553	(16)	95	44.5294	54.9262
(3)	105	68.0848	68.0848	(17)	105	4.4314	3.1454
(4)	95	11.6553	11.6553	(18)	95	5.3297	3.7704
(5)	105	9.3604	9.3604	(19)	105	27.5644	18.9896
(6)	95	11.2223	11.2223	(20)	95	38.7533	22.7755
(7)	105	64.8426	64.8426	(21)	105	4.8758	4.9081
(8)	95	77.7017	77.7017	(22)	95	0.0000	0.0407
(9)	105	4.9081	4.9081	(23)	105	39.9391	40.1574
(10)	95	3.0461	3.0461	(24)	95	0.0000	0.2676
(11)	105	40.1574	40.1574	(25)	105	0.0323	0.0000
(12)	95	17.2983	17.2983	(26)	95	3.0461	3.0054
(13)	105	4.9289	6.2150	(27)	105	0.2183	0.0000
(14)	95	5.3710	7.4519	(28)	95	17.2983	17.0306

2.12 ASIAN OPTIONS

Asian options are especially popular in the currency and commodity markets. An average is less volatile than the underlying asset itself and will lower the price of an average-rate option compared with a similar standard option.[10] If the option is based on an average, an attempt to manipulate the asset price just before expiration will normally have little or no effect on the option's value. Asian options should therefore be of particular interest in markets for thinly traded assets.

---

10. If the option is into the average period, the value of an average-rate option can naturally be higher than that of a similar standard option, depending on the realization of the asset price.

2.12.1 Geometric Average-Rate Options

If the underlying asset is assumed to be lognormally distributed, the geometric average $((x_1 \cdots x_n)^{1/n})$ of the asset will itself be lognormally distributed. As originally shown by Kemna and Vorst (1990), the geometric average option can be priced as a standard option by changing the volatility and cost-of-carry term:

$$c = Se^{(b_A - r)T}N(d_1) - Xe^{-rT}N(d_2) \tag{2.59}$$

$$p = Xe^{-rT}N(-d_2) - Se^{(b_A - r)T}N(-d_1), \tag{2.60}$$

where

$$d_1 = \frac{\ln(S/X) + (b_A + \sigma_A^2/2)T}{\sigma_A\sqrt{T}}, \qquad d_2 = d_1 - \sigma_A\sqrt{T},$$

and the adjusted volatility is equal to

$$\sigma_A = \frac{\sigma}{\sqrt{3}}.$$

Further, the adjusted cost of carry is set to

$$b_A = \frac{1}{2}\left(b - \frac{\sigma^2}{6}\right).$$

Example
What is the value of a geometric average-rate put option with three months to maturity? The strike is 85, the asset price is 80, the risk-free rate is 5%, the cost of carry is 8%, and the volatility is 20%. $S = 80$, $X = 85$, $T = 0.25$, $r = 0.05$, $b = 0.08$, $\sigma = 0.20$.

$$\sigma_A = \frac{0.20}{\sqrt{3}} = 0.1155, \qquad b_A = \frac{1}{2}\left(0.08 - \frac{0.20^2}{6}\right) = 0.0366$$

$$d_1 = \frac{\ln(80/85) + (0.0366 + 0.1155^2/2)0.25}{0.1155\sqrt{0.25}} = -0.8624$$

$$d_2 = d_1 - 0.1155\sqrt{0.25} = -0.9201$$

$$N(-d_1) = N(0.8624) = 0.8058, \qquad N(-d_2) = N(0.9201) = 0.8213$$

$$p = 85e^{-0.05 \times 0.25}N(-d_2) - 80e^{(0.0366-0.05)0.25}N(-d_1) = 4.6922$$

The value of a similar standard European put option is 5.2186.

2.12.2 Arithmetic Average-Rate Options

It is not possible to find a closed-form solution for the valuation of options on an arithmetic average ($\frac{x_1+\cdots+x_n}{n}$). The main reason for this is that when the asset is assumed to be lognormally distributed, the arithmetic average will not itself have a lognormal distribution. Arithmetic average-rate options can be priced by analytical approximations, as presented below, or with Monte Carlo simulations, presented in Chapter 3.

The Turnbull and Wakeman Approximation

The approximation formula below is based on the work of Turnbull and Wakeman (1991). The approximation adjusts the mean and variance so that they are consistent with the exact moments of the arithmetic average. The adjusted mean, b_A, and variance, σ_A^2, are then used as input in the generalized Black–Scholes formula:

$$c \approx Se^{(b_A-r)T_2}N(d_1) - Xe^{-rT_2}N(d_2) \tag{2.61}$$

$$p \approx Xe^{-rT_2}N(d_2) - Se^{(b_A-r)T_2}N(d_1) \tag{2.62}$$

$$d_1 = \frac{\ln(S/X) + (b_A + \sigma_A^2/2)T_2}{\sigma_A\sqrt{T_2}}, \qquad d_2 = d_1 - \sigma_A\sqrt{T_2},$$

where T_2 is the remaining time to maturity. In addition,

$$\sigma_A = \sqrt{\frac{\ln(M_2)}{T} - 2b_A}$$

$$b_A = \frac{\ln(M_1)}{T}.$$

The exact first and second moments of the arithmetic average are

$$M_1 = \frac{e^{bT} - e^{b\tau}}{b(T - \tau)}$$

$$M_2 = \frac{2e^{(2b+\sigma^2)T}}{(b+\sigma^2)(2b+\sigma^2)(T-\tau)^2} + \frac{2e^{(2b+\sigma^2)\tau}}{b(T-\tau)^2}\left[\frac{1}{2b+\sigma^2} - \frac{e^{b(T-\tau)}}{b+\sigma^2}\right],$$

where T is the original time to maturity, and τ is the time to the beginning of the average period. If the option is into the average period, the strike price must be replaced by $\hat{X}$, and the option value must be multiplied by $\frac{T_2}{T}$, where

$$\hat{X} = \frac{T}{T_2}X - \frac{T_1}{T_2}S_A,$$

where S_A is the average asset price during the realized or observed time period T_1 ($T_1 = T - T_2$). The formula doesn't work for trivial cost of carry ($b = 0$).

Computer algorithm

The computer code below calculates an adjusted cost-of-carry term, b_A, and volatility, v_A, and then calls the general Black–Scholes formula described in Chapter 1.

```
Function TurnbullWakemanAsian(CallPutFlag As String, S As Double, _
    SA As Double, X As Double, T As Double, T2 As Double, _
    tau As Double, r As Double, b As Double, v As Double) As Double

    Dim M1 As Double, M2 As Double, T1 As Double
    Dim bA As Double, vA As Double

    M1 = (Exp(b * T) − Exp(b * tau))/(b * (T − tau))
    M2 = 2 * Exp((2 * b + v^2) * T)/((b + v^2) * (2 * b + v^2) * (T − tau)^2) _
    +2 * Exp((2 * b + v^2) * tau)/(b * (T − tau)^2) * (1/(2 * b + v^2) − _
    Exp(b * (T − tau))/(b + v^2))
    bA = Log(m1)/T
    vA = Sqr(Log(m2)/T − 2 * bA)
    T1 = T − T2
    If T1 > 0 Then
        X = T/T2 * X − T1/T2 * SA
        TurnbullWakemanAsian = GBlackScholes(CallPutFlag, S, X, T2, _
        r, bA, vA) * T2/T
    Else
            TurnbullWakemanAsian = GBlackScholes(CallPutFlag, S, X, T2, _
            r, bA, vA)
    End If
End Function
```

Example: *TurnbullWakemanAsian*("p", 90, 88, 95, 0.5, 0.25, 0, 0.07, 0.02, 0.25) will return an arithmetic average put value of 5.8482.

Levy's Approximation

An alternative to the Turnbull and Wakeman formula is the Levy (1992) Asian option approximation:

$$c_{Asian} \approx S_E N(d_1) - X^* e^{-rT_2} N(d_2), \tag{2.63}$$

where

$$S_E = \frac{S}{Tb}(e^{(b-r)T_2} - e^{-rT_2})$$

$$d_1 = \frac{1}{\sqrt{V}}\left[\frac{\ln(D)}{2} - \ln(X^*)\right], \qquad d_2 = d_1 - \sqrt{V}$$

$$X^* = X - \frac{T-T_2}{T}S_A, \qquad V = \ln(D) - 2[rT_2 + \ln(S_E)], \qquad D = \frac{M}{T^2}$$

$$M = \frac{2S^2}{b+\sigma^2}\left[\frac{e^{(2b+\sigma^2)T_2}-1}{2b+\sigma^2} - \frac{e^{bT_2}-1}{b}\right]$$

The Asian put value can be found by using the following put–call parity:

$$p_{Asian} = c_{Asian} - S_E + X^* e^{-rT_2}$$

where

S_A = Arithmetic average of the known asset price fixings.
S = Asset price.
X = Strike price of option.
r = Risk-free interest rate.
b = Cost of carry rate.
T_2 = Remaining time to maturity.
T = Original time to maturity.
σ = Volatility of natural logarithms of return
   of the underlying asset.

The formula does not allow for $b = 0$. The Levy formula should be a bit more accurate than the Turnbull–Wakeman formula. For practical purposes, the difference is quite small. Table 2–19 illustrates this.[11]

Example
Consider an arithmetic average currency option with a time to expiration of six months. The spot price is 6.80, the strike is 6.90, the domestic risk-free interest rate is 7% per annum, the foreign interest rate is 9% per annum, and the volatility of the spot rate is 14%. The option is on the average of the next six months. $S = 6.80$, $S_A = 6.80$, $X = 6.90$, $T = 0.5$, $T_2 = 0.5$, $r = 0.07$, $b = r - r_f = 0.07 - 0.09 = -0.02$, $\sigma = 0.14$.

---

11. For more comparisons between Asian option approximations, see Levy and Turnbull (1992).

TABLE 2–19

Examples of Arithmetic Average Call Options Values
$(S = S_A = 100, T = 0.75, r = 0.10, b = 0.05)$

X	$\sigma = 0.15$			$\sigma = 0.35$		
	$T_2 = 0.75$	$T_2 = 0.50$	$T_2 = 0.25$	$T_2 = 0.75$	$T_2 = 0.50$	$T_2 = 0.25$
	Turnbull and Wakeman Approximation					
95	7.0544	5.6748	5.0810	10.1213	6.9793	5.1432
100	3.7845	1.9996	0.6745	7.5038	4.0795	1.4299
105	1.6729	0.3584	0.0005	5.4071	2.1461	0.1587
	Levy's Approximation					
95	7.0544	5.6731	5.0806	10.1213	6.9705	5.1411
100	3.7845	1.9964	0.6722	7.5038	4.0687	1.4222
105	1.6729	0.3565	0.0004	5.4071	2.1359	0.1552

$$S_E = \frac{6.8}{0.5(-0.02)}(e^{(-0.02-0.07)\times 0.5} - e^{-0.07\times 0.5}) = 6.5334$$

$$X^* = 6.90 - \frac{0.5 - 0.5}{0.5}6.80 = 6.9000$$

$$M = \frac{2 \times 6.80^2}{-0.02 + 0.14^2}$$
$$\times \left[\frac{e^{(2(-0.02)+0.14^2)0.5} - 1}{2(-0.02) + 0.14^2} - \frac{e^{(-0.02)0.5} - 1}{-0.02}\right] = 11.4825$$

$$D = \frac{11.4825}{0.5^2} = 45.9298$$

$$V = \ln(45.9298) - 2[0.07 \times 0.5 + \ln(6.5334)] = 0.0033$$

$$d_1 = \frac{1}{\sqrt{0.0033}}\left[\frac{\ln(45.9298)}{2} - \ln(6.9000)\right] = -0.3146$$

$$d_2 = d_1 - \sqrt{0.0033} = -0.3717$$

$$N(d_1) = N(-0.3146) = 0.3765, \qquad N(d_2) = N(-0.3717) = 0.3551$$

$$c \approx 6.5334N(d_1) - 6.9000e^{-0.07\times 0.5}N(d_2) \approx 0.0944$$

$$p \approx 0.0944 - 6.5334 + 6.9000e^{-0.07\times 0.5} \approx 0.2237$$

Curran's Approximation

Curran (1992)[12] has developed an approximation method for pricing Asian options based on the geometric conditioning approach. Curran (1992) claims that this method is more accurate than other closed-form approximations presented earlier.

$$c \approx e^{-rT} \left[\frac{1}{n} \sum_{i=1}^{n} e^{\mu_i + \sigma_i^2/2} N \left(\frac{\mu - \ln(\hat{X})}{\sigma_x} + \frac{\sigma_{xi}}{\sigma_x} \right) \right.$$

$$\left. -XN \left(\frac{\mu - \ln(\hat{X})}{\sigma_x} \right) \right], \qquad (2.64)$$

where

$S =$ Initial asset price.
$X =$ Strike price of option.
$r =$ Risk-free interest rate.
$b =$ Cost of carry.
$T =$ Time to expiration in years.
$t_1 =$ Time to first averaging point.
$\Delta t =$ Time between averaging points.
$n =$ Number of averaging points.
$\sigma =$ Volatility of asset.
$N(x) =$ The cumulative normal distribution function.

$$\mu_i = \ln(S) + (b - \sigma^2/2)t_i$$

$$\sigma_i = \sqrt{\sigma^2[t_1 + (i-1)\Delta t]}$$

$$\sigma_{xi} = \sigma^2\{t_1 + \Delta t[(i-1) - i(i-1)/(2n)]\}$$

$$\mu = \ln(S) + (b - \sigma^2/2)[t_1 + (n-1)\Delta t/2]$$

$$\sigma_x = \sqrt{\sigma^2[t_1 + \Delta t(n-1)(2n-1)/6n]}$$

and

---

12. For more on Asian options valuation, see Geman and Yor (1993), Haykov (1993), Curran (1994b), Bouaziz, Briys, and Grouhy (1994), Zhang (1994), Geman and Eydeland (1995), and Zhang (1995a).

$$\hat{X} = 2X - \frac{1}{n}\sum_{i=1}^{n}\exp\left\{\mu_i + \frac{\sigma_{xi}[\ln(X) - \mu]}{\sigma_x^2} + \frac{\sigma_i^2 - \sigma_{xi}^2/\sigma_x^2}{2}\right\}.$$

Table 2–20 reports Asian option values based on Curran's approximation method.

T A B L E 2–20

Asian Call Options Using the Geometric Conditioning Approach

($X = 100$, $T = 26$ weeks, $\Delta t = 1$ week, $r = 0.08$, $b = 0.03$, $n = 27$)

t_1	S	$\sigma = 0.10$	$\sigma = 0.20$	$\sigma = 0.30$	$\sigma = 0.40$	$\sigma = 0.50$
	95	0.2758	1.4262	2.8099	4.2581	5.7298
0 weeks	100	1.9466	3.4899	5.0395	6.5878	8.1320
	105	5.7110	6.7024	8.0489	9.5053	11.005
	95	0.8956	2.9260	5.0916	7.2866	9.4866
10 weeks	100	3.0019	5.2739	7.5597	9.8425	12.1171
	105	6.6074	8.4137	10.5604	12.7983	15.0669
	95	1.5308	4.1925	6.9307	9.6780	12.4172
20 weeks	100	3.8838	6.6982	9.5350	12.3667	15.1844
	105	7.4609	9.8449	12.5693	15.3776	18.2081

2.13   CURRENCY-TRANSLATED OPTIONS

2.13.1   Foreign Equity Options Struck in Domestic Currency

As the name indicates, this is an option on foreign equity where the strike is denominated in domestic currency. At expiry, the foreign equity is translated into the domestic currency.

The payoff to a U.S. investor where the option is linked to the Nikkei index is:

$$c_{(\$/share)} = \max(E_{(\$/yen)}S^*_{(yen/share)} - X_{(\$/share)}, 0)$$

$$p_{(\$/share)} = \max(X_{(\$/share)} - E_{(\$/yen)}S^*_{(yen/share)}, 0)$$

Valuation of these options is achieved using the formula attributed to Reiner (1992).[13]

---

13. Valuation of this option is based on the same technique as developed by Margrabe (1978).

Option value in domestic currency (i.e., USD)

$$c = ES^* e^{-qT} N(d_1) - X e^{-rT} N(d_2) \tag{2.65}$$

$$p = X e^{-rT} N(-d_2) - ES^* e^{-qT} N(-d_1), \tag{2.66}$$

where

$$d_1 = \frac{\ln(ES^*/X) + (r - q + \sigma_{ES^*}^2/2)T}{\sigma_{ES^*}\sqrt{T}}$$

$$d_2 = d_1 - \sigma_{ES^*}\sqrt{T}$$

$$\sigma_{ES^*} = \sqrt{\sigma_E^2 + \sigma_{S^*}^2 + 2\rho_{ES^*}\sigma_E\sigma_{S^*}}.$$

Option value in foreign currency (i.e., JPY)

$$c = S^* e^{-qT} N(d_1) - E^* X e^{-rT} N(d_2) \tag{2.67}$$

$$p = E^* X e^{-rT} N(-d_2) - S^* e^{-qT} N(-d_1), \tag{2.68}$$

where

$$d_1 = \frac{\ln(S^*/(E^*X)) + (r - q + \sigma_{E^*S^*}^2/2)T}{\sigma_{E^*S^*}\sqrt{T}}$$

$$d_2 = d_1 - \sigma_{E^*S^*}\sqrt{T}$$

$$\sigma_{E^*S^*} = \sqrt{\sigma_{E^*}^2 + \sigma_{S^*}^2 - 2\rho_{E^*S^*}\sigma_{E^*}\sigma_{S^*}}$$

S^* = Underlying asset price in foreign currency.
X = Delivery price in domestic currency.
r = Domestic interest rate.
q = Instantaneous proportional dividend payout rate of the underlying asset.
E = Spot exchange rate specified in units of the domestic currency per unit of the foreign currency.
E^* = Spot exchange rate specified in units of the foreign currency per unit of the domestic currency.
σ_{S^*} = Volatility of the underlying asset.
σ_E = Volatility of the domestic exchange rate.
σ_E^* = Volatility of the foreign exchange rate.
ρ_{ES^*} = Correlation between asset and domestic exchange rate.
$\rho_{E^*S^*}$ = Correlation between asset and foreign exchange rate.

Example

Consider a foreign-equity call option struck in domestic currency with six months to expiry. The stock index is 100, the strike is 160, the spot exchange rate is 1.5, the domestic interest rate is 8% per annum, the dividend yield is 5% per annum, the volatility of the stock index is 20%, the volatility of the currency is 12% per annum, and the correlation between the stock index and the currency rate is 0.45. $S^* = 100$, $X = 160$, $T = 0.5$, $E = 1.5$, $r = 0.08$, $q = 0.05$, $\sigma_{S^*} = 0.20$, $\sigma_E = 0.12$, $\rho_{E,S^*} = 0.45$.

$$\sigma_{ES^*} = \sqrt{0.12^2 + 0.20^2 + 2 \times 0.45 \times 0.12 \times 0.20} = 0.2757$$

$$d_1 = \frac{\ln(1.5 \times 100/160) + (0.08 - 0.05 + 0.2757^2/2)0.5}{0.2757\sqrt{0.5}} = -0.1567$$

$$d_2 = d_1 - 0.2757\sqrt{0.5} = -0.3516$$

$$N(d_1) = N(-0.1567) = 0.4378 \qquad N(d_2) = N(-0.3516) = 0.3626$$

$$c = 1.5 \times 100e^{-0.05 \times 0.5}N(d_1) - 160e^{-0.08 \times 0.5}N(d_2) = 8.3056$$

2.13.2   Fixed Exchange-Rate Foreign-Equity Options

A fixed exchange-rate foreign-equity option (quanto) is denominated in another currency than that of the underlying equity exposure. The face value of the currency protection expands or contracts to cover changes in the foreign currency value of the underlying asset. Quanto options are traded on stock indexes on several exchanges as well as in the OTC equity market.

The payoff to a U.S. investor where the option is linked to the Nikkei index is:

$$c_{(\$/share)} = E_{P(\$/yen)} \max(S^*_{(yen/share)} - X^*_{(yen/share)}, 0)$$

$$p_{(\$/share)} = E_{P(\$/yen)} \max(X^*_{(yen/share)} - S^*_{(yen/share)}, 0)$$

Valuation of quanto options was originally introduced by Derman, Karasinski, and Wecker (1990) and was later extended and discussed by Reiner (1992), Dravid, Richardson, and Sun (1993), and others.

Option value in domestic currency (i.e., USD)

$$c = E_p[S^* e^{(r_f - r - q - \rho \sigma_{S^*} \sigma_E)T} N(d_1) - X^* e^{-rT} N(d_2)] \qquad (2.69)$$

$$p = E_p[X^* e^{-rT} N(-d_2) - S^* e^{(r_f - r - q - \rho \sigma_{S^*} \sigma_E)T} N(-d_1)] \qquad (2.70)$$

Option value in foreign currency (i.e., JPY)

$$c = E^* E_p[S^* e^{(r_f - r - q - \rho \sigma_{S^*} \sigma_E)T} N(d_1) - X^* e^{-rT} N(d_2)] \qquad (2.71)$$

$$p = E^* E_p[X^* e^{-rT} N(-d_2) - S^* e^{(r_f - r - q - \rho \sigma_{S^*} \sigma_E)T} N(-d_1)], \qquad (2.72)$$

where

$$d_1 = \frac{\ln(S^*/X^*) + (r_f - q - \rho \sigma_{S^*} \sigma_E + \sigma_{S^*}^2/2)T}{\sigma_{S^*} \sqrt{T}}$$

$$d_2 = d_1 - \sigma_{S^*} \sqrt{T}$$

$S^* =$ Underlying asset price in foreign currency.
$X^* =$ Delivery price in foreign currency.
$r =$ Domestic interest rate.
$r_f =$ Foreign interest rate.
$q =$ Instantaneous proportional dividend payout rate
of the underlying asset.
$E_p =$ Predetermined exchange rate specified in units of domestic
currency per unit of foreign currency.
$E^* =$ Spot exchange rate specified in units of foreign
currency per unit of domestic currency.
$\sigma_{S^*} =$ Volatility of the underlying asset.
$\sigma_E =$ Volatility of the domestic exchange rate.
$\rho =$ Correlation between asset and domestic exchange rate.

Note that if the exchange rate had been been specified in, for example, yen per dollar, the sign of ρ would be reversed. $\rho_{(Nikkei, yen/\$)} = -\rho_{(Nikkei, \$/yen)}$.

Example
Consider a fixed exchange-rate foreign-equity call option with six months to expiry. The stock index is 100, the strike is 105, the predetermined exchange rate is 1.5, the domestic interest rate is 8% per annum, the foreign interest rate is 5% per annum, the average dividend yield is 4% per annum, the volatility of the stock index is 20%, the volatility of the currency is 10% per annum, and the correlation between the stock index and the currency rate is 0.30. $S^* = 100$, $X^* = 105$, $T = 0.5$, $E_p = 1.5$, $r = 0.08$, $r_f = 0.05$, $q = 0.04$, $\sigma_S^* = 0.20$, $\sigma_E = 0.10$, $\rho = 0.30$. What is the value in domestic currency?

$$d_1 = \frac{\ln(100/105) + (0.05 - 0.04 - 0.30 \times 0.20 \times 0.10 + 0.20^2/2)0.5}{0.20\sqrt{0.5}} = -0.2601$$

$$d_2 = d_1 - 0.20\sqrt{0.5} = -0.4016$$

$$N(d_1) = N(-0.2601) = 0.3974 \qquad N(d_2) = N(-0.4016) = 0.3440$$

$$
\begin{aligned}
c &= 1.5[100e^{(0.05-0.08-0.04-0.30\times0.2\times0.10)0.5}N(d_1) \\
&\quad - 105e^{-0.08\times0.5}N(d_2)] = 5.3280
\end{aligned}
$$

Computer algorithm

The code returns the value of a call or put quanto option quoted in the domestic currency.

```
Function Quanto(CallPutFlag As String, Ep As Double, S As Double, X As Double, _
        T As Double, r As Double, rf As Double, q As Double, vs As Double, _
        ve As Double, rho As Double) As Double

    Dim d1 As Double, d2 As Double

    d1 = (Log(S/X) + (rf - q - rho * vs * ve + vs^2/2) * T)/(vs * Sqr(T))
    d2 = d1 - vs * Sqr(T)
    If CallPutFlag = "c" Then
        Quanto = Ep * (S * Exp((rf - r - q - rho * vs * ve) * T) * CND(d1) - _
        X * Exp(-r * T) * CND(d2))
    ElseIf CallPutFlag = "p" Then
            Quanto = Ep * (X * Exp(-r * T) * CND(-d2) - _
            S * Exp((rf - r - q - rho * vs * ve) * T) * CND(-d1))
    End If
End Function
```

2.13.3   Equity-Linked Foreign-Exchange Options

In an equity-linked foreign-exchange option, the quantity of the face value will be linked to the level of the forward price of a stock or equity index. This is an ideal option for an investor who wants to speculate directly in a foreign equity market but wishes to place a floor on the currency exposure.

The payoff to a U.S. investor where the option is linked to the Nikkei index is:

$$c_{(\$/share)} = S^*_{(yen/share)}\max(E_{(\$/yen)} - X_{(\$/yen)}, 0)$$

$$P_{(\$/share)} = S^*_{(yen/share)}\max(X_{(\$/yen)} - E_{(\$/yen)}, 0)$$

Valuation of these options has been described by Reiner (1992).

Option value in domestic currency (i.e., USD)

$$c = ES^* e^{-qT} N(d_1) - X S^* e^{(r_f - r - q - \rho \sigma_{S^*} \sigma_E)T} N(d_2) \qquad (2.73)$$

$$p = X S^* e^{(r_f - r - q - \rho \sigma_{S^*} \sigma_E)T} N(-d_2) - ES^* e^{-qT} N(-d_1) \qquad (2.74)$$

Option value in foreign currency (i.e., JPY)

$$c = S^* e^{-qT} N(d_1) - E^* X S^* e^{(r_f - r - q - \rho \sigma_{S^*} \sigma_E)T} N(d_2) \qquad (2.75)$$

$$p = E^* X S^* e^{(r_f - r - q - \rho \sigma_{S^*} \sigma_E)T} N(-d_2) - S^* e^{-qT} N(-d_1), \qquad (2.76)$$

where

$$d_1 = \frac{\ln(E/X) + (r - r_f + \rho \sigma_{S^*} \sigma_E + \sigma_E^2/2)T}{\sigma_E \sqrt{T}}$$

$$d_2 = d_1 - \sigma_E \sqrt{T}$$

$S^* = $ Underlying asset price in foreign currency.
$X = $ Currency strike price in domestic currency.
$r = $ Domestic interest rate.
$r_f = $ Foreign interest rate.
$q = $ Instantaneous proportional dividend payout rate of the underlying asset.
$E = $ Spot exchange rate specified in units of the domestic currency per unit of the foreign currency.
$E^* = $ Spot exchange rate specified in units of the foreign currency per unit of the domestic currency.
$\sigma_{S^*} = $ Volatility of the underlying asset.
$\sigma_E = $ Volatility of the domestic exchange rate.
$\rho = $ Correlation between asset and the domestic exchange rate.

Example
Consider an equity-linked foreign-exchange put option with three months to expiry. The stock index is 100, the exchange rate is 1.5, the strike is 1.52, the domestic interest rate is 8% per annum, the foreign interest rate is 5% per annum, the dividend yield is 4% per annum, the volatility of the stock index is 20%, the volatility of the currency is 12% per annum, and the correlation between the stock index and the currency rate is -0.40. $S^* = 100$, $E = 1.5$, $X = 1.52$, $T = 0.25$, $r = 0.08$, $r_f = 0.05$, $q = 0.04$, $\sigma_S^* = 0.20$, $\sigma_E = 0.12$, $\rho = -0.40$. What is the value in domestic currency?

$$d_1 = \frac{\ln(1.5/1.52) + (0.08 - 0.05 - 0.4 \times 0.20 \times 0.12 + 0.12^2/2)0.25}{0.12\sqrt{0.25}} = -0.1057$$

$$d_2 = d_1 - 0.12\sqrt{0.25} = -0.1657$$

$$N(-d_1) = N(0.1057) = 0.5421 \qquad N(-d_2) = N(0.1657) = 0.5658$$

$$
\begin{aligned}
p \; &= \; 1.52 \times 100 e^{(0.05 - 0.08 - 0.04 + 0.40 \times 0.20 \times 0.12)0.25} N(-d_2) \\
&- 1.50 \times 100 e^{-0.04 \times 0.25} N(-d_1) = 4.2089
\end{aligned}
$$

2.13.4   Takeover Foreign-Exchange Options

A takeover foreign exchange call gives the buyer the right to buy B units of a foreign currency at the strike price X if, and only if, the corporate takeover is successful. A successful takeover is defined as having occurred when the value of the foreign firm, V, in the foreign currency is less than or equal to the number of currency units, B, at the option expiration. The value of this option can be found by using the Schnabel and Wei (1994) formula:

$$
\begin{aligned}
c \; &= \; B[E e^{-r_f T} M(a_2 + \sigma_E \sqrt{T}, -a_1 - \rho \sigma_E \sqrt{T}; -\rho) \\
&- X e^{-rT} M(-a_1, a_2; -\rho)],
\end{aligned}
$$

where

$$a_1 = \frac{\ln(V/B) + (r_f - \rho \sigma_E \sigma_V - \sigma_V^2/2)T}{\sigma_V \sqrt{T}}, \quad a_2 = \frac{\ln(E/X) + (r - r_f - \sigma_E^2/2)T}{\sigma_E \sqrt{T}}.$$

Both the strike price, X, and the currency price, E, are quoted in units of the domestic currency per unit of the foreign currency.

2.14   USE OF PUT–CALL SYMMETRY

The European put–call symmetry published by Carr (1994) and later extended and discussed by Carr and Bowie (1994), and Carr and Ellis (1995)[14] states that a call with strike X when the spot is at H must have the same value as $\frac{X}{He^{bT}}$ number of puts with strike $\frac{(He^{bT})^2}{X}$.

---

14. For more on static option replication, see Derman, Ergener, and Kani (1995).

$$c(S,X,T,r,b,\sigma) = \frac{X}{Se^{bT}} \times p(S, \frac{(Se^{bT})^2}{X}, T, r, b, \sigma)$$

The put–call symmetry is useful to construct a static hedge consisting of standard options when hedging exotic options, such as barrier options. Barrier options often have complex and high gamma risk when the asset is close to the barrier. In that case, a static hedge consisting of plain vanilla options will cover the risk far better than dynamic delta hedging.

The put–call symmetry is based on assumptions that the volatility smile (implied volatilities for different strikes) is symmetric in the natural logarithm of $\frac{X}{Se^{bT}}$. As a result, a put with strike $\frac{(He^{bT})^2}{X}$ will have the same volatility as a call with strike X. Put options will have higher volatility than calls equidistant from the forward price.

Example
Consider a down-and-in call option on a futures contract with barrier $H = 120$ and strike $X = 140$. A static hedge can be constructed by using the put–call symmetry:

- Buy $\frac{140}{120e^{0 \times T}} = 1.1667$ standard put options.

- Choose a strike of $\frac{(120e^{0 \times T})^2}{140} = 102.8571$.

If the asset price closes above the barrier, both the down-and-out call and the standard put option will expire worthless. If the asset price hits the barrier before expiration, the puts will have the same value as one standard call option with strike 140. So by selling the put options at a barrier hit and at the same time buying the call option, the put–call symmetry will ensure a zero net cost.

⑥ **NUMERICAL METHODS
IN OPTIONS PRICING**

$\mathbf{T}$his chapter deals with numerical methods frequently used to price options and other derivative securities. The numerical methods are more flexible than analytical solutions and can be used to price a wide range of options contracts. The chapter starts out with binomial and trinomial trees for pricing options dependent on one underlying asset. Next the chapter covers a method for pricing options on two correlated assets: the three-dimensional binomial model. The chapter then moves on to some of the latest development in option pricing, so-called implied trees. The last section of the chapter illustrates how to implement Monte Carlo simulation.

3.1 BINOMIAL OPTION PRICING

The binomial method is certainly the most widely used numerical method to price American options on stocks, futures, and currencies. The binomial method was first published by Cox, Ross, and Rubinstein (1979) and Rendleman and Bartter (1979). They introduced how to construct a recombining binomial tree that discretize the geometric Brownian motion. At the limit, a binomial tree (with a very large number of time steps) is equivalent to the continuous-time Black–Scholes formula when pricing European options. More interesting, the binomial model handles the pricing of American options, where no closed-form solution exists, as well as several exotic options.

To price European call or put options, the binomial model can be expressed as

$$c = e^{-rT} \sum_{i=a}^{n} \left(\frac{n!}{i!(n-i)!} \right) p^i (1-p)^{n-i} (Su^i d^{n-i} - X) \tag{3.1}$$

$$p = e^{-rT} \sum_{i=0}^{a-1} \left(\frac{n!}{i!(n-i)!} \right) p^i (1-p)^{n-i} (X - Su^i d^{n-i}) \tag{3.2}$$

The asset price can either increase by a fixed amount u with a probability p, or decrease by a fixed amount d with probability $1 - p$. The number of time steps[1] is n, and a is the smallest nonnegative integer greater than $\frac{\ln(X/Sd^n)}{\ln(u/d)}$.

3.1.1   Cox–Ross–Rubinstein Binomial Tree

The binomial model described in this subsection is a version of the well-known Cox–Ross–Rubinstein binomial tree. Including a cost of carry term b, the model can be used to price European and American options on stocks $(b = r)$, stocks and stock indexes paying a continuous dividend yield q $(b = r - q)$, futures $(b = 0)$, and currency options with foreign interest rate r_f $(b = r - r_f)$. The asset price at each node is set equal to

$$Su^i d^{j-i}, \qquad i = 0, 1, \ldots, j,$$

where the up and down jump size that the asset price can take at each time step Δt apart is given by

$$u = e^{\sigma\sqrt{\Delta t}}, \qquad d = e^{-\sigma\sqrt{\Delta t}},$$

where $\Delta t = T/n$ is the size of each time step, and n is the number of time steps. The probability of the stock price increasing at the next time step is

$$p = \frac{e^{b\Delta t} - d}{u - d}.$$

The probability of going down must be $1 - p$ since the probability of going either up or down equals unity. The up-and-down jump size and the-up-and-down probability are chosen to match the first two moments of the stock price distribution (mean and variance). This ensures that the binomial tree will be a discretization of the geometric Brownian motion.

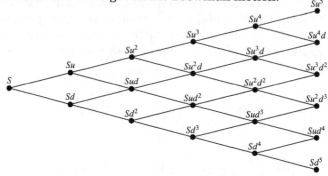

---

1. In all of the chapter's tree models, we will start counting from zero.

Example

Consider an American stock put option with six months to expiry. The stock price is 100, the strike price is 95, the risk-free interest rate is 8%, and the volatility is 30%. The option is priced in a binomial tree with five time steps. $S = 100, X = 95, T = 0.5, r = b = 0.08, \sigma = 0.30, n = 5$.

$$\Delta t = \frac{0.5}{5} = 0.1$$

$$u = e^{0.30\sqrt{0.1}} = 1.0995, \qquad d = e^{-0.30\sqrt{0.1}} = 0.9095$$

$$p = \frac{e^{0.08 \times 0.1} - 0.9095}{1.0995 - 0.9095} = 0.5186$$

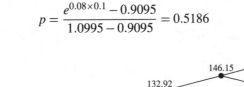

The value of the American put option can now easily be found by standard backward induction.

$$P_{j,i} = \max\{X - Su^i d^{j-i}, e^{-r\Delta t}[pP_{j+1,i+1} + (1-p)P_{j+1,i}]\}$$

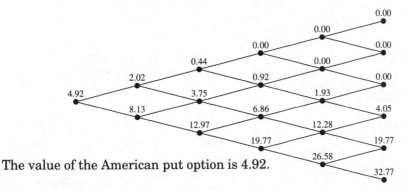

The value of the American put option is 4.92.

Computer algorithm

The computer code returns the value of a European or American call or put option. Setting the *AmeEurFlag* ="a" gives American option values, *AmeEurFlag* ="e" gives European values.

Similarly, setting the *CallPutFlag* ="c" returns a call value, and *CallPutFlag* ="p" returns a put value. In the computer code $v = \sigma$ and $dt = \Delta t$.

The computer code starts with the statement "Option Base 0." This statement forces the arrays to start counting from zero.

```
Option Base 0

Function CRRBinomial(AmeEurFlag As String, CallPutFlag As String, _
            S As Double, X As Double, T As Double, r As Double, _
            b As Double, v As Double, n As Integer) As Double

        Dim OptionValue() As Double
        Dim u As Double, d As Double, p As Double
        Dim dt As Double, Df As Double
        Dim i As Integer, j As Integer, z As Integer

        ReDim OptionValue(n + 1)

        If CallPutFlag = "c" Then
          z = 1
        ElseIf CallPutFlag = "p" Then
              z = -1
        End If
        dt = T/n
        u = Exp(v * Sqr(dt))
        d = 1/u
        a = Exp(b * dt)
        p = (a - d)/(u - d)
        Df = Exp(-r * dt)
        For i = 0 To n
            OptionValue(i) = Max(0, z * (S * u^i * d^(n - i) - X))
        Next
        For j = n - 1 To 0 Step - 1 :
            For i = 0 To j
                If AmeEurFlag = "e" Then
                    OptionValue(i) = (p * OptionValue(i + 1) + (1 - p) * _
                    OptionValue(i)) * Df
                ElseIf AmeEurFlag = "a" Then
                        OptionValue(i) = Max((z * (S * u^i * d^(Abs(i - j)) - X)), _
                        (p * OptionValue(i + 1) + (1 - p) * OptionValue(i)) * Df)
                End If
            Next
        Next
        CRRBinomial = OptionValue(0)
End Function
```

3.1.2 Options on a Stock Paying a Known Dividend Yield

In a binomial tree, it is also possible to price options on a stock that at certain points in time pays a known dividend yield. Before the stock goes exdividend, the stock price at each node is set equal to

$$Su^i d^{j-i}, \qquad i = 0, 1, \ldots, j$$

After the stock goes exdividend, the stock price corresponds to

$$S(1 - \delta_j) u^i d^{j-i}, \qquad i = 0, 1, \ldots, j,$$

where δ_j is the total dividend yield from all exdividend dates between time zero and the relevant time step in the binomial tree. The binomial tree will still be recombining.

Another possibility is that the dividends are paid in lump sums. The binomial tree will not recombine after a payment of such dividends. Implementations thus tend to be demanding in terms of computer time.

3.1.3 Barrier Options in Binomial Trees

The analytical barrier options pricing formulas presented in Chapter 2 are applicable only to European options. American barrier options, on the other hand, can be priced in binomial trees. The accuracy will in general increase with the number of time steps in the tree when pricing standard options in binomial trees. However, when pricing barrier options, this is not necessarily true. If the barrier does not coincide with the nodes, monitoring of the barrier in the tree will be inaccurate. Boyle and Lau (1994) show that it is possible to adjust the number of time steps to make the barrier fall exactly on or very close to the nodes. To achieve this, the number of time steps should be set equal to

$$F(i) = \frac{i^2 \sigma^2 T}{\left[\ln\left(\frac{S}{H}\right)\right]^2} \qquad i = 1, 2, 3 \cdots \tag{3.3}$$

Example
Consider valuing a down-and-out option by the Cox–Ross–Rubinstein binomial lattice. Time to expiration is six months, the stock price is 50, the barrier is 45, and the volatility is 36%. How many time steps should you use to get an accurate value? Using Equation 3.3 and the input parameters above results in the values shown in Table 3–1 to attain maximum accuracy for the value of this specific barrier option one should use 5, 23, 52, ... time steps for the corresponding 1, 2, 3, ... steps i used.

TABLE 3-1

Number of Time Steps to Use in a Down-and-Out Option

($S = 50, H = 45, T = 0.5, \sigma = 0.36$)

i	1	2	3	4	5	6	7	8	9	10
$F(i)$	5	23	52	93	145	210	286	373	472	583

3.1.4   Convertible Bonds in Binomial Trees

A convertible bond can be seen as a combination of a plain bond and a stock option. If the stock price is far below the strike (conversion price), the convertible behaves like a straight bond. If the stock price is far above the strike, the convertible behaves like a stock. This should also affect the discounting of the cash flows. When the convertible is deep out-of-the money, the future cash flows should be discounted by a rate that takes into account the credit spread k above the treasury rate of the particular bond. If the convertible is deep-in-the-money, it is almost certain to be converted, and the cash flows should be discounted at the risk-free rate.

Goldman-Sachs (1993) has incorporated these effects by using a discounting rate that is a function of a variable conversion probability. The model starts out with a standard binomial stock price tree. The convertible bond price is then found by starting at the end of the stock price tree. At each end node, the convertible value must be equal to the maximum of the value of converting the bond into stocks or the face value plus the final coupon. One next rolls backwards through the tree, using backward induction. If it is optimal to convert the bond, the value is set equal to the conversion value at that node, or else the convertible bond value $P_{n,i}$ is set equal to

$$P_{n,i} = \max[mS, pP_{n+1,i+1}e^{-r_{n+1,i+1}\Delta t} + (1-p)P_{n+1,i}e^{-r_{n+1,i}\Delta t}], \qquad (3.4)$$

where m is the conversion ratio. In some convertible bonds, there is an initial lockout period where the investor is not allowed to convert the bond. The convertible bond value at these nodes can be simplified to

$$P_{n,i} = pP_{n+1,i+1}e^{-r_{n+1,i+1}\Delta t} + (1-p)P_{n+1,i}e^{-r_{n+1,i}\Delta t}.$$

Instead of using a constant discount rate r, the discount rate $r_{n,i}$ is set to fluctuate with the conversion probability $q_{n,i}$ at each node.

The conversion probabilities $q_{n,i}$, where n is the time step and i the number of up movements (the state), are calculated by starting at the end of the stock price tree. If it is optimal to convert the bond, the conversion probability is set to one; otherwise, the conversion probability is set to zero. For time steps before the end of the tree, the conversion probability is set equal to one if it is optimal to convert at that node; otherwise,

$$q_{n,i} = pq_{n+1,i+1} + (1-p)q_{n+1,i}. \qquad (3.5)$$

The credit-adjusted discount rate is set equal to a conversion probability weighted mixture of the risk-free rate and the credit-adjusted rate. This gives a discount rate for up movements equal to

$$r_{n,i} = q_{n,i}r + (1 - q_{n,i})(r+k). \qquad (3.6)$$

So if the conversion probability is one, the discount rate is set equal to the constant risk-free rate r, and if the conversion probability is zero, the discount rate is set equal to the risk-free rate plus the credit spread $r + k$. For conversion probabilities between zero and one, the discount rate will move smoothly between the risk-free rate and the credit-adjusted rate.

Example

Consider a convertible corporate bond with five years to maturity. The continuously compounding yield on a five-year treasury bond is 7%, the credit spread on the corporate bond is 3% above treasury, the face value is 100, the annual coupon is 6, the conversion ratio is 1, the current stock price is 75, and the volatility of the stock is 20%. What is the value of the convertible bond? $S = 75, T = 5, r = b = 0.07, k = 0.03, m = 1, \sigma = 0.20$.

To price the convertible bond, we need to build a standard binomial stock price tree. With the number of time steps $n = 5$, we get $\Delta t = 1$ and up-and-down jump sizes

$$u = e^{\sigma\sqrt{\Delta t}} = e^{0.20\sqrt{1}} = 1.2214, \qquad d = \frac{1}{u} = 0.8187.$$

The up transition probability is thus given by

$$p = \frac{e^{b\Delta t} - d}{u - d} = \frac{e^{0.07\times1} - 0.8187}{1.2214 - 0.8187} = 0.6302,$$

and we obtain the following binomial stock price tree:

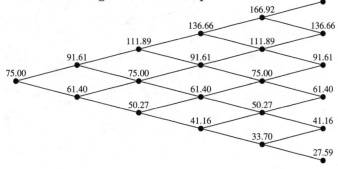

The next step is to find the convertible bond values and the conversion probabilities at each node in the tree. To see how this works, let's look at the calculation of several nodes.

At the end node with stock price 203.87, it is better to convert the bond into one stock and receive the stock price 203.87 than to get the notional plus the coupon $100 + 6$. The probability of conversion at this node, $q_{5,5}$, is 100%, which we write as 1.00 in the conversion probability tree.

At the end node, with a stock price of 91.61, it is better not to convert the bond and receive the face value plus the coupon of 106. The probability of conversion is $q_{5,3} = 0$.

For the node at year four ($n = 4$) with stock price 111.89, the convertible bond value of 121.77 is found by using equation (3.4):

$$P_{4,4} = \max[1 \times 111.89, 0.6302 \times 136.66e^{-r_{n+1,i+1} \times 1} + (1 - 0.6302)106.00e^{-r_{n+1,i} \times 1}]$$

The credit-adjusted discount rates are found by using equation (3.6):

$$r_{n+1,i+1} = 1 \times 0.07 + (1 - 1)(0.07 + 0.03) = 0.07$$

$$r_{n+1,i} = 0 \times 0.07 + (1 - 0)(0.07 + 0.03) = 0.10$$

The conversion probability of 0.63 at this node is found by equation (3.5):

$$q_{4,4} = 0.6302 \times 1 + (1 - 0.6302) \times 0$$

The same procedure can be used to find any convertible bond value and conversion probability.

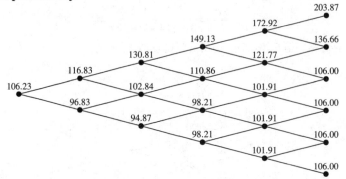

Conversion probability tree

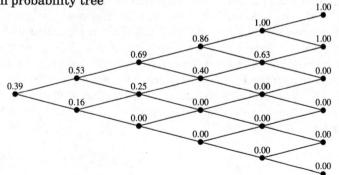

Several convertible bonds allow the issuer to force investors to convert the bond if the stock price reaches a certain prespecified level (barrier). To include a barrier in the convertible binomial model, the number of time steps should be chosen to make the barrier fall exactly on the nodes. The conversion probability is then set to one if the stock price is larger than or equal to the barrier.

3.2 TRINOMIAL TREES

Trinomial trees in option pricing, introduced by Boyle (1986), are similar to binomial trees. Trinomial trees can be used to price both European and American options on a single underlying asset.[2]

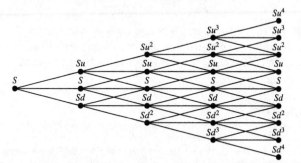

Because the asset price can move in three directions from a given node, compared with only two in a binomial tree, the number of time steps can be reduced to attain the same accuracy as in the binomial tree. This makes trinomial trees more efficient than binomial trees. Trinomial trees also offer

---

2. One-dimensional trinomial trees can also be used to price some derivatives on two correlated assets. However, a more efficient method, the three-dimensional lattice model, will be introduced later.

more flexibility than binomial trees. The extra flexibility is useful when pricing complex derivatives, such as American barrier options.[3]

There are several ways to choose jump size and move probabilities in a trinomial tree that give the same result when the number of time steps is large. To discretize a geometric Brownian motion, the jump sizes and probabilities must match the first two moments of the distribution (the mean and variance). One possibility is to build a trinomial tree where the asset price at each node can go up, stay at the same level, or go down. In that case, the up-and-down jump sizes are:

$$u = e^{\sigma\sqrt{2\Delta t}}, \qquad d = e^{-\sigma\sqrt{2\Delta t}},$$

and the probability of going up and down respectively are:

$$p_u = \left(\frac{e^{b\Delta t/2} - e^{-\sigma\sqrt{\Delta t/2}}}{e^{\sigma\sqrt{\Delta t/2}} - e^{-\sigma\sqrt{\Delta t/2}}} \right)^2$$

$$p_d = \left(\frac{e^{\sigma\sqrt{\Delta t/2}} - e^{b\Delta t/2}}{e^{\sigma\sqrt{\Delta t/2}} - e^{-\sigma\sqrt{\Delta t/2}}} \right)^2 .$$

The probabilities must sum to unity. Thus the probability of staying at the same asset price level is

$$p_m = 1 - p_u - p_d$$

T is the time to maturity in years, b is the cost of carry, $\Delta t = T/n$ is the size of each time step, and n is the number of time steps. After building the asset price tree, the value of the option can be found in the standard way by using backward induction.

Computer algorithm

The following function can be used to price European and American options on stocks, futures, and currencies. In the computer code, $v = \sigma$ and $dt = \Delta t$.

The computer code starts with the statement "Option Base 0." This statement forces the arrays to start counting from 0.

Option Base 0

Function *TrinomialTree*(*AmeEurFlag* As String, *CallPutFlag* As String, _
    S As Double, *X* As Double, *T* As Double, *r* As Double, _

---

3. See Ritchken (1995) and Cheuk and Vorst (1996).

b As Double, v As Double, n As Integer) As Double

Dim *OptionValue*() As Double
Dim *dt* As Double, *u* As Double, *d* As Double
Dim *pu* As Double, *pd* As Double, *pm* As Double
Dim *i* As Integer, *j* As Integer, *z* As Integer
Dim *Df* As Double

ReDim *OptionValue*($n * 2 + 1$)

If *CallPutFlag* = "c" Then
  $z = 1$
ElseIf *CallPutFlag* = "p" Then
    $z = -1$
End If
$dt = T/n$
$u = Exp(v * Sqr(2 * dt))$
$d = Exp(-v * Sqr(2 * dt))$
$pu = ((Exp(b * dt/2) - Exp(-v * Sqr(dt/2)))/(Exp(v * Sqr(dt/2)) - $ _
$Exp(-v * Sqr(dt/2))))^{\wedge}2$
$pd = ((Exp(v * Sqr(dt/2)) - Exp(b * dt/2))/(Exp(v * Sqr(dt/2)) - $ _
$Exp(-v * Sqr(dt/2))))^{\wedge}2$
$pm = 1 - pu - pd$
$Df = Exp(-r * dt)$
For $i = 0$ To $(2 * n)$
    $OptionValue(i) = Max(0, z * (S * u^{\wedge}Max(i - n, 0) * $ _
    $d^{\wedge}Max(n * 2 - n - i, 0) - X))$
Next
For $j = n - 1$ To 0 Step -1
    For $i = 0$ To $(j * 2)$
        If *AmeEurFlag* = "e" Then
          $OptionValue(i) = (pu * OptionValue(i + 2) + $ _
          $pm * OptionValue(i + 1) + pd * OptionValue(i)) * Df$
        ElseIf *AmeEurFlag* = "a" Then
            $OptionValue(i) = Max((z * (S * u^{\wedge}Max(i - j, 0) * $ _
            $d^{\wedge}Max(j * 2 - j - i, 0) - X)), (pu * OptionValue(i + 2) + $ _
            $pm * OptionValue(i + 1) + pd * OptionValue(i)) * Df)$
        End If
    Next
Next
$TrinomialTree = OptionValue(0)$
End Function

Example

To price an American put option with stock price 100, strike price 110, time to maturity of six months, risk-free rate equal to the cost of carry of 10%, volatility 27%, and 30 time steps: *TrinomialTree*("a", "p", 100, 110, 0.5, 0.1, 0.1, 0.27, 30). This will return an American put value of 11.6493.

3.3   THREE-DIMENSIONAL BINOMIAL TREES

Rubinstein (1994b) has published a method to construct a three-dimensional binomial model that can be used to price most types of options that depend on two assets, both European and American.[4] Examples of options that can be valued are as follows:

Spread options:	call: $\max[0, Q_1 S_1 - Q_2 S_2 - X]$,
	put: $\max[0, X + Q_2 S_2 - Q_1 S_1]$.
Options on the maximum:	call: $\max[0, \max(Q_1 S_1, Q_2 S_2) - X]$,
	put $\max[0, X - \max(Q_1 S_1, Q_2 S_2)]$.
Options on the minimum:	call: $\max[0, \min(Q_1 S_1, Q_2 S_2) - X]$,
	put $\max[0, X - \min(Q_1 S_1, Q_2 S_2)]$.
Dual-strike options:	call: $\max[0, (Q_1 S_1 - X_1), (Q_2 S_2 - X_2)]$,
	put: $\max[0, (X_1 - Q_1 S_1), (X_2 - Q_2 S_2)]$.
Reverse dual-strike options:	call: $\max[0, (Q_1 S_1 - X_1), (X_2 - Q_2 S_2)]$,
	put: $\max[0, (X_1 - Q_1 S_1), (Q_2 S_2 - X_2)]$.
Portfolio options:	call: $\max[0, (Q_1 S_1 + Q_2 S_2) - X]$,
	put: $\max[0, X - (Q_1 S_1 + Q_2 S_2)]$.
Options to exchange one asset for another:	$\max[0, Q_2 S_2 - Q_1 S_1]$.

where Q_1 and Q_2 are the fixed quantities of the two different assets. In the three-dimensional binomial model, asset 1 can move up to u or down to d at each time step. If asset 1 moves to u, asset 2 can move to A or B. If asset 1 moves down to d, asset 2 can move to C or D. By setting $A \neq C$ and $B \neq D$, it is possible to construct nonzero correlation between the two assets.

$$u = \exp(\mu_1 \Delta t + \sigma_1 \sqrt{\Delta t}), \qquad d = \exp(\mu_1 \Delta t - \sigma_1 \sqrt{\Delta t}),$$

where

$$\mu_1 = b_1 - \sigma_1^2/2, \qquad \mu_2 = b_2 - \sigma_2^2/2,$$

and

$$A = \exp[\mu_2 \Delta t + \sigma_2 \sqrt{\Delta t}(\rho + \sqrt{1 - \rho^2})]$$

$$B = \exp[\mu_2 \Delta t + \sigma_2 \sqrt{\Delta t}(\rho - \sqrt{1 - \rho^2})]$$

---

4. An alternative would be to use a three-dimensional trinomial tree as described by Boyle (1988) and later simplified by Cho and Lee (1995).

$$C = \exp[\mu_2 \Delta t - \sigma_2 \sqrt{\Delta t}(\rho - \sqrt{1 - \rho^2})]$$

$$D = \exp[\mu_2 \Delta t - \sigma_2 \sqrt{\Delta t}(\rho + \sqrt{1 - \rho^2})].$$

Table 3–2 shows European and American spread option values generated using a three-dimensional binomial tree with 100 time steps.

T A B L E   3–2

Examples of Call Values

$(S_1 = 122, S_2 = 120, X = 3, r = 0.10, b_1 = b_2 = 0, n = 100)$

		$T = 0.1$			$T = 0.50$		
σ_1	σ_2	$\rho = -0.5$	$\rho = 0$	$\rho = 0.5$	$\rho = -0.5$	$\rho = 0$	$\rho = 0.5$
		European Values					
0.20	0.20	4.7554	3.8008	2.5551	10.7566	8.7080	6.0286
0.25	0.20	5.4297	4.3732	3.0098	12.2031	9.9377	7.0097
0.20	0.25	5.4079	4.3469	2.9743	12.1521	9.8811	6.9323
		American Values					
0.20	0.20	4.7630	3.8067	2.5590	10.8754	8.8029	6.0939
0.25	0.20	5.4385	4.3802	3.0145	12.3383	10.0468	7.0858
0.20	0.25	5.4166	4.3538	2.9790	12.2867	9.9897	7.0082

Application

American spread options are traded on the New York Mercantile Exchange on oil products. The heating oil crack is an option on the spread between heating oil and crude oil. The gasoline crack is an option on the spread between unleaded gasoline and crude oil. Crack spread options are useful to oil refineries for hedging purposes.

Maximum, minimum, and dual-strike options have been traded in the OTC market on commodities and stock indexes. The three-dimensional binomial model is extremely flexible. Adding a new type of option to the model can in most cases be achieved by a small adjustment in the payoff function.

Computer algorithm

The function can be used to build a complete three-dimensional binomial tree. Setting the value of *TypeFlag* determines what kind of option value that is estimated: *TypeFlag* = 1 returns the value of a spread option, *TypeFlag* = 2 returns the value of an option on the maximum of two assets, *TypeFlag* = 3 returns the value of an option on the minimum of two assets, *TypeFlag* = 4 returns the value of a dual-strike option, *TypeFlag* = 5 returns the value of a reverse dual-strike option, *TypeFlag* = 6 gives the value of a two-asset portfolio option, while *TypeFlag* = 7 returns the value of an option to exchange one asset for another. Setting the *AmeEurFlag* equal to "e" gives European option values, and "a" American option values. Setting the *CallPutFlag* equal to "c" or "p" gives a call or put value, respectively.

The computer code starts with the statement "Option Base 0." This statement forces the arrays to start counting from zero.

Option Base 0

Function *ThreeDimensionalBinomial(TypeFlag* As Integer, *AmeEurFlag* As String, _
    CallPutFlag As String, *S*1 As Double, *S*2 As Double, *Q*1 As Double, _
    *Q*2 As Double, *X*1 As Double, *X*2 As Double, *T* As Double, _
    r As Double, *b*1 As Double, *b*2 As Double, *v*1 As Double, _
    *v*2 As Double, *rho* As Double, *n* As Integer) As Double

    Dim *OptionValue*() As Double
    Dim *dt* As Double, *u* As Double, *d* As Double
    Dim *mu*1 As Double, *mu*2 As Double
    Dim *Y*1 As Double, *y*2
    Dim *NodeValueS*1 As Double, *NodeValueS*2 As Double
    Dim *i* As Integer, *j* As Integer, *m* As Integer

    ReDim *OptionValue*($n+1, n+1$)

    $dt = T/n$
    $mu1 = b1 - v1\hat{\ }2/2$
    $mu2 = b2 - v2\hat{\ }2/2$
    $u = Exp(mu1 * dt + v1 * Sqr(dt))$
    $d = Exp(mu1 * dt - v1 * Sqr(dt))$
    For $j = 0$ To n
        $y1 = (2 * j - n) * Sqr(dt)$
        $NodeValueS1 = S1 * u\hat{\ }j * d\hat{\ }(n-j)$
        For $i = 0$ To n
            $y2 = rho * y1 + Sqr(1 - rho\hat{\ }2) * (2 * i - n) * Sqr(dt)$
            $NodeValueS2 = S2 * Exp(mu2 * n * dt) * Exp(v2 * (rho * y1 + \_$
            $Sqr(1 - rho\hat{\ }2) * (2 * i - n) * Sqr(dt)))$
            $OptionValue(j, i) = PayoffFunction(TypeFlag, CallPutFlag, \_$
            $NodeValueS1, NodeValueS2, Q1, Q2, X1, X2)$
        Next
    Next
    For $m = n - 1$ To 0 Step -1
        For $j = 0$ To m
            $y1 = (2 * j - m) * Sqr(dt)$
            $NodeValueS1 = S1 * u\hat{\ }j * d\hat{\ }(m-j)$
            For $i = 0$ To m
                $y2 = rho * y1 + Sqr(1 - rho\hat{\ }2) * (2 * i - m) * Sqr(dt)$
                $NodeValueS2 = S2 * Exp(mu2 * m * dt) * Exp(v2 * y2)$
                $OptionValue(j, i) = 1/4 * (OptionValue(j, i) + \_$
                $OptionValue(j+1, i) + OptionValue(j, i+1) + \_$
                $OptionValue(j+1, i+1)) * Exp(-r * dt)$
                If *AmeEurFlag* $=$ "a" Then
                    $OptionValue(j, i) = Max(OptionValue(j, i), \_$
                    $PayoffFunction(TypeFlag, CallPutFlag, NodeValueS1, \_$
                    $NodeValueS2, Q1, Q2, X1, X2))$
                End If

           Next
         Next
      Next
      $ThreeDimensionalBinomial = OptionValue(0,0)$
End Function

Function $PayoffFunction(TypeFlag$ As Integer, $CallPutFlag$, $S1$ As Double, _
      $S2$ As Double, $Q1$ As Double, $Q2$ As Double, _
      $X1$ As Double, $X2$ As Double) As Double

    Dim z As Integer

    If $CallPutFlag = "c"$ Then
      $z = 1$
    ElseIf $CallPutFlag = "p"$ Then
        $z = -1$
    End If
    If $TypeFlag = 1$ Then '// Spread option
      $PayoffFunction = Max(0, z*(Q1*S1 - Q2*S2) - z*X1)$
    ElseIf $TypeFlag = 2$ Then '// Options on the maximum of two assets
        $PayoffFunction = Max(0, z*Max(Q1*S1, Q2*S2) - z*X1)$
    ElseIf $TypeFlag = 3$ Then '// Options on the minimum of two assets
        $PayoffFunction = Max(0, z*Min(Q1*S1, Q2*S2) - z*X1)$
    ElseIf $TypeFlag = 4$ Then '// Dual-strike option
        $PayoffFunction = Max(0, z*(Q1*S1 - X1), z*(Q2*S2 - X2))$
    ElseIf $TypeFlag = 5$ Then '// Reverse dual-strike option
        $PayoffFunction = Max(0, z*(Q1*S1 - X1), z*(X2 - Q2*S2))$
    ElseIf $TypeFlag = 6$ Then '// Portfolio option
        $PayoffFunction = Max(0, z*(Q1*S1 + Q2*S2) - z*X1)$
    ElseIf $TypeFlag = 7$ Then '// Exchange option
       $PayoffFunction = Max(0, Max(0, Q1*S1 - Q2*S2))$
    End If
End Function

3.4 RECENT DEVELOPMENTS

A recent development in option pricing that has received a lot of attention both from practitioners and academics is the implied tree model. The main idea is to use information from liquid options with different strikes and maturities to build an arbitrage-free model that contains all the information given by market prices. The idea of implied tree models was published in 1994 by Dupire (1994), Derman and Kani (1994), and Rubinstein (1994a). The method was later discussed and extended by Barle and Cakici (1995), Rubinstein (1995a), Derman, Kani, and Chriss (1996), Buchen and Kelly (1996), Chriss (1996), Jackwerth and Rubinstein (1996), and others.

The implied tree model is a discretization of a stock price process where the local volatility is a function of both the price level of the underlying asset and time:

$$dS = \mu(T)Sdt + \sigma(S,T)Sdz$$

This differs from the geometric Brownian motion assumed in the Black–Scholes economy:

$$dS = \mu Sdt + \sigma Sdz$$

The local volatility is here constant throughout the lifetime of the option. The volatility function in the implied tree $\sigma(S,T)$ is deduced numerically from the volatility smile given by the prices of liquid options. In this way, the implied tree model is calibrated to be arbitrage-free relative to observed option prices. The model can be used to price exotic options and other derivatives. The next two subsections show how to build implied binomial and trinomial trees.

3.4.1   Implied Binomial Trees

In this section, we will concentrate on the Derman and Kani (1994) implied binomial model. The following figure illustrates an implied binomial tree where the stock prices for time step $n = 1$ have already been solved for.

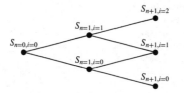

In general, if we stand at time step n and wish to find the unknown parameters at time $n+1$, there are $2n+3$ unknown parameters to solve for:[5]

- $n+2$ stock prices $S_{n+1,i}$.
- $n+1$ unknown risk-neutral transition probabilities $p_{n,i}$ from node (n,i) to node $(n+1,i+1)$.

There are $2n+2$ known quantities:

---

5. This is somewhat different from the Derman and Kani (1994) paper, which has $2n+1$ unknown parameters. The reason for this is that we start counting the initial node as time step zero, not one as in the Derman and Kani paper. The result is naturally the same. We do this to get consistency with the other tree models described in this chapter.

- $n+1$ forward prices $F_{n,i} = S_{n,i}e^{b\Delta t}$
- $n+1$ option prices $c_{n,i}$ expiring at time T_{n+1}

where n is the time step and i the state. The remaining degree of freedom is used to center the implied binomial tree around the center of the standard Cox, Ross, and Rubinstein (1979) binomial tree.

The implied binomial tree is constructed by forward induction and the use of Arrow–Debreu prices λ. Arrow–Debreu prices represent prices of primitive securities. $\lambda_{n,i}$ is the price today of a security that has a cash flow of unity at period n and state i and a cash flow of zero elsewhere. The Arrow–Debreu price for the next step $n+1$ are given by

$$e^{r\Delta t}\lambda_{n+1,i} = \begin{cases} p_{n,n}\lambda_{n,n} & \text{when} \quad i = n+1 \\ p_{n,i-1}\lambda_{n,i-1} + (1-p_{n,i})\lambda_{n,i} & \text{when} \quad 1 \leq i \leq n+1 \\ (1-p_{n,0})\lambda_{n,0} & \text{when} \quad i = 0 \end{cases}$$

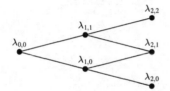

By solving the $(2n+3)$ unknown parameters using the $(2n+2)$ known parameters and by centering the tree around the center of the Cox–Ross–Rubinstein tree, Derman and Kani get the following equations for the stock prices above the central node

$$S_{n+1,i+1} = \frac{S_{n+1,i}[e^{r\Delta t}c(S_{n,i};\,T_{n+1}) - \Sigma] - \lambda_{n,i}S_{n,i}(F_{n,i} - S_{n+1,i})}{[e^{r\Delta t}c(S_{n,i};\,T_{n+1}) - \Sigma] - \lambda_{n,i}(F_{n,i} - S_{n+1,i})}, \tag{3.7}$$

where $\Sigma = \sum_{j=i+1}^{n} \lambda_{n,j}(F_{n,j} - S_{n,i})$ and $F_{n,j} = S_{n,j}e^{b\Delta t}$. The term $c(S_{n,i};\,T_{n+1})$ is the price of a European call with strike equal to the known stock price $S_{n,i}$ and time to maturity T_{n+1}. The stock prices below the central node is given by

$$S_{n+1,i} = \frac{S_{n+1,i+1}[e^{r\Delta t}p(S_{n,i};\,T_{n+1}) - \Sigma] + \lambda_{n,i}S_{n,i}(F_{n,i} - S_{n+1,i+1})}{[e^{r\Delta t}p(S_{n,i};\,T_{n+1}) - \Sigma] + \lambda_{n,i}(F_{n,i} - S_{n+1,i+1})}, \tag{3.8}$$

where $\Sigma = \sum_{j=0}^{i-1} \lambda_{n,j}(S_{n,i} - F_{n,j})$, and $p(S_{n,i};\,T_{n+1})$ is the price of a European put with strike equal to the known stock price $S_{n,i}$ and time to maturity T_{n+1} (not to be confused with the probability $p_{n,i}$). The transition probability at any time step is given by

$$p_{n,i} = \frac{F_{n,i} - S_{n+1,i}}{S_{n+1,i+1} - S_{n+1,i}}. \tag{3.9}$$

How to Start Building a New Level of the Tree

If we know $S_{n+1,i}$ at one initial node, we can use these equations to find the implied stock price for all nodes above and below the center of the tree.

1. If the number of time steps n already solved for is odd, $(n+1)$ is even: The initial central node $S_{n+1,i}$ is set equal to the central node of the Cox–Ross–Rubinstein tree.

2. If the number of time steps n already solved for is even, $(n+1)$ is odd: Use the logarithmic Cox–Ross–Rubinstein centering condition $S_{n+1,i}$ $= S^2/S_{n+1,i+1}$ where S is today's stock price. Substituting this relation into (3.7) gives

$$S_{n+1,i+1} = \frac{S[e^{r\Delta t}c(S; T_{n+1}) + \lambda_{n,i}S - \Sigma]}{\lambda_{n,i}F_{n,i} - e^{r\Delta t}c(S; T_{n+1}) + \Sigma}, \tag{3.10}$$

where

$$\Sigma = \sum_{j=i+1}^{n} \lambda_{n,j}(F_{n,j} - S_{n,i}).$$

From the implied stock prices and probabilities, we can find the implied local volatilities at each node:

$$\sigma_{n,i} = \frac{1}{\sqrt{\Delta t}} \sqrt{p_{n,i}(1 - p_{n,i})} \ln(S_{n+1,i+1}/S_{n+1,i}).$$

Implied Binomial Tree Example

Construct a five-year implied binomial tree with annual time steps. Assume that the stock price is 100, the risk-free rate is 5%, and the at-the-money volatility is 15% and increases (decreases) 0.5% with every 10-point drop (rise) in the strike price. The 90 strike will trade for 15.5% volatility, and the 110 strike for 14.5% volatility. The results below show a standard binomial tree together with the implied binomial tree, its transition probabilities, Arrow–Debreu prices, and local volatilities at each node.

Cox–Ross–Rubinstein binomial tree with constant volatility 15% where $u = e^{0.15\sqrt{1}} = 1.162$, $d = \frac{1}{u} = 0.861$ and a constant up probability equal to $p = \frac{e^{0.05 \times 1} - 0.861}{1.162 - 0.861} = 0.633$:

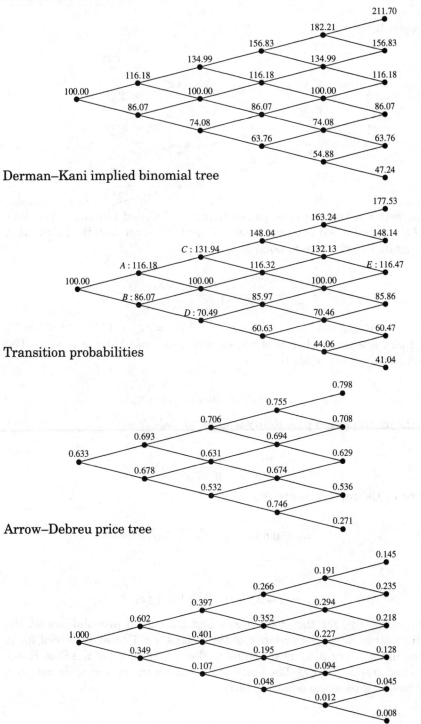

Derman–Kani implied binomial tree

Transition probabilities

Arrow–Debreu price tree

Local volatilities

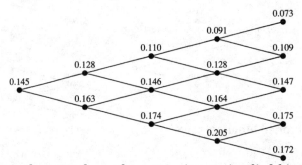

To illustrate the procedure of constructing an implied binomial tree, let's look at the calculations of a few nodes in detail. We start with the calculation of the implied stock price at node A:

$$S_A = S_{1,1} = \frac{100[e^{0.05 \times 1}c(S; T_{n+1}) + 1 \times 100 - \Sigma]}{1 \times F_{n,i} - e^{0.05 \times 1}c(S; T_{n+1}) + \Sigma} = 116.18,$$

where $c(X = 100; T = 1; \sigma = 15\%) = 9.74$ and $F_{n,i} = F_{0,0} = 100e^{0.05 \times 1} = 105.13$. Since there are no stock prices above this node, the Σ term is zero. The implied stock price at node B is

$$S_B = S_{1,0} = S^2/S_{1,1} = 100^2/116.18 = 86.07,$$

while the up transition probability leading to node A is

$$p_{0,0} = \frac{105.13 - 86.07}{116.18 - 86.07} = 0.633.$$

The Arrow–Debreu prices are thus

$$\lambda_{1,1} = 0.633 \times 1e^{-0.05 \times 1} = 0.602$$

and

$$\lambda_{1,0} = (1 - 0.633)1e^{-0.05 \times 1} = 0.349.$$

We can now solve for the stock prices and transition probabilities at the next time step. Since the number of time steps $n = 1$ already solved for is odd, the initial stock price is set equal to the central node of the Cox–Ross–Rubinstein tree $S_{2,1} = 100$. The stock prices above the center node can now easily be found by using equation (3.7).

$$S_C = S_{2,2} = \frac{100[e^{0.05 \times 1} c(S_{n,i}; T_{n+1}) - \Sigma] - 0.602 \times 116.18(F_{n,i} - 100)}{[e^{0.05 \times 1} c(S_{n,i}; T_{n+1}) - \Sigma] - 0.0602(F_{n,i} - 100)}$$

$$= 131.94,$$

where $c(X = 116.18; T = 2; \sigma = 14.19\%) = 6.25$, and $F_{n,i} = F_{1,1} = 116.18e^{0.05 \times 1} = 122.14$. Since there are no stock prices above this node, the Σ term is zero. Below the central node we get

$$S_D = S_{2,0} = \frac{100[e^{0.05 \times 1} p(S_{n,i}; T_{n+1}) - \Sigma] + 0.349 \times 86.07(F_{n,i} - 100)}{[e^{0.05 \times 1} p(S_{n,i}; T_{n+1}) - \Sigma] + 0.349(F_{n,i} - 100)}$$

$$= 70.49,$$

where $p(X = 86.07; T = 2; \sigma = 15.70\%) = 1.67$ and $F_{n,i} = F_{1,0} = 86.07e^{0.05 \times 1} = 90.48$. Since there are no stock prices below this node, the Σ term is zero. The two transition probabilities leading to these nodes are

$$p_{1,1} = \frac{122.14 - 100.00}{131.94 - 100.00} = 0.693$$

$$p_{1,0} = \frac{90.48 - 70.49}{100.00 - 70.49} = 0.678.$$

At node E, the number of time steps $n + 1 = 5$ is odd. We can now find the implied stock price using equation (3.10).

$$S_E = S_{5,3} = \frac{100[e^{0.05 \times 1} c(S; T_{n+1}) + 0.227 \times 100 - \Sigma]}{0.227F_{n,i} - e^{0.05 \times 1} c(S; T_{n+1}) + \Sigma} = 116.47$$

where $c(X = 100.00; T = 5; \sigma = 15.00\%) = 26.17$ and $F_{n,i} = 100e^{0.05 \times 1} = 105.13$. Since there are two nodes above this node, the Σ term is equal to:

$$\Sigma = \sum_{j=2+1}^{4} = 0.294(132.13e^{0.05 \times 1} - 100)$$

$$+ 0.191 \times (163.24e^{0.05 \times 1} - 100) = 25.15$$

3.4.2 Implied Trinomial Trees

The implied binomial model can run into problems when matching some common volatility structures. In several cases, negative transition probabilities can occur. In case of negative transition probabilities, one will need to override the input data. However, the more data one has to override, the less information from market prices will be reflected in the model.

A trinomial tree offers more flexibility and can match a larger class of volatility structures than its binomial counterpart. In an implied trinomial model, the state space can be chosen independently of the probabilities. The option prices are then used only to solve for the transition probabilities. We concentrate on constructing an implied trinomial tree using the method described by Derman, Kani, and Chriss (1996).

The transition probabilities above the center node of the tree are given by

$$p_{n,i} = \frac{e^{r\Delta T} c(S_{n+1,i+1}, T_{n+1}) - \sum_{j=i+1}^{2n} \lambda_{n,j}(F_{n,j} - S_{n+1,i+1})}{\lambda_{n,i}(S_{n+1,i+2} - S_{n+1,i+1})} \tag{3.11}$$

$$q_{n,i} = \frac{F_{n,i} - p_{n,i}(S_{n+1,i+2} - S_{n+1,i+1}) - S_{n+1,i+1}}{S_{n+1,i} - S_{n+1,i+1}} \tag{3.12}$$

The transition probabilities below and including the center node of the tree are given by

$$q_{n,i} = \frac{e^{r\Delta T} p(S_{n+1,i+1}, T_{n+1}) - \sum_{j=0}^{i-1} \lambda_{n,j}(S_{n+1,i+1} - F_{n,j})}{\lambda_{n,i}(S_{n+1,i+1} - S_{n+1,i})} \tag{3.13}$$

$$p_{n,i} = \frac{F_{n,i} + q_{n,i}(S_{n+1,i+1} - S_{n+1,i}) - S_{n+1,i+1}}{S_{n+1,i+2} - S_{n+1,i+1}} \tag{3.14}$$

In case of negative transition probabilities, one should try to choose another state space that better fits the volatility structure. Alternatively, one can override the negative probabilities. One way to ensure that the probabilities lie between zero and one is to set the probabilities equal to

If $S_{n+1,i+1} < F_{n,i} < S_{n+1,i+2}$

$$p_{n,i} = \frac{1}{2}\left(\frac{F_{n,i} - S_{n+1,i+1}}{S_{n+1,i+2} - S_{n+1,i+1}} + \frac{F_{n,i} - S_{n+1,i}}{S_{n+1,i+2} - S_{n+1,i}}\right)$$

$$q_{n,i} = \frac{1}{2}\left(\frac{S_{n+1,i+2} - F_{n,i}}{S_{n+1,i+2} - S_{n+1,i}}\right),$$

and if $S_{n+1,i} < F_{n,i} < S_{n+1,i+1}$

$$p_{n,i} = \frac{1}{2}\left(\frac{F_{n,i} - S_{n+1,i}}{S_{n+1,i+2} - S_{n+1,i}}\right)$$

$$q_{n,i} = \frac{1}{2}\left(\frac{S_{n+1,i+2} - F_{n,i}}{S_{n+1,i+2} - S_{n+1,i}} + \frac{S_{n+1,i+1} - F_{n,i}}{S_{n+1,i+1} - S_{n+1,i}}\right).$$

The transition probabilities at each time step can be used to calculate implied local volatilities for corresponding nodes in the tree.

$$
\sigma_{n,i} = \{[p_{n,i}(S_{n+1,i+2} - F_0)^2 + (1 - p_{n,i} - q_{n,i})(S_{n+1,i+1} - F_0)^2
$$
$$
+ q_{n,i}(S_{n+1,i} - F_0)^2]/(F_0^2 \Delta t)\}^{\frac{1}{2}}, \tag{3.15}
$$

where $F_0 = p_{n,i}S_{n+1,i+2} + (1 - p_{n,i} - q_{n,i})S_{n+1,i+1} + q_{n,i}S_{n+1,i}$.

Example

Assume the stock price is 100, the time to maturity is two years, the risk-free rate is 8%, the dividend yield is 6%, the at-the-money volatility is 12%. Assume, further, a volatility structure where the volatility increases (decreases) with 0.04% for every one-point decrease (increase) in the strike price. A strike price of 110 would then trade for 11.6% and a strike of 90 for 12.4% volatility. Build a two-year implied trinomial tree model with four time steps. $S = 100$, $T = 2$, $r = 0.08$, $b = 0.08 - 0.06 = 0.02$, $\sigma = 0.12$, $n = 4$, $\Delta t = 2/4 = 0.5$

By choosing a trinomial equivalent Cox–Ross–Rubinstein binomial tree ($u = e^{\sigma\sqrt{2\Delta t}}$ and $d = \frac{1}{u}$), we get the following stock price tree (state space):

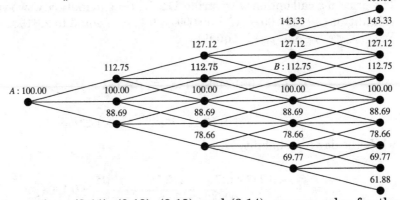

By using equations (3.11), (3.12), (3.13), and (3.14), we can solve for the transition probabilities, the Arrow–Debreu prices, and the local volatilities at each node. To illustrate the calculation procedure, let's look at the calculation at node A:

$$
q_{0,0} = \frac{e^{0.08 \times 0.5} p(100, 0.5) - \sum_{j=0}^{i-1} \lambda_{n,j}(S_{n+1,i+1} - F_{n,j})}{1(100 - 88.69)} = 0.2240
$$

The put price with strike 100, time to maturity six months, and volatility 12% is equal to 2.4333 in a standard trinomial tree with the same state space. The sum term $\sum_{j=0}^{i-1} \lambda_{n,j}(S_{n+1,i+1} - F_{n,j})$ is equal to zero since there are no nodes below this node.

$$p_{0,0} = \frac{F_{n,i} + 0.2240(100.00 - 88.69) - 100.00}{112.75 - 100.00} = 0.2775$$

$F_{n,i} = F_{0,0} = 100e^{0.02 \times 0.5} = 101.01$. The local volatility at this node is:

$$\sigma_{0,0} = \{[0.2775(112.75 - F_0)^2 + (1 - 0.2775 - 0.2240)(100.00 - F_0)^2$$

$$+ 0.2240(88.69 - F_0)^2]/(F_0^2 \times 0.5)\}^{\frac{1}{2}} = 0.1191,$$

where

$$F_0 = (0.2775 \times 112.75 + 0.2240 \times 88.69$$

$$+ (1 - 0.2775 - 0.2240)100.00)e^{0.02 \times 0.5} = 102.02$$

As a last example, let's look at the calculations at node B:

$$p_{3,4} = \frac{e^{0.08 \times 0.5}c(112.75, 2) - \sum_{j=i+1}^{2n} \lambda_{n,j}(F_{n,j} - S_{n+1,i+1})}{0.2440(127.12 - 112.75)} = 0.2476$$

The price of a call option with strike 112.75, time to maturity two years, and volatility $0.12 + (100.00 - 112.75)0.0004 = 0.1149$ is equal to 2.8198. $\sum_{j=i+1}^{2n} \lambda_{n,j}(F_{n,j} - S_{n+1,i+1})$ is equal to

$$\sum_{j=4+1}^{2 \times 3} = 0.1024(127.12e^{0.02 \times 0.5} - 112.75)$$

$$+ 0.0145(143.33e^{0.02 \times 0.5} - 112.75) = 2.07,$$

while the down probability equals

$$q_{3,4} = \frac{F_{n,i} - 0.2476(127.12 - 112.75) - 112.75}{100.00 - 112.75} = 0.1903 \qquad (3.16)$$

$F_{n,i} = F_{3,4} = 112.75^{0.02 \times 0.5} = 113.88$. The local volatility is

$$\sigma_{n,i} = \{[0.2476(127.12 - F_0)^2 + (1 - 0.2476 - 0.1903)(112.75 - F_0)^2$$

$$+ 0.1903(100.00 - F_0)^2]/(F_0^2 \times 0.5)\} = 0.1114,$$

where

$$F_0 = (0.2476 \times 127.12 + 0.1903 \times 100.00$$

$$+ (1 - 0.2476 - 0.1903)112.75)e^{0.02 \times 0.5} = 115.03.$$

Up-transition probabilities

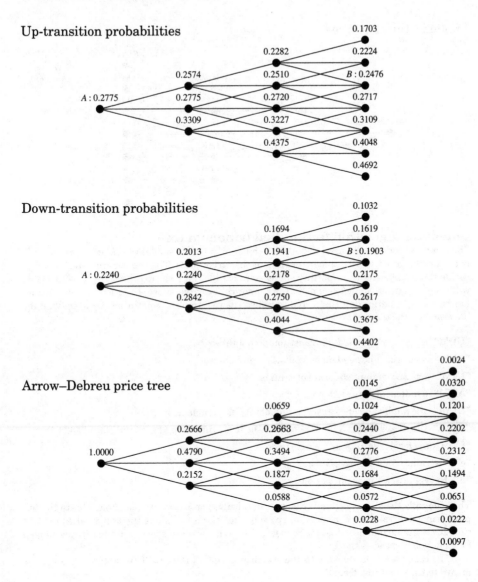

Down-transition probabilities

Arrow–Debreu price tree

Implied local volatilities

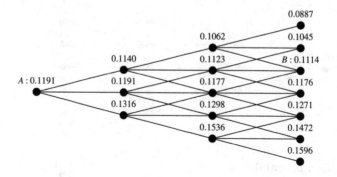

Computer algorithm for implied trinomial tree

The computer code can be used to build a complete implied trinomial tree. The volatility smile is for simplicity set to be a linear function of the strike price. The input parameter *Skew* will decide the steepness of the volatility smile/skew. For instance, setting the *Skew* equal to 0.0004 will give a volatility smile/skew as in the numerical example above. In practice, the volatility function should naturally be adjusted to reflect the real implied volatilities. By specifying the "*ReturnFlag*," the code will return

"UPM" a matrix of implied up transition probabilities.

"DPM" a matrix of implied down transition probabilities.

"LVM" a matrix of implied local volatilities.

"ADM" a matrix of Arrow–Debreu prices.

"DPni" the implied down transition probability at a single node.

"ADni" the Arrow–Debreu price at a single node (at time step $STEPn$ and state $STATEn$).

"LVni" the local volatility at a single node.

"c" the value of a European call option.

"p" the value of a European put option.

The code calls the $TrinomialTree(\cdot)$ function to calculate option prices used to calibrate the implied trinomial tree. The chosen state space in the computer code is the trinomial equivalent Cox–Ross–Rubinstein binomial state space. However, the state space could easily be changed by modifying the code slightly.

The computer code starts with the statement "Option Base 0." This statement forces the arrays to start counting from 0.

Option Base 0

```
Function ImpliedTrinomialTree(ReturnFlag As String, STEPn As Integer,
            STATEi As Integer, S As Double, X As Double, T As Double, _
            r As Double, b As Double, v As Double, Skew As Double, nSteps As Integer)

        Dim ArrowDebreuPrice() As Double, LocalVolatility() As Double
        Dim UpProbability() As Double, DownProbability() As Double
        Dim OptionValueNode() As Double
```

```
Dim dt As Double, u As Double, d As Double
Dim Si1 As Double, Si As Double, Si2 As Double
Dim vi As Double, Fj As Double, Fi As Double, Fo As Double
Dim Sum As Double, OptionValue As Double
Dim Df As Double, pi As Double, qi As Double
Dim i As Integer, j As Integer, n As Integer, z As Integer

ReDim OptionValueNode(nSteps * 2) As Double
ReDim ArrowDebreu(nSteps, nSteps * 2) As Double
ReDim UpProbability(nSteps − 1, nSteps * 2 − 2) As Double
ReDim DownProbability(nSteps − 1, nSteps * 2 − 2) As Double
ReDim LocalVolatility(nSteps − 1, nSteps * 2 − 2) As Double


dt = T/nSteps
u = Exp(v * Sqr(2 * dt))
d = 1/u
Df = Exp(−r * dt)
ArrowDebreu(0,0) = 1
For n = 0 To nSteps − 1
    For i = 0 To n * 2
        Sum = 0
        Si1 = S * u^Max(i − n,0) * d^Max(n * 2 − n − i,0)
        Si = Si1 * d
        Si2 = Si1 * u
        Fi = Si1 * Exp(b * dt)
        vi = v + (S − Si1) * Skew'// Linear volatility smile function


        '// Calculates the probabilities below and including the central node:
        If i < (n * 2)/2 + 1 Then
            For j = 0 To i − 1
                Fj = S * u^Max(j − n,0) * d^Max(n * 2 − n − j,0) * Exp(b * dt)
                Sum = Sum + ArrowDebreu(n, j) * (Si1 − Fj)
            Next
            OptionValue = TrinomialTree("e","p",S,Si1,(n + 1) * dt,r,b,vi,n + 1)
            qi = (Exp(r * dt) * OptionValue − Sum)/(ArrowDebreu(n,i) * (Si1 − Si))
            pi = (Fi + qi * (Si1 − Si) − Si1)/(Si2 − Si1)
            If pi < 0 Or pi > 1 Or qi < 0 Or qi > 1 Then
                pi = 1/2 * ((Fi − Si1)/(Si2 − Si1) + (Fi − Si)/(Si2 − Si))
                qi = 1/2 * ((Si2 − Fi)/(Si2 − Si))
        End If


        '// Calculates the probabilities above the central node:
        Else
            OptionValue = TrinomialTree("e","c",S,Si1,(n + 1) * dt,r,b,vi,n + 1)
            Sum = 0
            For j = i + 1 To n * 2
                Fj = S * u^Max(j − n,0) * d^Max(n * 2 − n − j,0) * Exp(b * dt)
                Sum = Sum + ArrowDebreu(n, j) * (Fj − Si1)
            Next
            pi = (Exp(r * dt) * OptionValue − Sum)/(ArrowDebreu(n,i) * (Si2 − Si1))
            qi = (Fi − pi * (Si2 − Si1) − Si1)/(Si − Si1)
            If pi < 0 Or pi > 1 Or qi < 0 Or qi > 1 Then
```

$$pi = 1/2*((Fi - Si1)/(Si2 - Si1) + (Fi - Si)/(Si2 - Si))$$
$$qi = 1/2*((Si2 - Fi)/(Si2 - Si))$$
    End If
End If
'// Replacing negative probabilities:
If $pi < 0$ **Or** $pi > 1$ **Or** $qi < 0$ **Or** $qi > 1$ **Then**
  If $Fi > Si1$ **And** $Fi < Si2$ **Then**
$$pi = 1/2*((Fi - Si1)/(Si2 - Si1) + (Fi - Si)/(Si2 - Si))$$
$$qi = 1/2*((Si2 - Fi)/(Si2 - Si))$$
  ElseIf $Fi > Si$ **And** $Fi < Si1$ **Then**
$$pi = 1/2*((Fi - Si)/(Si2 - Si))$$
$$qi = 1/2*((Si2 - Fi)/(Si2 - Si) + (Si1 - Fi)/(Si1 - Si))$$
  End If
End If
$DownProbability(n, i) = qi$
$UpProbability(n, i) = pi$

'// Calculation of local volatilities:
$$Fo = (pi*Si2 + qi*Si + (1 - pi - qi)*Si1)*Exp(b*dt)$$
$$LocalVolatility(n, i) = Sqr((pi*(Si2 - Fo)\string^2 + (1 - pi - qi)*\_$$
$$(Si1 - Fo)\string^2 + qi*(Si - Fo)\string^2)/(Fo\string^2*dt))$$

'// Calculates the Arrow–Debreu prices:
If $n = 0$ **Then**
  $ArrowDebreu(n + 1, i) = qi*ArrowDebreu(n, i)*Df$
  $ArrowDebreu(n + 1, i + 1) = (1 - pi - qi)*ArrowDebreu(n, i)*Df$
  $ArrowDebreu(n + 1, i + 2) = pi*ArrowDebreu(n, i)*Df$
ElseIf $n > 0$ **And** $i = 0$ **Then**
  $ArrowDebreu(n + 1, i) = qi*ArrowDebreu(n, i)*Df$
ElseIf $n > 0$ **And** $i = n*2$ **Then**
  $ArrowDebreu(n + 1, i) = UpProbability(n, i - 2)*\_$
  $ArrowDebreu(n, i - 2)*Df + (1 - UpProbability(n, i - 1) - \_$
  $DownProbability(n, i - 1))*ArrowDebreu(n, i - 1)*Df + \_$
  $qi*ArrowDebreu(n, i)*Df$
  $ArrowDebreu(n + 1, i + 1) = UpProbability(n, i - 1)*\_$
  $ArrowDebreu(n, i - 1)*Df + (1 - pi - qi)*ArrowDebreu(n, i)*Df$
  $ArrowDebreu(n + 1, i + 2) = pi*ArrowDebreu(n, i)*Df$
ElseIf $n > 0$ **And** $i = 1$ **Then**
  $ArrowDebreu(n + 1, i) = (1 - UpProbability(n, i - 1) - \_$
  $DownProbability(n, i - 1))*ArrowDebreu(n, i - 1)*Df \_$
  $+qi*ArrowDebreu(n, i)*Df$
Else
  $ArrowDebreu(n + 1, i) = UpProbability(n, i - 2)*\_$
  $ArrowDebreu(n, i - 2)*Df + (1 - UpProbability(n, i - 1) - \_$
  $DownProbability(n, i - 1))*ArrowDebreu(n, i - 1)*Df \_$
  $+qi*ArrowDebreu(n, i)*Df$
End If
  Next
Next

'// Returns output dependent on the settings of the: $ReturnFlag$
If $ReturnFlag = "DPM"$ **Then**

$ImpliedTrinomialTree = Application.Transpose(DownProbability)$
ElseIf $ReturnFlag = "UPM"$ **Then**
  $ImpliedTrinomialTree = Application.Transpose(UpProbability)$
ElseIf $ReturnFlag = "DPni"$ **Then**
  $ImpliedTrinomialTree = (DownProbability(STEPn, STATEi))$
ElseIf $ReturnFlag = "UPni"$ **Then**
  $ImpliedTrinomialTree = (UpProbability(STEPn, STATEi))$
ElseIf $ReturnFlag = "ADM"$ **Then**
  $ImpliedTrinomialTree = Application.Transpose(ArrowDebreu)$
ElseIf $ReturnFlag = "LVM"$ **Then**
  $ImpliedTrinomialTree = Application.Transpose(LocalVolatility)$
ElseIf $ReturnFlag = "LVni"$ **Then**
  $ImpliedTrinomialTree = Application.\_$
  $Transpose(LocalVolatility(STEPn, STATEi))$
ElseIf $ReturnFlag = "ADni"$ **Then**
  $ImpliedTrinomialTree = (ArrowDebreu(STEPn, STATEi))$
Else
    '// Calculates the value of a call or put option using the implied tree:
    If $ReturnFlag = "c"$ **Then**
      $z = 1$
    ElseIf $ReturnFlag = "p"$ **Then**
      $z = -1$
    End If
    For $i = 0$ **To** $(2 * nSteps)$
      $OptionValueNode(i) = Max(0, z * (S * u\hat{\ }Max(i - nSteps, 0) * \_$
      $d\hat{\ }Max(nSteps - i, 0) - X))$
    Next
    For $n = nSteps - 1$ **To** 0 **Step** -1
      For $i = 0$ **To** $(n * 2)$
        $OptionValueNode(i) = (UpProbability(n, i) * \_$
        $OptionValueNode(i + 2) + (1 - UpProbability(n, i) - \_$
        $DownProbability(n, i)) * OptionValueNode(i + 1) + \_$
        $DownProbability(n, i) * OptionValueNode(i)) * Df$
      Next
    Next
    $ImpliedTrinomialTree = OptionValueNode(0)$
  End If
End Function

3.5 MONTE CARLO SIMULATION

Monte Carlo simulation is another numerical method that is often useful when no closed-form solution is available. Monte Carlo simulating in option pricing, originally introduced by Boyle (1977), can be used to value most types of European[6] options (e.g., arithmetic average-rate options where only

---

6. In general, Monte Carlo simulation can only be used to price European options. Recently, however, several papers have shown that Monte Carlo simulation also can be used to price American options, for example, Barraquand and Martineau (1995).

closed-form approximations are available). The Monte Carlo method can be used to simulate a wide range of stochastic processes. To illustrate the use of Monte Carlo simulation, we will here limit ourselves to processes where the natural logarithm of the underlying asset follows geometric Brownian motion. That is, the process governing the asset price S is given by

$$S + dS = S \exp\left[\left(\mu - \frac{1}{2}\sigma^2\right) dt + \sigma dz\right],$$

where dz is a Wiener process with a standard deviation one and mean zero. To simulate the process, we split it up at discrete time intervals, Δt apart.

$$S + \Delta S = S \exp\left[\left(\mu - \frac{1}{2}\sigma^2\right) \Delta t + \sigma \epsilon_t \sqrt{\Delta t}\right],$$

where ΔS is a discrete change in S in the chosen time interval Δt, and ϵ_t is a random drawing from a standard normal distribution. Most computer languages have built-in functions that draw randomly from a standard normal distribution. If the computer languages only have a function to draw randomly a number Z between zero and one, this can easily be transformed into a random number from a standard normal distribution ϵ by using the relationship

$$\epsilon = \sum_{i=1}^{12} Z_i - 6$$

The main drawback of Monte Carlo simulation is that it is computer-intensive. 10 thousand simulations are typically necessary to price an option with satisfying accuracy.[7] The computer code in this book is written in Visual Basic. Implementing the same code in C (or most other lower-level computer languages) will increase the speed dramatically and is recommended for serious, large-scale use of Monte Carlo simulation.

Computer algorithm for standard European options
This function can be used to price standard European call and put options.

Function *MonteCarloStandardOption(CallPutFlag* As String,S As Double, _
    X As Double, T As Double, r As Double, b As Double, _
    v As Double, *nStep* As Integer,*nSimulations* As Integer) As Double

---

7. Several techniques are available to speed up the Monte Carlo simulation, for example, Duffie and Glynn (1992), Curran (1994a), Moro (1995), and Brotherton-Ratcliffe (1994).

```
Dim dt As Double, St As Double
Dim Sum As Double, Drift As Double, vSqrdt As Double
Dim i As Integer, j As Integer, z As Integer

dt = T/nSteps
Drift = (b − v^2/2) * dt
vSqrdt = v * Sqr(dt)
If CallPutFlag = "c" Then
    z = 1
ElseIf CallPutFlag = "p" Then
        z = −1
End If
For i = 1 To nSimulations
    St = S
    For j = 1 To nSteps
        St = St * Exp(Drift + vSqrdt * Application.NormInv(Rnd(),0,1))
    Next
    Sum = Sum + Max(z * (St − X),0)
Next
MonteCarloStandardOption = Exp(−r * T) * (Sum/nSimulations)
End Function
```

Two Assets

Monte Carlo simulation can easily be extended to options on two underlying assets.

$$S_1 + \Delta S_1 = S_1 \exp\left[\left(\mu_1 - \frac{1}{2}\sigma_1^2\right)\Delta t + \sigma_1 \alpha_{1,t}\sqrt{\Delta t}\right]$$

$$S_2 + \Delta S_2 = S_2 \exp\left[\left(\mu_2 - \frac{1}{2}\sigma_2^2\right)\Delta t + \sigma_2 \alpha_{2,t}\sqrt{\Delta t}\right]$$

Correlation between the two assets is allowed by setting

$$\alpha_{1,t} = \epsilon_{1,t}$$

$$\alpha_{2,t} = \rho\epsilon_{1,t} + \epsilon_{2,t}\sqrt{1 - \rho^2},$$

where $\epsilon_{1,t}$ and $\epsilon_{2,t}$ are two independently random numbers from a standard normal distribution.

Most options on two correlated assets can more efficiently be priced analytically or in a three-dimensional binomial lattice, shown earlier in this chapter. One example where two-asset Monte Carlo simulation is useful is in the pricing of European Asian spread options.[8] These are options whose

---

8. For pricing Asian Spread options, see Heenk, Kemna, and Vorst (1990).

payoff depends on the difference between the arithmetic average of the two assets at expiration.

Computer algorithm for two-asset Asian spread options

The computer code below shows how to price a European arithmetic average spread call or put option. The code is limited to pricing the option at the beginning of the averaging period. It is easy to extend the code to price the option before or into the averaging period.

```
Function MonteCarloAsianSpreadOption(CallPutFlag As String, S1 As Double, _
        S2 As Double, X As Double, T As Double, r As Double, b1 As Double, _
        b2 As Double, v1 As Double, v2 As Double, As Double, _
        nSteps As Integer, nSimulations As Integer) As Double

    Dim dt As Double, St1 As Double, St2 As Double
    Dim i As Integer, j As Integer, z As Integer
    Dim Sum As Double, Drift1 As Double, Drift2 As Double
    Dim v1Sqrdt As Double, v2Sqrdt As Double
    Dim Epsilon1 As Double, Epsilon2 As Double
    Dim Average1 As Double, Average2 As Double

    If CallPutFlag = "c" Then
        z = 1
    ElseIf CallPutFlag = "p" Then
        z = -1
    End If
    dt = T/nSteps
    Drift1 = (b1 - v1^2/2) * dt
    Drift2 = (b2 - v2^2/2) * dt
    v1Sqrdt = v1 * Sqr(dt)
    v2Sqrdt = v2 * Sqr(dt)
    For i = 1 To nSimulations
        Average1 = 0
        Average2 = 0
        St1 = S1
        St2 = S2
        For j = 1 To nSteps
            Epsilon1 = Application.NormInv(Rnd(),0,1)
            Epsilon2 = rho * Epsilon1 + _
            Application.NormInv(Rnd(),0,1) * Sqr(1 - rho^2)
            St1 = St1 * Exp(Drift1 + v1Sqrdt * Epsilon1)
            St2 = St2 * Exp(Drift2 + v2Sqrdt * Epsilon2)
            Average1 = Average1 + St1
            Average2 = Average2 + St2
        Next
        Average1 = Average1/nSteps
        Average2 = Average2/nSteps
        Sum = Sum + Max(z * (Average1 - Average2 - X),0)
    Next
    MonteCarloAsianSpreadOption = Exp(-r * T) * (Sum/nSimulations)
End Function
```

CHAPTER

4

⑥ INTEREST-RATE OPTIONS

4.1 PRICING INTEREST-RATE OPTIONS USING BLACK-76

The Black-76 modified Black–Scholes model is probably the most widely used model to price interest-rate options. The formula was originally developed to price options on forwards and assumes that the underlying asset is lognormally distributed. When used to price a cap, for example, the underlying forward rates of the cap are thus assumed to be lognormal. Similarly, when used to price a swaption (an option on a swap), the underlying swap rate is assumed to be lognormal. This can be justified when pricing these types of options independently (Jamshidian (1996), Miltersen, Sandmann, and Sondermann (1997)). Still, a simultaneous valuation of both a cap and a swaption with the Black-76 formula is theoretically inconsistent. Both the forward rate of the cap and the swap rate cannot be lognormal simultaneously. However, the great popularity of this model for pricing both caps and swaptions indicates that any problems due to this inconsistency are negligible in an economic sense.[1]

The same is true with bond prices and swap rates: they cannot be lognormal at the same time. For instance, if the bond price is assumed to be lognormal, the continuously compounded swap rate must be normally distributed. Using the same model (Black-76) for pricing swaptions and bond options is then inconsistent.

4.1.1 Caps and Floors

An interest-rate cap consists of a series of individual European call options, called *caplets*. Each caplet can be priced by using a modified version of the Black-76 formula. This is accomplished by using the implied forward rate, F, at each caplet maturity as the underlying asset. The price of the cap is

---

1. Traders often adjust inconsistencies by adjusting the volatility slightly, based on experience from the particular market in which they operate.

the sum of the price of the caplets that make up the cap. Similarly, the value of a floor is the sum of the sequence of individual put options, often called floorlets, that make up the floor.

$$Cap = \sum_{i=1}^{n} Caplet_i, \qquad Floor = \sum_{i=1}^{n} Floorlet_i,$$

where

$$\begin{aligned} \text{Caplet value} \quad &= \quad \frac{\text{Notional} \times \frac{d}{Basis}}{\left(1 + F\frac{d}{Basis}\right)} \times \text{Black-76 call value} \\ &= \quad \frac{\text{Notional} \times \frac{d}{Basis}}{\left(1 + F\frac{d}{Basis}\right)} e^{-rT} [FN(d_1) - XN(d_2)] \end{aligned}$$

d is the number of days in the forward rate period. *Basis* is the day basis or number of days per year used in the market (i.e. 360 or 365).

$$\text{Floorlet value} = \frac{\text{Notional} \times \frac{d}{Basis}}{\left(1 + F\frac{d}{Basis}\right)} e^{-rT} [XN(-d_2) - FN(-d_1)],$$

where

$$d_1 = \frac{\ln(F/X) + (\sigma^2/2)T}{\sigma\sqrt{T}}$$

$$d_2 = \frac{\ln(F/X) - (\sigma^2/2)T}{\sigma\sqrt{T}} = d_1 - \sigma\sqrt{T}.$$

Miltersen, Sandmann, and Sondermann (1997) recently developed an interesting closed-form lognormal yield-based model for the valuation of caps and floors. Their model is an extension of the modified Black-76 caps and floor model that allows for stochastic discount rates and time-dependent volatility.

Example
What is the value of a caplet with six months to expiry on a 182-day forward rate and a notional principle of 100 million? The six-month forward rate is 8% ($\frac{Act}{360}$ basis), the strike is 8%, the risk-free interest rate is 7%, and the volatility of the forward rate is 28% per annum. $F = 0.08$, $X = 0.08$, $T = 0.5$, $r = 0.07$, $\sigma = 0.28$.

$$d_1 = \frac{\ln(0.08/0.08) + (0.28^2/2)0.5}{0.28\sqrt{0.5}} = 0.0990, \quad d_2 = d_1 - 0.28\sqrt{0.5} = -0.0990$$

$$N(d_1) = N(0.0990) = 0.5394, \qquad N(d_2) = N(-0.0990) = 0.4606$$

$$\text{Caplet value} = \frac{100,000,000 \times \frac{182}{360}}{\left(1 + 0.08\frac{182}{360}\right)} e^{-0.07 \times 0.5}[0.08N(d_1) - 0.08N(d_2)] = 295.995$$

4.1.2 Swaptions

It is usual to distinguish between the following:

- **Payer swaptions.** The right but not the obligation to pay fixed rate and receive floating rate in the underlying swap.
- **Receiver swaptions.** The right but not the obligation to receive fixed rate and pay floating rate in the underlying swap.

European swaptions[2] are normally priced by using the forward swap rate as input in the Black-76 option pricing model. The Black-76 value is multiplied by a factor adjusting for the tenor of the swaption, as shown by Smith (1991). This is the practitioner's benchmark swaption model. As illustrated by Jamshidian (1996), the model is arbitrage-free under the assumption of a lognormal swap rate.

$$c = \left[\frac{1 - \frac{1}{\left(1+\frac{F}{m}\right)^{t_1 \times m}}}{F} \right] e^{-rT}[FN(d_1) - XN(d_2)] \tag{4.1}$$

$$p = \left[\frac{1 - \frac{1}{\left(1+\frac{F}{m}\right)^{t_1 \times m}}}{F} \right] e^{-rT}[XN(-d_2) - FN(-d_1)], \tag{4.2}$$

where

$$d_1 = \frac{\ln(F/X) + (\sigma^2/2)T}{\sigma\sqrt{T}}, \quad d_2 = d_1 - \sigma\sqrt{T},$$

where c indicates a payer swaption, and p is a receiver swaption.

---

2. More than 90% of the swaption market consists of European swaptions. To price American swaptions, look at section 4.2 for yield-based models.

t_1 = Tenor of swap in years.
F = Forward rate of underlying swap.
X = Strike rate of swaption.
r = Risk-free interest rate.
T = Time to expiration in years.
σ = Volatility of the forward-starting swap rate.
m = Compoundings per year in swap rate.

Example

Consider a two-year payer swaption on a four-year swap with semiannual compounding. The forward swap rate of 7% starts two years from now and ends six years from now. The strike is 7.5%, the risk-free interest rate is 6%, and the volatility of the forward starting swap rate is 20% per annum. $t_1 = 4$, $m = 2$, $F = 0.07$, $X = 0.075$, $T = 2$, $r = 0.06$, $\sigma = 0.20$.

$$d_1 = \frac{\ln(0.07/0.075) + (0.20^2/2)2}{0.20\sqrt{2}} = -0.1025, \quad d_2 = d_1 - 0.20\sqrt{2} = -0.3853$$

$$N(d_1) = N(-0.1025) = 0.4592, \qquad N(d_2) = N(-0.3853) = 0.3500$$

$$c = e^{-0.06 \times 2}[0.07 N(d_1) - 0.075 N(d_2)] = 0.5227\%$$

With a semiannual forward swap rate, the up-front value of the payer swaption in per cent of the notional is

$$c \times \left[\frac{1 - \frac{1}{\left(1 + \frac{0.07}{2}\right)^{4 \times 2}}}{0.07} \right] = 1.7964\%$$

4.1.3   Convexity Adjustments

A standard bond or interest-rate swap has a convex price-yield relationship. To price options with the Black-76 model when the underlying asset is a derivative security with a payoff function linear in the bond or swap yield, the yield should be adjusted for lack of convexity value.

Examples of derivatives where the payoff is a linear function of the bond or swap yield are Constant Maturity Swaps (CMS) and Constant Maturity Treasury Swaps (CMT). The closed-form formula published by Brotherton-Ratcliffe and Iben (1993) assumes that the forward yield is lognormally distributed.[3]

---

3. The original formula published by Brotherton-Ratcliffe and Iben (1993) is slightly different.

$$\text{Convexity adjustment} = -\frac{1}{2}\frac{\frac{\partial^2 P}{\partial y_F^2}}{\frac{\partial P}{\partial y_F}}y_F^2(e^{\sigma^2 T} - 1), \qquad (4.3)$$

where

$$P = \text{Bond or fixed side swap value.}$$
$$y_F = \text{Forward yield.}$$
$$T = \text{Time to payment date in years.}$$
$$\sigma = \text{Volatility of the forward yield.}$$

Example

Consider a derivative instrument with a single payment five years from now that is based on the the notional principal times the yield of a standard four-year swap with annual payments. The forward yield of the four-year swap starting five years in the future and ending nine years in the future is 7%. The volatility of the forward swap yield is 18%. What is the convexity adjustment of the swap yield? The value of the fixed side of the swap with annual yield is equal to the value of a bond where the coupon is equal to the forward swap rate/yield y_f:

$$P = \frac{c}{1 + y_F} + \frac{c}{(1 + y_F)^2} + \frac{c}{(1 + y_F)^3} + \frac{1 + c}{(1 + y_F)^4}$$

The partial derivative of the swap with respect to the yield is

$$\frac{\partial P}{\partial y_F} = -\frac{c}{(1 + y_F)^2} - \frac{2c}{(1 + y_F)^3} - \frac{3c}{(1 + y_F)^4} - \frac{4(1 + c)}{(1 + y_F)^5}$$

$$= -\frac{0.07}{(1 + 0.07)^2} - \frac{2 \times 0.07}{(1 + 0.07)^3} - \frac{3 \times 0.07}{(1 + 0.07)^4} - \frac{4(1 + 0.07)}{(1 + 0.07)^5} = -3.3872,$$

and the second partial derivative with respect to the forward swap rate is

$$\frac{\partial^2 P}{\partial y_F^2} = \frac{2c}{(1 + y_F)^3} + \frac{6c}{(1 + y_F)^4} + \frac{12c}{(1 + y_F)^5} + \frac{20(1 + c)}{(1 + y_F)^6}$$

$$= \frac{2 \times 0.07}{(1 + 0.07)^3} + \frac{6 \times 0.07}{(1 + 0.07)^4} + \frac{12 \times 0.07}{(1 + 0.07)^5} + \frac{20(1 + 0.07)}{(1 + 0.07)^6} = 15.2933.$$

The convexity adjustment can now be found by using equation (4.3):

$$\text{Convexity adjustment} = -\frac{1}{2}\frac{15.2933}{-3.3872}0.07^2(e^{0.18^2 \times 5} - 1) = 0.0019$$

The convexity adjusted rate is then equal to 7.19% $(0.07 + 0.0019)$.

Vega of the convexity adjustment
The convexity adjustment's sensitivity to a small change in volatility is given by

$$Vega = -\frac{\frac{\partial^2 P}{\partial y_F^2}}{\frac{\partial P}{\partial y_F}} y_F^2 \sigma T e^{\sigma^2 T} \tag{4.4}$$

Implied volatility from the convexity value in a bond
If the convexity adjustment is known, it is possible to calculate the implied volatility by simply rearranging the convexity adjustment formula:

$$\sigma = \sqrt{\ln\left(\frac{\text{Convexity adjustment}}{-\frac{1}{2}\frac{\partial^2 P}{\partial y_F^2} y_F^2} + 1\right)\frac{1}{T}} \tag{4.5}$$

4.1.4   European Short-Term Bond Options

European bond options can be priced in the Black-76 model by using the forward price of the bond at expiration as the underlying asset.

$$c = e^{-rT}[FN(d_1) - XN(d_2)] \tag{4.6}$$

$$p = e^{-rT}[XN(-d_2) - FN(-d_1)], \tag{4.7}$$

where F is the forward price of the bond at the expiration of the option, and

$$d_1 = \frac{\ln(F/X) + (\sigma^2/2)T}{\sigma\sqrt{T}}, \qquad d_2 = d_1 - \sigma\sqrt{T}.$$

This model does not take into consideration the pull to par effect of the bond. At maturity, the bond price must be equal to principal plus the coupon. For this reason, the uncertainty of a bond will first increase and then decrease.

The Black-76 model assumes that the uncertainty (variance) of the underlying asset increases linearly with time to maturity. Pricing of European bond options using this approach should thus be limited to options with short time to maturity relative to the time to maturity of the bond. A rule of thumb used by some traders is that the time to maturity of the option should be no longer than one-fifth of the time to maturity on the underlying bond.

Example

Consider a European put option with six months to expiry and strike price 122 on a bond with forward price at option expiration equal to 122.5. The volatility of the forward price is 4%, and the risk-free discount rate is 5%. What is the option's value? $F = 122.5, X = 122, T = 0.5, r = 0.05, \sigma = 0.04$.

$$d_1 = \frac{\ln(122.5/122) + (0.04^2/2)0.5}{0.04\sqrt{0.5}} = 0.1587$$

$$d_2 = 0.1587 - 0.04\sqrt{0.5} = 0.1305$$

$$N(-d_1) = N(-0.1587) = 0.4369, \quad N(-d2) = N(-0.1305) = 0.4481$$

$$p = e^{-0.05 \times 0.5}[122 \times 0.4481 - 122.5 \times 0.4369] = 1.1155$$

4.1.5 The Schaefer and Schwartz Model

The Schaefer and Schwartz (1987) modified Black–Scholes model for pricing bond options takes into consideration that the price volatility of a bond increases with duration:

$$c = Se^{(b-r)T}N(d_1) - Xe^{-rT}N(d_2)$$

$$p = Xe^{-rT}N(-d_2) - Se^{(b-r)T}N(-d_1),$$

where

$$\sigma = (KS^{\alpha-1})D$$

$$d_1 = \frac{\ln(S/X) + (b + \sigma^2/2)T}{\sigma\sqrt{T}}$$

$$d_2 = d_1 - \sigma\sqrt{T},$$

where D is the duration of the bond after the option expires. K is estimated from the observed price volatility σ_o of the bond. α is a constant that Schaefer and Schwartz suggest should be set to 0.5.

$$K = \frac{\sigma_o}{S^{\alpha-1}D^*},$$

where D^* is the duration of the bond today.

Example

Assume that the duration of the bond is eight years and that the observed price volatility of the bond is 12%. This gives

$$K = \frac{0.12}{100^{0.5-1}8} = 0.15$$

Table 4–1 uses this value and compares the option prices from the Schaefer and Schwartz formula with option prices from the Black-76 formula.

T A B L E   4–1

Comparison of the Black-76 Formula with the Schaefer and Schwartz Volatility-Adjusted Black-76 Formula

$(F = 100, X = 100, T = 2, r = 0.10, b = 0)$

Bond Duration	Base Volatility	Adjusted Volatility	Black-76 Value	Modified Black-76 Value
1	12.0 %	1.5 %	5.5364	0.6929
2	12.0 %	3.0 %	5.5364	1.3857
3	12.0 %	4.5 %	5.5364	2.0783
4	12.0 %	6.0 %	5.5364	2.7707
5	12.0 %	7.5 %	5.5364	3.4628
6	12.0 %	9.0 %	5.5364	4.1545
7	12.0 %	10.5 %	5.5364	4.8457
8	12.0 %	12.0 %	5.5364	5.5364

4.2   ONE-FACTOR TERM-STRUCTURE MODELS

4.2.1   The Rendleman and Bartter Model

The Rendleman and Bartter (1980) model is a one-factor equilibrium model that assumes that the short-term interest rate is lognormal, that is, that it follows a geometric Brownian motion:

$$dr = \mu r dt + \sigma r dz,$$

where μ is a constant drift of the instantaneous change in the short-term interest rate, and σ is the instantaneous variance of the change in the rate. The model can be implemented by a binomial tree similar to the Cox–Ross–Rubinstein tree described in Chapter 3. The up and down step sizes are set to

$$u = e^{\sigma\sqrt{\Delta t}}, \qquad d = e^{-\sigma\sqrt{\Delta t}}$$

The probability of moving up is

$$p = \frac{e^{\mu \Delta t} - d}{u - d}$$

4.2.2 The Vasicek Model

The Vasicek (1977) model is a yield-based one-factor equilibrium model that assumes that the short rate is normal. The model contains mean reversion and is popular in the academic community (mainly due to its analytic tractability). Because the model is not necessarily arbitrage-free with respect to the actual underlying securities in the marketplace, the model is not used much.

$$dr = \kappa(\theta - r)dt + \sigma dz \tag{4.8}$$

κ is the speed of the mean reversion, and θ is the mean reversion level.

Bond prices
The price at time t of a discount bond maturing at time T is $P(t,T)$ where

$$P(t,T) = A(t,T)e^{-B(t,T)r(t)}$$

where $r(t)$ is the rate at time t and

$$B(t,T) = \frac{1 - e^{-\kappa(T-t)}}{\kappa}$$

$$A(t,T) = \exp\left[\frac{(B(t,T) - T + t)(\kappa^2\theta - \sigma^2/2)}{\kappa^2} - \frac{\sigma^2 B(t,T)^2}{4\kappa}\right].$$

European options
The value of a European option maturing at time T on a zero-coupon bond that matures at time τ is

$$c = P(t,\tau)N(h) - XP(t,T)N(h - \sigma_P) \tag{4.9}$$

$$p = XP(t,T)N(-h + \sigma_P) - P(t,\tau)N(-h), \tag{4.10}$$

where

$$h = \frac{1}{\sigma_P}\ln\left[\frac{P(t,\tau)}{P(t,T)X}\right] + \frac{\sigma_P}{2}$$

$$\sigma_P = B(T,\tau)\sqrt{\frac{\sigma^2(1 - e^{-2\kappa(T-t)})}{2\kappa}}.$$

Example

Consider a European call option on a zero-coupon bond. Time to expiration is two years, the strike price is 92, the volatility is 3%, the mean-reverting level is 9%, and the mean reverting rate is 0.05. The face value of the bond is 100 with time to maturity three years, and initial risk-free rate of 8%.
$F = 100$, $\quad X = 92$, $\quad T = 2$, $\quad \tau = 3$, $\quad \theta = 0.09$, $\quad \kappa = 0.05$, $\quad r = 0.08$, $\quad \sigma = 0.03$.

$$B(t,T) = B(0,2) = \frac{1 - e^{-0.05(2-0)}}{0.05} = 1.9032$$

$$B(T,\tau) = B(2,3) = \frac{1 - e^{-0.05(3-2)}}{0.05} = 0.9754$$

$$B(t,\tau) = B(0,3) = \frac{1 - e^{-0.05(3-0)}}{0.05} = 2.7858$$

$$A(t,T) = A(0,2) \quad = \quad \exp\left[\frac{(B(0,2) - 2 + 0)(0.05^2 \times 0.09 - 0.03^2/2)}{0.05^2}\right.$$
$$\left. -\frac{0.03^2 B(0,2)^2}{4 \times 0.05}\right] = 0.9924$$

$$A(t,\tau) = A(0,3) \quad = \quad \exp\left[\frac{(B(0,3) - 3 + 0)(0.05^2 \times 0.09 - 0.03^2/2)}{0.05^2}\right.$$
$$\left. -\frac{0.03^2 B(0,3)^2}{4 \times 0.05}\right] = 0.9845$$

$$P(t,T) = P(0,2) = A(0,2)e^{-B(0,2)0.08} = 0.8523$$

$$P(t,\tau) = P(0,3) = A(0,3)e^{-B(0,3)0.08} = 0.7878$$

$$\sigma_P = B(2,3)\sqrt{\frac{0.03^2(1 - e^{-2 \times 0.05 \times 2})}{2 \times 0.05}} = 0.0394$$

$$h = \frac{1}{\sigma_P}\ln\left[\frac{P(0,3)}{P(0,2)92}\right] + \frac{\sigma_P}{2} = 0.1394$$

The call value for one USD in face value is

$$c = P(0,3)N(h) - 92P(0,2)N(h - \sigma_P) = 0.0143$$

With a face value of 100 the call value is 1.43 USD (100×0.0143).

Jamshidian's approach for coupon bonds

Jamshidian (1989) has shown that a European option on a coupon bond can be decomposed into a portfolio of options on zero-coupon bonds, where each coupon is treated as a zero-coupon bond. One proceeds by finding the value of the risk-free interest rate $\hat{r}$ at time T that causes the value of the coupon bond to equal the strike price.

Example

Consider a European call option on a coupon bond. Time to expiration is four years, the strike price 99.5, the volatility is 3%, the mean-reverting level is 10%, and the mean-reverting rate is 0.05. The face value of the bond is 100, and it pays a semiannual coupon of four. Time to maturity is seven years, and the risk-free rate is initially 9%.

First find the rate $\hat{r}$ that makes the value of the coupon bond equal to the strike price at the option's expiry. Trial and error gives $\hat{r} = 8.0050\%$. To find the value of the option, we have to determine the value of six different options:

1. A four-year option with strike price 3.8427 on a 4.5-year zero-coupon bond with a face value of four.

2. A four-year option with strike price 3.6910 on a five-year zero-coupon bond with a face value of four.

3. A four-year option with strike price 3.5452 on a 5.5-year zero-coupon bond with a face value of four.

4. A four-year option with strike price 3.4055 on a six-year zero-coupon bond with a face value of four.

5. A four-year option with strike price 3.2717 on a 6.5-year zero-coupon bond with a face value of four.

6. A four-year option with strike price 81.7440 on a seven-year zero-coupon bond with a face value of 104.

The value of the six options are, respectively, 0.0256, 0.0493, 0.0713, 0.0917, 0.1105, and 3.3219. This gives a total value of 3.6703.

4.2.3   The Ho and Lee Model

Ho and Lee (1986) published the first arbitrage-free yield-based model. It assumes a normally distributed short-term rate. This enables analytical solutions for European bond options. The short rate's drift depends on time, thus making the model arbitrage-free with respect to observed prices (the input to the model). The model does not incorporate mean reversion.

$$dr = \theta(t)dt + \sigma dz \tag{4.11}$$

where $\theta(t)$ is a time-dependent drift.

Bond prices
The price at time t of a discount bond maturing at time T is $P(T)$, given by

$$P(t,T) = A(t,T)e^{-r(t)(T-t)},$$

where $r(t)$ is the rate at time t and

$$\ln A(t,T) = \ln\left(\frac{P(0,T)}{P(0,t)}\right) - (T-t)\frac{\partial \ln P(0,t)}{\partial t} - \frac{1}{2}\sigma^2 t(T-t)^2$$

European options
The value of a European option maturing at time T on a zero-coupon bond maturing at time τ is

$$c = P(t,\tau)N(h) - XP(t,T)N(h - \sigma_P) \tag{4.12}$$

$$p = XP(t,T)N(h - \sigma_P) - P(t,\tau)N(h), \tag{4.13}$$

where

$$h = \frac{1}{\sigma_P}\ln\left[\frac{P(t,\tau)}{P(t,T)X}\right] + \frac{\sigma_P}{2}$$

$$\sigma_P = \sigma(\tau - T)\sqrt{T - t}$$

4.2.4 The Hull and White Model

The Hull and White (1990) model[4] is simply the Ho and Lee model with mean reversion.[5] The Hull and White model allows closed-form solutions for European options on zero-coupon bonds. Jamshidian's approach can be used to price options on coupon bonds.

$$dr = \kappa \left(\frac{\theta(t)}{\kappa} - r \right) dt + \sigma dz, \tag{4.14}$$

where κ is the speed of mean reversion. $\frac{\theta(t)}{\kappa}$ is a time-dependent mean-reversion level.

Bond prices
The price at time t of a discount bond maturing at time T is $P(t,T)$:

$$P(t,T) = A(t,T)e^{-B(t,T)r(t)}$$

where $r(t)$ is the rate at time t and

$$B(t,T) = \frac{1 - e^{-\kappa(T-t)}}{\kappa}$$

$$\ln A(t,T) = \ln \left[\frac{P(0,T)}{P(0,t)} \right] - B(t,T)\frac{\partial P(0,t)}{\partial t} - \frac{v(t,T)^2}{2}$$

$$v(t,T)^2 = \frac{1}{2\kappa^3}\sigma^2(e^{-\kappa T} - e^{-\kappa t})^2(e^{2\kappa t} - 1)$$

European options
The value of a European option maturing at time T on a zero-coupon bond maturing at time τ is

$$c = P(0,\tau)N(h) - XP(0,T)N(h - v(T,\tau)) \tag{4.15}$$

$$p = XP(0,T)N(-h + v(T,\tau)) - P(0,\tau)N(-h), \tag{4.16}$$

where

---

4. For more on this model, see also Hull and White (1992, 1993).
5. Alternatively, it can be seen as an extension of the Vasicek (1977) model, with time-dependent drift.

$$h = \frac{1}{v(T,\tau)} \ln\left[\frac{P(0,\tau)}{P(0,T)X}\right] + \frac{v(T,\tau)}{2}$$

4.2.5   The Black–Derman–Toy Model

The Black, Derman, and Toy (1990)[6] one-factor model is one of the most used yield-based models to price bonds and interest-rate options. The model is arbitrage-free and thus consistent with the observed term structure of interest rates. Short rates are lognormally distributed at all times. This makes it difficult to find closed-form solutions for the options prices. The model must be implemented in a recombining binomial tree, for example. The short-rate volatility $\sigma(t)$ is potentially time dependent, and the continuous process of the short-term interest rate is

$$d\ln(r) = \left[\theta(t) + \frac{\partial\sigma(t)/\partial t}{\sigma(t)} \ln(r)\right] dt + \sigma(t)dz, \qquad (4.17)$$

where $\frac{\partial\sigma(t)/\partial t}{\sigma(t)}$ is the speed of mean reversion ("gravity"), and $\theta(t)$ divided by the speed of mean reversion is a time-dependent mean-reversion level. The following example shows how to calibrate the Black–Derman–Toy binomial tree to the current term structure of zero-coupon yields and zero-coupon volatilities.

Example
What is the value of an American call option on a five-year zero-coupon bond with time to expiration of four years and a strike price of 85.50? The term structure of zero-coupon rates and volatilities is shown in Table 4–2. From the rates and volatilities, we will calibrate the Black–Derman–Toy interest-rate tree.
To price the option by using backward induction, we build a tree for the bond prices, as shown below.

---

6. Black and Karasinski (1991) generalize the Black–Derman–Toy model.

T A B L E 4–2

Input to Black–Derman–Toy

Years to Maturity	Zero-Coupon Rates	Zero-Coupon Volatilities
1	9.0%	24%
2	9.5%	22%
3	10.0%	20%
4	10.5%	18%
5	11.0%	16%

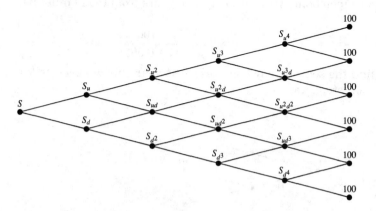

To build the price tree, we have to build the rate tree below:

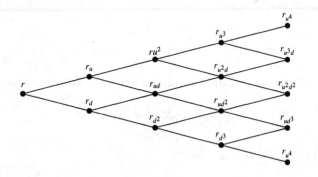

We start by finding the price of a zero-coupon bond with maturity one year in the future:

$$91.74 = \frac{100 \times 0.5 + 100 \times 0.5}{(1 + 0.09)}$$

This gives us the one-period price tree:

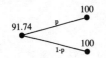

The next step is to build a two-period price tree. From the term structure of zero-coupon rates in Table 4–2, it is clear that the price today of a two-year zero-coupon bond with maturity two years from today must be

$$83.40 = \frac{100}{(1+0.095)^2}$$

To find the second-year bond prices at year one, we need to know the short rates at step one:

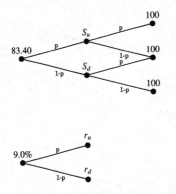

Appealing to risk-neutral valuation, the following relationship must hold:

$$83.40 = \frac{0.5S_u + 0.5S_d}{(1+0.09)} \qquad (4.18)$$

In a standard binomial tree, we have

$$u = e^{\sigma\sqrt{T/n}}, \qquad d = e^{-\sigma\sqrt{T/n}}$$

$$
\begin{aligned}
u/d &= e^{2\sigma\sqrt{T/n}} \\
\ln(u/d) &= 2\sigma\sqrt{T/n} \\
\sigma &= \frac{1}{2\sqrt{T/n}}\ln\left(\frac{u}{d}\right)
\end{aligned}
$$

Similarly, in the Black–Derman–Toy tree, the rates are assumed to be log-normally distributed. This implies that

$$\sigma_n = \frac{1}{2\sqrt{T/n}}\ln\left(\frac{r_u}{r_d}\right) = 0.22$$

$$0.5\ln\left(\frac{r_u}{r_d}\right) = 0.22 \tag{4.19}$$

and

$$S_d = \frac{100}{1+r_u} \tag{4.20}$$

$$S_u = \frac{100}{1+r_d} \tag{4.21}$$

Now, substitute (4.20) and (4.21) into (4.18) to obtain

$$83.40 = \frac{0.5\left(\frac{100}{1+r_u}\right) + 0.5\left(\frac{100}{1+r_d}\right)}{(1+0.09)} \tag{4.22}$$

We are left with two equations, (4.19) and (4.22), in two unknowns, r_u and r_d. We know that $r_u = r_d e^{0.22\times 2}$, which leads to the following quadratic equation

$$83.40 = \frac{0.5\left(\frac{100}{1+r_d e^{0.22\times 2}}\right) + 0.5\left(\frac{100}{1+r_d}\right)}{(1+0.09)}$$

By solving this equation, we get the following rates at step one

$$r_d = 7.87\%, \qquad r_u = 12.22\%$$

Using these solutions, it is now possible to calculate the bond prices that correspond to these rates. The two-step tree of prices then becomes:

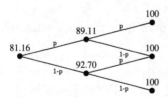

The next step is to fill in the two-period rate tree.

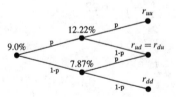

Last time, there were two unknown rates, and two sources of information:

1. Zero-coupon rates.

2. The volatility of the zero-coupon rates.

This time, we have three unknown rates, but still only two sources of information. To get around this problem, remember that the Black–Derman–Toy model is built on the following assumptions:

- Rates are lognormally distributed.

- The volatility is only dependent on time, not on the level of the short rates. There is thus only one level of volatility at the same time step in the rate tree.

Hence,

$$0.5\ln(r_{uu}/r_{ud}) = 0.5\ln(r_{ud}/r_{dd})$$
$$\frac{r_{uu}}{r_{ud}} = \frac{r_{ud}}{r_{dd}}$$
$$r_{dd} = \frac{r_{ud}^2}{r_{uu}}$$

and we are left with only two unknowns. As with the one-period tree, we start by finding the bond price at the start of the price tree. In three years, the price of the bond must be 100, and the price today must be

$$75.13 = \frac{100}{(1+0.10)^3}$$

Based on the risk-neutral valuation principle, the following relationships must hold:

$$S_{uu} = \frac{100}{1+r_{uu}}, \quad S_{ud} = \frac{100}{1+r_{ud}}, \quad S_{dd} = \frac{100}{1+r_{dd}} \qquad (4.23)$$

$$S_u = \frac{0.5S_{uu} + 0.5S_{ud}}{(1 + 0.1222)}, \qquad S_d = \frac{0.5S_{dd} + 0.5S_{ud}}{(1 + 0.0787)} \qquad (4.24)$$

$$75.13 = \frac{0.5S_u + 0.5S_d}{(1 + 0.09)} \qquad (4.25)$$

If the bond only has two years left to maturity, the bond yield or rate of return must satisfy

$$S_u = \frac{100}{(1 + y_u)^2} \quad \text{or} \quad S_d = \frac{100}{(1 + y_d)^2} \qquad (4.26)$$

By solving equation (4.26) with respect to the bond yield, we get

$$y_u = \sqrt{\frac{100}{S_u}} - 1, \quad y_d = \sqrt{\frac{100}{S_d}} - 1 \qquad (4.27)$$

As the bond yields must be approximately lognormally distributed, it also follows that

$$0.5 \ln\left(\frac{y_u}{y_d}\right) = 0.20$$

$$\ln\left(\frac{y_u}{y_d}\right) = 0.40$$

$$\frac{y_u}{y_d} = e^{0.40} \qquad (4.28)$$

By using equations (4.27), and (4.28), y_u can be expressed as

$$y_u = \frac{y_u}{y_d} y_d$$

$$y_u = e^{0.40}\left(\sqrt{\frac{100}{S_d}} - 1\right),$$

and S_u can be expressed in terms of S_d

$$S_u = \frac{100}{\left[1 + e^{0.40}\left(\sqrt{\frac{100}{S_d}} - 1\right)\right]^2} \qquad (4.29)$$

This equation must be solved by trial and error (possible, but not recommended) or, more efficiently, by the Newton–Raphson algorithm. The solution is

$$S_u = 78.81, \quad S_d = 84.98$$

$$r_{dd} = 7.47\%, \quad r_{ud} = r_{du} = 10.76\%, \quad r_{uu} = 15.50\%$$

This gives the missing information in the two-period rate tree.

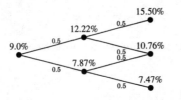

Now it is time to estimate the three-period price tree:

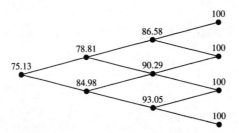

The consecutive time steps can be computed by forward induction, as introduced by Jamshidian (1991), or more easily with the Bjerksund and Stensland (1996) analytical approximation of the short-rate interest-rate tree. Finally, we get the four-year short-rate tree:

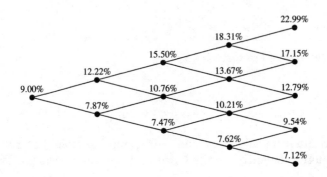

From the short-rate tree, we can calculate the short-rate volatilities by using the relationship $\sigma_n = \frac{1}{2\sqrt{T/n}} \ln\left(\frac{r_u}{r_d}\right)$

$$\sigma_0 = 24.00\%, \quad \sigma_1 = 22.00\%, \quad \sigma_2 = 18.24\%, \quad \sigma_3 = 14.61\%, \quad \sigma_4 = 14.66\%$$

The four-year rate tree supplies input to the solution to the five-year price tree:

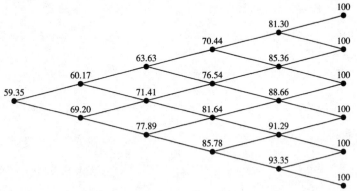

The value of the American call option with strike 85.50 and time to expiration of four years can now easily be found by standard backward induction. It follows that

$$C_{j,i} = \max\left[S_{j,i} - 85.50, \frac{(0.5 \times C_{j+1,i+1} + 0.5 \times C_{j+1,i})}{(1 + r_{j,i})}\right]$$

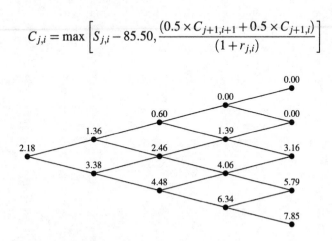

The price of the American call option on the five-year bond is thus 2.18.

5

VOLATILITY AND CORRELATION

This chapter deals with different ways to calculate volatility and correlation—an important topic, as these parameters are central in the valuation of most option contracts.

5.1 THE BLACK–SCHOLES MODEL ADJUSTED FOR TRADING-DAY VOLATILITY

The formula of French (1984) takes into consideration that volatility is usually higher on trading days than on nontrading days.[1]

$$c = SN(d_1) - Xe^{-rT}N(d_2) \tag{5.1}$$

$$p = Xe^{-rT}N(-d_2) - SN(-d_1), \tag{5.2}$$

where

$$d_1 = \frac{\ln(S/X) + rT + \sigma^2 t/2}{\sigma\sqrt{t}}$$

$$d_2 = \frac{\ln(S/X) + rT - \sigma^2 t/2}{\sigma\sqrt{t}} = d_1 - \sigma\sqrt{t}$$

$$t = \frac{\text{Trading days until maturity}}{\text{Trading days per year}}$$

$$T = \frac{\text{Calendar days until maturity}}{\text{Calendar days per year}}.$$

---

1. This has been supported by several empirical studies, for example, French (1980), Gibbons and Hess (1981), and French and Roll (1986).

Example

Consider a European put option with 146 calendar days and 104 trading days to expiry, assuming 365 calendar days per year and 253 trading days per year. The stock price is 70, the strike price is 75, the risk-free interest rate is 8% per annum, and the volatility is 30% per annum. $S = 70, X = 72, T = 0.4(146/365)$, $t = 0.4111(104/253), r = 0.08, \sigma = 0.30$. Thus,

$$d_1 = \frac{\ln(70/72) + 0.08 \times 0.4 + 0.30^2 \times 0.4111/2}{0.30\sqrt{0.4111}} = -0.0962$$

$$d_2 = d_1 - 0.30\sqrt{0.4111} = -0.2885$$

$$N(-d_1) = N(0.0962) = 0.5383 \qquad N(-d_2) = N(0.2885) = 0.6135$$

$$p = 75e^{-0.08 \times 0.4} N(-d_2) - 70N(-d_1) = 5.9910$$

5.2   HISTORICAL VOLATILITY

5.2.1   Historical Volatility from Close Prices

Calculation of the annualized standard deviation is definitely the most widely used method for estimating historical volatility. Standard deviation is simply the square root of the mean of the squared deviations of members of a sample (population) from their mean.

$$\sigma = \sqrt{\frac{1}{n-1}\sum_{i=1}^{n}\ln\left(\frac{Close_i}{Close_{i-1}}\right)^2 - \frac{1}{n(n-1)}\left[\sum_{i=1}^{n}\ln\left(\frac{Close_i}{Close_{i-1}}\right)\right]^2}, \qquad (5.3)$$

where n is the number of observations.

Example

Calculate the annualized volatility based on the close prices in Table 5–1.

$$\sigma = \sqrt{\frac{1}{20-1}\sum_{i=1}^{20}\ln\left(\frac{Close_i}{Close_{i-1}}\right)^2 - \frac{1}{20(20-1)}\left[\sum_{i=1}^{20}\ln\left(\frac{Close_i}{Close_{i-1}}\right)\right]^2} = 0.0173$$

When assuming 252 trading days in a year, the annualized close volatility is

$$\sigma = 0.0173\sqrt{252} = 0.2743$$

T A B L E 5-1

High, Low, and Close Prices

Day	Close	High	Low	$\ln(\text{Close}_i/\text{Close}_{i-1})$	$\ln(\text{High}/\text{Low})$
01.Oct.XX	132.5	132.5	131.0		0.011385
04.Oct.XX	133.5	134.0	131.0	0.007519	0.022642
05.Oct.XX	135.0	136.0	134.0	0.011173	0.014815
06.Oct.XX	133.0	137.0	133.0	−0.014926	0.029632
07.Oct.XX	133.0	136.0	133.0	0.000000	0.022306
08.Oct.XX	137.0	137.0	133.0	0.029632	0.029632
11.Oct.XX	135.0	136.5	135.0	−0.014706	0.011050
12.Oct.XX	135.0	136.0	135.0	0.000000	0.007380
13.Oct.XX	142.5	143.5	137.0	0.054067	0.046354
14.Oct.XX	143.0	145.0	142.0	0.003503	0.020907
15.Oct.XX	144.5	147.0	142.0	0.010435	0.034606
18.Oct.XX	145.0	147.5	145.0	0.003454	0.017094
19.Oct.XX	146.0	147.0	143.0	0.006873	0.027588
20.Oct.XX	149.0	150.0	148.0	0.020340	0.013423
21.Oct.XX	148.0	149.0	146.5	−0.006734	0.016921
22.Oct.XX	147.0	149.5	147.0	−0.006780	0.016864
25.Oct.XX	147.0	147.5	146.0	0.000000	0.010222
26.Oct.XX	147.0	149.0	146.5	0.000000	0.016921
27.Oct.XX	145.0	147.5	144.5	−0.013699	0.020549
28.Oct.XX	145.0	145.0	144.0	0.000000	0.006920
29.Oct.XX	150.0	150.0	143.5	0.033902	0.044300

5.2.2 High/Low Volatility

Parkinson (1980) suggests estimating the standard deviation by

$$\sigma = \frac{1}{2n\sqrt{\ln(2)}} \sum_{i=1}^{n} \ln\left(\frac{High_i}{Low_i}\right) \tag{5.4}$$

Example

Calculate the annualized volatility based on the high and low prices found in Table 5–1.

$$\sigma = \frac{1}{2 \times 21 \sqrt{\ln(2)}} \sum_{i=1}^{21} \ln\left(\frac{High_i}{Low_i}\right) = 0.0126$$

When assuming 252 trading days in a year, the annualized high-low volatility is

$$\sigma = 0.0126\sqrt{252} = 0.2004$$

The high-low method is statistically much more efficient than the standard close method.[2] However, it assumes continuous trading and observations of high and low prices. The method can therefore underestimate the true volatility.[3] The same is true for the high–low–close method described next.

5.2.3   High–Low–Close Volatility

Garman and Klass (1980) suggest using the estimator

$$\sigma = \sqrt{\frac{1}{n}\sum_{i=1}^{n}\frac{1}{2}\left[\ln\left(\frac{High_i}{Low_i}\right)\right]^2 - \frac{1}{n}\sum_{i=1}^{n}[2\ln(2)-1]\left[\ln\left(\frac{Close_i}{Close_{i-1}}\right)\right]^2} \qquad (5.5)$$

Example
Calculate the annualized volatility based on the high, low, and close prices reported in Table 5–1.

$$\sigma = \sqrt{\frac{1}{20}\sum_{i=1}^{20}\frac{1}{2}\left[\ln\left(\frac{High_i}{Low_i}\right)\right]^2 - \frac{1}{20}\sum_{i=1}^{20}[2\ln(2)-1]\left[\ln\left(\frac{Close_i}{Close_{i-1}}\right)\right]^2}$$

$$= 0.0128$$

Assuming 252 trading days in a year, the annualized high–low–close volatility is

$$\sigma = 0.0128\sqrt{252} = 0.2038$$

5.2.4   Confidence Intervals for the Volatility Estimate

The next formula can be used to find the confidence intervals around the estimated close volatility (standard deviation), s, based on the number of observations, n, used in the estimate. The formula uses the chi-square distribution and is based on the assumption that the percentage changes in the asset price are normally distributed.

---

2. In terms of number of observations needed to get the same confidence interval compared with the standard close method.
3. See Marsh and Rosenfield (1986). To get around some of its shortcomings, the high–low and the high–low–close methods have later been extended by Beckers (1983), Rogers and Satchell (1991), and Kunitomo (1992), as well as others.

$$P\left[s\sqrt{\frac{(n-1)}{\chi^2_{(n-1;\,\alpha/2)}}} \le \sigma \le s\sqrt{\frac{(n-1)}{\chi^2_{(n-1;\,1-\alpha/2)}}}\right] = 1-\alpha, \qquad (5.6)$$

where $\chi^2_{(n-1;\,\alpha/2)}$ is the value of the chi-square distribution with $n-1$ degrees of freedom and a confidence level of $1-\alpha$.

Example
Consider the 27.43% volatility estimate from the close prices in Table 5–1. The estimate is based on 21 close prices and 20 price changes. What is the 95% confidence interval ($\alpha = 0.05$) of this estimate? $s = 0.2743$, $\alpha = 0.05$, $n = 20$.

$$P\left[0.2743\sqrt{\frac{(20-1)}{\chi^2_{(20-1;\,0.05/2)}}} \le \sigma \le 0.2743\sqrt{\frac{(20-1)}{\chi^2_{(20-1;\,1-0.05/2)}}}\right] = 0.95$$

$$P[0.2086 \le \sigma \le 0.4006] = 0.95$$

With 20 observations there is 95% probability that the real volatility will lie between 20.86% and 40.06%, based on an estimate of 27.43%.[4]

5.3 IMPLIED VOLATILITY

5.3.1 The Newton–Raphson Method

The Newton–Raphson method is an efficient way to find the implied volatility of an option contract. The method seldom spends more than two to three searches before it converges to the implied volatility. Let

$$\sigma_{i+1} = \sigma_i - \frac{c(\sigma_i) - c_m}{\partial c / \partial \sigma_i} \qquad (5.7)$$

until $|c_m - c(\sigma_{i+1})| \le \epsilon$, at which point σ_{i+1} is the implied volatility, ϵ is the desired degree of accuracy, c_m is the market price of the option, and $\partial c / \partial \sigma_i$ is the vega of the option evaluated at σ_i (the sensitivity of the option value for a small change in volatility).

Manaster and Koehler start value
Manaster and Koehler (1982) have developed an efficient seed value when the Newton–Raphson method is used to compute implied volatility. The seed

---

4. That is, if we estimate the true volatility 100 times, with independent samples of size 20, the true volatility will lie within the confidence interval in approximately 95 out of the 100 estimations—given the viability of the assumptions.

value will guarantee convergence (if the implied volatility exists) for European Black–Scholes stock options. The seed value is simply

$$\sigma_1 = \left[|\ln(S/X) + rT| \frac{2}{T} \right]^{1/2} \tag{5.8}$$

Computer algorithm

This function returns the implied volatility of a European plain vanilla call or a put stock option.

Function *NewtonRaphsonAlgorithm(CallPutFlag* As String, *S* As Double, _
        X As Double, *T* As Double, *r* As Double, *cm* As Double) As Double

    Dim *vi* As Double, *ci* As Double
    Dim *Vegai* As Double, *epsilon* As Double

    '// Manaster and Koehler seed value (vi)
    vi = (*Abs*(*Log*(*S/X*) + *r* * *T*) * 2/*T*)^0.5
    ci = *GBlackScholes*(*CallPutFlag, S, X, T, r, r, vi*)
    Vegai = *GVega*(*S, X, T, r, r, vi*)
    epsilon = 0.00000000001
    While *Abs*(*cm − ci*) > *epsilon*
        vi = *vi* − (*ci − cm*)/*Vegai*
        ci = *GBlackScholes*(*CallPutFlag, S, X, T, r, r, vi*)
        Vegai = *GVega*(*S, X, T, r, r, vi*)
    Wend
    NewtonRaphsonAlgorithm = *vi*
End Function

5.3.2 The Bisection Method

When using the Newton–Raphson method to calculate implied volatility, it is necessary to know the partial derivative of the option-pricing formula with respect to volatility (vega). In some types of options (in particular exotic and American options), vega is not known analytically. The bisection method is an efficient method to estimate implied volatility when vega is unknown. The bisection method requires two initial volatility estimates (seed values):

1. A "low" estimate of the implied volatility, σ_L, corresponding to an option value, c_L.

2. A "high" volatility estimate, σ_H, corresponding to an option value, c_H.

The option market price, c_m, lies between c_L and c_H. The bisection estimate is given as the linear interpolation between the two estimates:

$$\sigma_{i+1} = \sigma_L + (c_m - c_L)\frac{\sigma_H - \sigma_L}{c_H - c_L} \tag{5.9}$$

Replace σ_L with σ_{i+1} if $c(\sigma_{i+1}) < c_m$, or else replace σ_H with σ_{i+1} if $c(\sigma_{i+1}) > c_m$ until $|c_m - c(\sigma_{i+1})| \leq \epsilon$, at which point σ_{i+1} is the implied volatility, and ϵ is the desired degree of accuracy.

Computer algorithm

This function returns the implied volatility of a European plain vanilla call or put option. With small modifications, the function can also be used to find the implied volatility for American and exotic options.

```
Function BisectionAlgorithm(CallPutFlag As String, S As Double, X As Double, _
        T As Double, r As Double, b As Double, cm As Double) As Double

        Dim vLow As Double, vHigh As Double, vi As Double
        Dim cLow As Double, cHigh As Double, epsilon As Double

        vLow = 0.01
        vHigh = 1
        epsilon = 0.000001
        cLow = GBlackScholes(CallPutFlag, S, X, T, r, b, vLow)
        cHigh = GBlackScholes(CallPutFlag, S, X, T, r, b, vHigh)
        vi = vLow + (cm - cLow) * (vHigh - vLow)/(cHigh - cLow)
        While Abs(cm - GBlackScholes(CallPutFlag, S, X, T, r, b, vi)) > epsilon
            If GBlackScholes(CallPutFlag, S, X, T, r, b, vi) < cm Then
                vLow = vi
            Else
                vHigh = vi
            End If
            cLow = GBlackScholes(CallPutFlag, S, X, T, r, b, vLow)
            cHigh = GBlackScholes(CallPutFlag, S, X, T, r, b, vHigh)
            vi = vLow + (cm - cLow) * (vHigh - vLow)/(cHigh - cLow)
        Wend
        BisectionAlgorithm = vi
End Function
```

5.3.3   Implied Volatility Approximations

At-the-Money Forward Approximation

Brenner and Subrahmanyam (1988) and Feinstein (1988) suggest a simple formula that can be used to find the implied volatility of a plain vanilla option that is at-the-money forward:

$$\sigma \approx \frac{c_m\sqrt{2\pi}}{Se^{(b-r)T}\sqrt{T}}, \tag{5.10}$$

where c_m is the market price of an at-the-money-forward call or put option. At-the-money-forward is defined as $S = Xe^{-bT}$.

Example
Consider an at-the-money-forward stock call option with three months to expiry. The stock price is 59, the strike price is 60, the risk-free interest rate is 6.7% per annum, and the market price of the option is 2.82. $S = 59, X = 60$, $T = 0.25, r = b = 0.067, c_m = 2.82$. What is the implied volatility?

$$\sigma \approx \frac{2.82\sqrt{2\pi}}{59e^{(0.067-0.067)0.25}\sqrt{0.25}} = 23.96\%$$

For comparison, the exact implied volatility is 23.99%.

Extended moneyness approximation
The implied volatility approximation due to Corrado and Miller (1996a) extends the range of accuracy to a band of option moneyness.[5] For a call option, the approximation is

$$\sigma \approx \frac{\sqrt{2\pi}}{Se^{(b-r)T} + Xe^{-rT}} \left\{ c_m - \frac{Se^{(b-r)T} - Xe^{-rT}}{2} \right.$$
$$+ \left[\left(c_m - \frac{Se^{(b-r)T} - Xe^{-rT}}{2} \right)^2 \right.$$
$$\left. \left. - \frac{(Se^{(b-r)T} - Xe^{-rT})^2}{\pi} \right]^{\frac{1}{2}} \right\} / \sqrt{T}, \tag{5.11}$$

where c_m is the market price for a call option. The approximation for a put option is

---

5. See also Corrado and Miller (1996b).

$$\sigma \approx \frac{\sqrt{2\pi}}{Se^{(b-r)T} + Xe^{-rT}} \left\{ p_m - \frac{Xe^{-rT} - Se^{(b-r)T}}{2} \right.$$

$$+ \left[\left(p_m - \frac{Xe^{-rT} - Se^{(b-r)T}}{2} \right)^2 \right.$$

$$\left. \left. - \frac{(Xe^{-rT} - Se^{(b-r)T})^2}{\pi} \right]^{\frac{1}{2}} \right\} / \sqrt{T}, \qquad (5.12)$$

where p_m is the market price of a put option.

Example

Consider a put option with six months to expiry. The futures price is 108, the strike price is 100, the risk-free interest rate is 10.50% per annum, and the market price of the put option is 5.08. $S = 108, X = 100, T = 0.5, r = 0.105,$ $b = 0, p_m = 5.08$. What is the implied volatility?

$$\sigma \approx \frac{\sqrt{2\pi}}{108e^{(0-0.105)0.5} + 100e^{-0.105\times0.5}} \left\{ 5.08 - \frac{100e^{-0.105\times0.5} - 108e^{(0-0.105)0.5}}{2} \right.$$

$$+ \left[\left(5.08 - \frac{100e^{-0.105\times0.5} - 108e^{(0-0.105)0.5}}{2} \right)^2 \right.$$

$$\left. \left. - \frac{(100e^{-0.105\times0.5} - 108e^{(0-0.105)0.5})^2}{\pi} \right]^{\frac{1}{2}} \right\} / \sqrt{0.5} \approx 29.90\%$$

For comparison, the exact implied volatility is 30.00%.

5.3.4 Implied Forward Volatility

Implied volatility is often considered the market's best estimate of future volatility. Similarly, the implied forward volatility can be seen as the market's best estimate of the forward volatility at a future date:

$$\sigma_F = \sqrt{\frac{\sigma_2^2 T_2 - \sigma_1^2 T_1}{T_2 - T_1}} \qquad (5.13)$$

Haug and Haug (1996) show that implied forward volatility takes into consideration information embedded in the slope of the term structure of implied volatilities (in a Black–Scholes economy).

Example

Suppose we have a six-month option with 12% implied volatility, and a three-month option with 15% implied volatility. The implied three-month volatility three months forward is

$$\sigma_F = \sqrt{\frac{0.12^2 \times 0.5 - 0.15^2 \times 0.25}{0.5 - 0.25}} = 0.0794 = 7.94\%$$

By rearranging the implied forward volatility formula, it's possible to get a lower boundary of implied volatilities with time to maturity T_2, given an implied volatility with time to maturity T_1, where $T_2 > T_1$:

$$\sigma_2 = \sigma_1 \sqrt{\frac{T_1}{T_2}} \tag{5.14}$$

Example

Suppose we have a three-month option with 15% implied volatility. What is the lower boundary of the six-month implied volatility?

$$\sigma_2 = 0.15 \sqrt{\frac{0.25}{0.5}} = 0.1061$$

Breakage of this lower bound signals a possible arbitrage opportunity.

5.3.5   From Price to Yield Volatility in Bonds

The following formulas can be used to find the yield volatility of a bond if one knows the price volatility, and vice versa.

$$\sigma_y = \frac{\sigma_P}{\frac{\partial P}{\partial y} \frac{1}{P} y} = \frac{\sigma_P}{y \frac{\text{Duration}}{(1+y)}} \tag{5.15}$$

$$\sigma_P = \sigma_y \frac{\partial P}{\partial y} \frac{1}{P} y = \sigma_y \left[y \frac{\text{Duration}}{(1+y)} \right], \tag{5.16}$$

where σ_P is the price volatility of the bond price P, and σ_y is the yield volatility of the bond yield y.

Example

Consider a government bond where the implied price volatility is 9%. The bond has a duration of six years and a yield to maturity of 8%. What is the equivalent yield volatility of the bond?

$$\sigma_y = \frac{0.09}{0.08\frac{6}{1+0.08}} = 20.25\%$$

5.3.6 Price and Yield Volatility in Money Market Futures

The yield y of money market futures F (i.e., Eurodollar futures) is

$$y = 100 - F$$

The relation between price volatility and yield volatility is

$$\sigma_y = \sigma_F \frac{F}{100 - F} \tag{5.17}$$

$$\sigma_F = \sigma_y \frac{100 - F}{F} \tag{5.18}$$

Example
Consider a Eurodollar futures with price 94.53 and price volatility 1.5%.
What is the equivalent yield volatility? $F = 94.53$, $\sigma_F = 0.015$, $y = 5.47\%$.

$$\sigma_y = 0.015 \frac{94.53}{100 - 94.53} = 25.92\%$$

5.4 CONFIDENCE INTERVAL FOR THE ASSET PRICE

Given the assumption of lognormally distributed security prices, we can define the confidence interval for the asset price S by

$$S_{min} = Se^{(b-\sigma^2/2)T - n\sigma\sqrt{T}} \tag{5.19}$$

and

$$S_{max} = Se^{(b-\sigma^2/2)T + n\sigma\sqrt{T}}, \tag{5.20}$$

where n is the standard deviation around the expected price (some common standard deviations are $1 = 68.3\%$, $1.65 = 90.0\%$, $2 = 95.4\%$, $3 = 99.7\%$).

Example
What is the confidence interval six months from now, with two standard deviations, for a stock which trades at 80 today? Let the risk-free interest rate be 8% per annum and the volatility be 25% per annum. $S = 80$, $T = 0.5$, $r = b = 0.08$, $\sigma = 0.25$, $n = 2$.

$$S_{min} = 80e^{(0.08-0.25^2/2)0.5-2\times0.25\sqrt{0.5}} = 57.5612$$

$$S_{max} = 80e^{(0.08-0.25^2/2)0.5+2\times0.25\sqrt{0.5}} = 116.7407$$

5.5   HIGHER MOMENTS

5.5.1   Skewness

The skewness of a series of price data can be measured in terms of the third moment about the mean. If the distribution is symmetric, the skewness will be zero.

$$Skewness = \frac{\sum_{i=1}^{n}(x_i - \bar{x})^3/n}{\sigma^3} \tag{5.21}$$

5.5.2   Kurtosis

The kurtosis describes the relative peakedness of a distribution. The kurtosis is measured by the fourth moment about the mean. The normal distribution has a kurtosis of three. Distributions with kurtosis larger than three are called leptokurtic, indicating higher peaks and fatter tails than the normal distribution. A kurtosis smaller than three is called platykurtic.

$$Kurtosis = \frac{\sum_{i=1}^{n}(x_i - \bar{x})^4/n}{\sigma^4} \tag{5.22}$$

5.6   IMPLIED CORRELATIONS

5.6.1   Implied Correlation from Currency Options

Implied correlation from liquid currency options is useful as an estimate of correlation in the future.[6]

$$\sigma_{DEM/JPY} = \sqrt{\sigma_{USD/DEM}^2 + \sigma_{USD/JPY}^2 - 2\rho\sigma_{USD/DEM}\sigma_{USD/JPY}} \tag{5.23}$$

$$\rho_{DEM/JPY} = \frac{\sigma_{USD/DEM}^2 + \sigma_{USD/JPY}^2 - \sigma_{DEM/JPY}^2}{2\sigma_{USD/DEM}\sigma_{USD/JPY}} \tag{5.24}$$

---

6. See Haug (1996).

Example

Consider three currency options, all with six months to expiry. The implied volatility of the USD/DEM option is 14.90%, the implied volatility of the USD/JPY option is 15.30%, and the implied volatility of the DEM/JPY option is 12.30%. What is the implied correlation for the next six months between USD/DEM and USD/JPY? $\sigma_{USD/DEM} = 0.1490$, $\sigma_{USD/JPY} = 0.1530$, $\sigma_{DEM/JPY} = 0.1230$.

$$\rho_{DEM/JPY} = \frac{0.1490^2 + 0.1530^2 - 0.1230^2}{2 \times 0.1490 \times 0.1530} = 0.6685$$

5.6.2 Average Implied Index Correlation

The volatility of a portfolio containing two risky assets:

$$\sigma = \sqrt{\sigma_1^2 Q_1^2 + \sigma_2^2 Q_2^2 + 2Q_1 Q_2 \rho \sigma_1 \sigma_2}, \qquad \rho = \frac{\sigma^2 - \sigma_1^2 Q_1^2 - \sigma_2^2 Q_2^2}{2Q_1 Q_2 \sigma_1 \sigma_2},$$

where Q_1 is the quantity of asset 1, and Q_2 is the quantity of asset 2. ρ is the correlation between the return of assets 1 and 2. When the correlation coefficient is 0, 1, or -1, the formula for the volatility of a portfolio of two assets can be simplified to:

$$\rho = 0: \qquad \sigma = \sqrt{\sigma_1^2 Q_1^2 + \sigma_2^2 Q_2^2}$$

$$\rho = 1: \qquad \sigma = \sigma_1 Q_1 + \sigma_2 Q_2$$

$$\rho = -1: \qquad \sigma = \sigma_1 Q_1 - \sigma_2 Q_2$$

The volatility of a portfolio containing three risky assets is

$$\sigma^2 = \sigma_1^2 Q_1^2 + \sigma_2^2 Q_2^2 + \sigma_3^2 Q_3^2$$
$$+ 2Q_1 Q_2 \rho_{1,2} \sigma_1 \sigma_2 + 2Q_1 Q_3 \rho_{1,3} \sigma_1 \sigma_3 + 2Q_2 Q_3 \rho_{2,3} \sigma_2 \sigma_3$$

The volatility of a portfolio containing several risky assets is

$$\sigma_{\text{Index}} = \sqrt{\sum_{i=1}^{n} \sigma_i^2 Q_i^2 + 2 \sum_{i=1}^{n} \sum_{j=1, j \neq i}^{n} Q_i Q_j \rho_{i,j} \sigma_i \sigma_j}$$

$$\rho_{\text{Average}} = \frac{\sigma_{\text{Index}}^2 - \sum_{i=1}^{n} \sigma_i^2 Q_i^2}{2 \sum_{i=1}^{n} \sum_{j=1, j \neq i}^{n} Q_i Q_j \sigma_i \sigma_j}$$

6

6 SOME USEFUL FORMULAS

6.1 INTERPOLATION

6.1.1 Linear Interpolation

Linear interpolation is a line fitted between two data points. (Draw the line further, and you get an extrapolation.)

$$r_i = (r_2 - r_1)\frac{T_i - T_1}{T_2 - T_1} + r_1 \tag{6.1}$$

Example
Suppose we have a three-year interest rate of 6.3% and a four-year rate of 7.2%. What is the linear interpolated 3.5 year rate? $r_1 = 0.063$, $r_2 = 0.072$, $T_1 = 3$, $T_2 = 4$, $T_i = 3.5$.

$$r_i = (0.072 - 0.063)\frac{3.5 - 3}{4 - 3} + 0.063 = 6.7500\%$$

6.1.2 Log-Linear Interpolation

$$r_i = \left(\frac{r_2}{r_1}\right)^{\left(\frac{T_i - T_1}{T_2 - T_1}\right)} r_1 \tag{6.2}$$

Example
What is the log-linear interpolated 3.5 year rate with the same parameters as in the linear interpolation example?

$$r_i = \left(\frac{0.072}{0.063}\right)^{\left(\frac{3.5 - 3}{4 - 3}\right)} 0.063 = 6.7350\%$$

6.1.3 Cubic Interpolation; Lagrange's Formula

Cubic interpolation fits a third order curve to four data points in a row, with the interpolation being between the center two points. The cubic interpolation in Lagrangian form is given by

$$
\begin{aligned}
r_i = {} & \frac{(T_i - T_2)(T_i - T_3)(T_i - T_4)}{(T_1 - T_2)(T_1 - T_3)(T_1 - T_4)} r_1 + \frac{(T_i - T_1)(T_i - T_3)(T_i - T_4)}{(T_2 - T_1)(T_2 - T_3)(T_2 - T_4)} r_2 \\
& + \frac{(T_i - T_1)(T_i - T_2)(T_i - T_4)}{(T_3 - T_1)(T_3 - T_2)(T_3 - T_4)} r_3 \\
& + \frac{(T_i - T_1)(T_i - T_2)(T_i - T_3)}{(T_4 - T_1)(T_4 - T_2)(T_4 - T_3)} r_4
\end{aligned} \tag{6.3}
$$

Example

Suppose we have a two-year interest rate of 6.4%, a three-year rate of 6.3%, a four-year rate of 7.2%, and a five-year rate of 8.0%. What is the cubic interpolated 3.5 year rate? $r_1 = 0.064$, $r_2 = 0.063$, $r_3 = 0.072$, $r_4 = 0.080$, $T_1 = 2$, $T_2 = 3$, $T_3 = 4$, $T_4 = 5$, $T_i = 3.5$.

$$
\begin{aligned}
r_i = {} & \frac{(3.5 - 3)(3.5 - 4)(3.5 - 5)}{(2 - 3)(2 - 4)(2 - 5)} 0.064 + \frac{(3.5 - 2)(3.5 - 4)(3.5 - 5)}{(3 - 2)(3 - 4)(3 - 5)} 0.063 \\
& + \frac{(3.5 - 2)(3.5 - 3)(3.5 - 5)}{(4 - 2)(4 - 3)(4 - 5)} 0.072 \\
& + \frac{(3.5 - 2)(3.5 - 3)(3.5 - 4)}{(5 - 2)(5 - 3)(5 - 4)} 0.080 = 6.6938\%
\end{aligned}
$$

6.1.4 Two-Dimensional Interpolation

The formula below is a straight-line interpolation between four data points in the plane.

$$
\begin{aligned}
v_{t_i, T_i} = {} & \frac{(t_2 - t_i)(T_2 - T_i)v_{t_1, T_1} + (t_2 - t_i)(T_i - T_1)v_{t_1, T_2}}{(t_2 - t_1)(T_2 - T_1)} \\
& + \frac{(t_i - t_1)(T_2 - T_i)v_{t_2, T_1} + (t_i - t_1)(T_i - T_1)v_{t_2, T_2}}{(t_2 - t_1)(T_2 - T_1)}
\end{aligned} \tag{6.4}
$$

Example

Consider four bond options: Option 1 with three months to expiry, implied volatility 6%, on an underlying bond with three years to maturity; option 2 with three months to expiry, implied volatility 8% on an underlying bond with five years to maturity; option 3 with nine months to expiry, implied volatility 5% on an underlying bond with three years to maturity; and option 4 with nine months to expiry, implied volatility 7% on an underlying bond with five years to maturity. The two-dimensional interpolated volatility of an option with six months to expiry on a bond with four years to maturity is $t_1 = 0.25$, $t_2 = 0.75$, $T_1 = 3$, $T_2 = 5$, $v_{t_1,T_1} = 0.06^2$, $v_{t_1,T_2} = 0.08^2$, $v_{t_2,T_1} = 0.05^2$, $v_{t_2,T_2} = 0.07^2$, $t_i = 0.5$, $T_i = 4$.

$$
\begin{aligned}
v_{0.5,4} &= \frac{(0.75-0.5)(5-4)0.06^2 + (0.75-0.5)(4-3)0.08^2}{(0.75-0.25)(5-3)} \\
&+ \frac{(0.5-0.25)(5-4)0.05^2 + (0.5-0.25)(4-3)0.07^2}{(0.75-0.25)(5-3)} = 0.0044
\end{aligned}
$$

$$
\sigma_{0.5,4} = \sqrt{0.0044} = 0.0660 = 6.60\%
$$

6.2   INTEREST RATES

6.2.1   Future Value of Annuity

$$
FV = C + C(1+r) + C(1+r)^2 + \cdots + C(1+r)^{n-1} = C\left[\frac{(1+r)^n - 1}{r}\right], \qquad (6.5)
$$

where C is the cash flow, and n is the number of cash flows.

6.2.2   Net Present Value of Annuity

$$
NPV = \frac{C}{(1+r)} + \frac{C}{(1+r)^2} + \cdots + \frac{C}{(1+r)^n} = C\left\{\frac{1 - \left[\frac{1}{(1+r)^n}\right]}{r}\right\}, \qquad (6.6)
$$

where C is the cash flow, and n is the number of cash flows.

6.2.3   Continuous Compounding

From compounding m times per year to continuous compounding:

$$
r_c = m\ln\left(1 + \frac{r_m}{m}\right) \qquad (6.7)
$$

From continuous compounding to compounding m times per year:

$$
r_m = m(e^{r_c/m} - 1) \qquad (6.8)
$$

Example
Consider an interest rate that is quoted 8% per annum with quarterly compounding. The equivalent rate with continuous compounding is

$$r_c = 4\ln\left(1 + \frac{0.08}{4}\right) = 0.0792 = 7.92\%$$

Next, consider an interest rate that is quoted 12% per annum with continuous compounding. The equivalent rate with annual compounding is

$$r_1 = 1(e^{0.12/1} - 1) = 0.1275 = 12.75\%$$

6.2.4   Compounding Frequency

From compounding m times per annum to annual compounding

$$r = \left(1 + \frac{r_m}{m}\right)^m - 1 \tag{6.9}$$

From annual compounding to compounding m times per annum

$$r_m = \left[(1+r)^{(1/m)} - 1\right]m \tag{6.10}$$

Example
Consider an interest rate that is quoted 8% per annum with quarterly compounding. The equivalent rate with annual compounding is

$$r = \left(1 + \frac{0.08}{4}\right)^4 - 1 = 0.0824 = 8.24\% \tag{6.11}$$

From m to n compoundings per annum.
The formula below can be used to transform a rate r_n with n compoundings per year to a rate r_m with m compoundings per year.

$$r_n = \left[\left(1 + \frac{r_m}{m}\right)^{m/n} - 1\right]n \tag{6.12}$$

Example
Consider a rate with compounding frequency four times per year. If the rate is 7%, what is the equivalent rate with semianuual compounding?

$$r_2 = \left[\left(1 + \frac{0.07}{4}\right)^{4/2} - 1\right]2 = 0.0706$$

The equivalent rate with semiannual compounding is 7.06%.

6.2.5 Zero-Coupon Rates from Par Bonds/Par Swaps

To calculate zero-coupon rates from par bonds or swaps, the bootstrapping method originally introduced by Caks (1977) is often used.

$$100 \; = \; C_1 e^{-r_1 T_1} + C_2 e^{-r_2 T_2} \cdots + (100 + C) e^{-r_n T_n}$$

$$100 - C \sum_{i=1}^{n-1} e^{-r_i T_i} \; = \; (100 + C) e^{-r_n T_n}$$

$$r_n \; = \; -\ln\left(\frac{100 - C \sum_{i=1}^{n-1} e^{-r_i T_i}}{100 + C} \right) / T_n, \tag{6.13}$$

where C is the bond coupon and r_i is the continuous compounding zero-coupon rate with time to maturity T_i.

Example
What are the zero-coupon rates given the following five par coupon bonds?

1. A bond with one year to maturity and an annual coupon of 6.0%.
2. A bond with two years to maturity and an annual coupon of 7.0%.
3. A bond with three years to maturity and an annual coupon of 7.5%.
4. A bond with four years to maturity and an annual coupon of 8.0%.
5. A bond with five years to maturity and an annual coupon of 8.5%.

The continuous compounding zero rate at year 1 is $\ln(1 + 0.06) = 0.0583$. The continuous compounding zero-coupon rates at years 2, 3, 4, and 5 are

$$r_2 \; = \; -\ln\left(\frac{100 - 7.0 \sum_{i=1}^{2-1} e^{-r_i T_i}}{100 + 7.0} \right) / 2 = 0.0680$$

$$r_3 \; = \; -\ln\left(\frac{100 - 7.5 \sum_{i=1}^{3-1} e^{-r_i T_i}}{100 + 7.5} \right) / 3 = 0.0729$$

$$r_4 \; = \; -\ln\left(\frac{100 - 8.0 \sum_{i=1}^{4-1} e^{-r_i T_i}}{100 + 8.0} \right) / 4 = 0.0780$$

$$r_5 \; = \; -\ln\left(\frac{100 - 8.5 \sum_{i=1}^{5-1} e^{-r_i T_i}}{100 + 8.5} \right) / 5 = 0.0834$$

6.2.6   Simple Bond Mathematics

Bond Price and Yield Relationship

The bond price continuous compounded yield relationship is

$$P = \sum_{i=1}^{n} C_i e^{-yT_i}$$

P = Bond price.
y = Bond yield continuous compounding.
C_i = Cash flow (coupon) at time T_i.

The bond's sensitivity to a small change in yield is

$$\frac{\partial P}{\partial y} = \sum_{i=1}^{n} -C_i T_i e^{-yT_i}$$

The convexity of a bond is given by

$$\frac{\partial^2 P}{\partial y^2} = \sum_{i=1}^{n} C_i T_i^2 e^{-yT_i}$$

Price and Yield Relationship for a Bond

It is more common to quote the bond yield as annual compounding or with the same compounding as the number of coupons per year. Assuming annual compounding yield, the dirty price of a bond (clean price P + accrued interest rates) at any time is given by

$$
\begin{aligned}
P + C \frac{d_1}{Basis} &= \frac{C}{m} \left[\frac{1}{(1+y)^{\frac{d_2}{Basis}}} + \frac{1}{(1+y)^{\frac{d_2}{Basis}+\frac{1}{m}}} + \ldots + \frac{1}{(1+y)^{\frac{d_2}{Basis}+\frac{N-1}{m}}} \right] \\
&\quad + \frac{F}{(1+y)^{\frac{d_2}{Basis}+\frac{N-1}{m}}} \\
&= (1+y)^{\frac{1}{m}-\frac{d_2}{Basis}} \left[\frac{C}{m} \times \frac{(1+y)^{-\frac{N}{m}}-1}{1-(1+y)^{\frac{1}{m}}} + \frac{F}{(1+y)^{\frac{N}{m}}} \right], \quad (6.14)
\end{aligned}
$$

where N is the number of coupons left to maturity, m is the number of coupons per year, y is the yield to maturity, d_1 is the number of days since the last coupon payment, d_2 is the number of days to the next coupon payment, F is the face value of the bond, and *Basis* is the day basis (i.e., 365 or 360).

From Bond Price to Yield

The Newton–Raphson algorithm is useful to find the yield given the bond price:

$$y_{n+1} = y_n - \frac{P(y_n) - P_m}{\frac{\partial P}{\partial y_n}},$$

until $| P_m - P(y_{n+1}) | \leq \epsilon$, at which point y_{n+1} is the implied yield. ϵ is the desired degree of accuracy. P_m is the market price of the bond, and $\frac{\partial P}{\partial y_n}$ is the delta of the bond (the sensitivity of the bond value for a small change in the yield).

$$
\frac{\partial P}{\partial y} = a^{\frac{1}{m} - \frac{d_2}{Basis}} \left[\frac{\frac{1}{m} - \frac{d_2}{Basis}}{a} \left(\frac{C}{m} \frac{a^{-\frac{N}{m}} - 1}{1 - a^{\frac{1}{m}}} + F a^{-\frac{N}{m}} \right) \right.
$$
$$
\left. + \frac{C}{m^2} \left(\frac{a^{-\frac{N}{m}} [1 + (N+1)(a^{\frac{1}{m}} - 1)] - a^{\frac{1}{m}}}{a(1 - a^{\frac{1}{m}})^2} \right) - F \frac{N}{m} a^{-\frac{N}{m} - 1} \right],
$$

where $a = 1 + y$. Alternatively, assuming yield compounding equal to the number of coupons per year gives the dirty price of a bond (price + accrued interest rates) as a function of the yield:

$$
P + C \frac{d_1}{Basis} = \left(1 + \frac{y}{m} \right)^{1 - \frac{d_2}{Basis/m}} \left[\frac{C}{m} \times \frac{(1 + \frac{y}{m})^{-N} - 1}{1 - (1 + \frac{y}{m})} + \frac{F}{(1 + \frac{y}{m})^N} \right] \tag{6.15}
$$

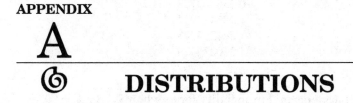

DISTRIBUTIONS

A.1 THE CUMULATIVE NORMAL DISTRIBUTION FUNCTION

The following approximation of the cumulative normal distribution function $N(x)$ produces values to within four decimal place accuracy.

$$N(x) = \frac{1}{\sqrt{2\pi}} \int_{-\infty}^{x} \exp(-z^2/2)dz$$

$$N(x) = \begin{cases} 1 - n(x)(a_1 k + a_2 k^2 + a_3 k^3) & \text{when} \quad x \geq 0 \\ 1 - N(-x) & \text{when} \quad x < 0 \end{cases},$$

where

$$k = \frac{1}{1 + 0.33267x}$$

$$\begin{aligned} a_1 &= 0.4361836 \\ a_2 &= -0.1201676 \\ a_3 &= 0.9372980 \end{aligned}$$

$$n(x) = \frac{1}{\sqrt{2\pi}} e^{-x^2/2}.$$

The next approximation produces values of $N(x)$ to within six decimal places of the true value.

$$N(x) = \begin{cases} 1 - n(x)(a_1 k + a_2 k^2 + a_3 k^3 + a_4 k^4 + a_5 k^5) & \text{when} \quad x \geq 0 \\ 1 - N(-x) & \text{when} \quad x < 0 \end{cases}$$

$$k = \frac{1}{1 + 0.2316419x}$$

$$a_1 = 0.319381530$$
$$a_2 = -0.356563782$$
$$a_3 = 1.781477937$$
$$a_4 = -1.821255978$$
$$a_5 = 1.330274429$$

Example

Calculate the cumulative normal probability for d_1 when $S = 88$, $X = 90$, $T = 0.5$, $r = 0.10$, $b = 0.10$, $\sigma = 0.4$.

$$d_1 = \frac{\ln(S/X) + (b + \sigma^2/2)T}{\sigma\sqrt{T}}$$

$$d_1 = \frac{\ln(88/90) + (0.10 + 0.40^2/2)0.5}{0.40\sqrt{0.5}} = 0.2387$$

$$k = \frac{1}{1 + 0.33267 \times 0.2387} = 0.9264$$

$$n(d_1) = n(0.2387) = \frac{1}{\sqrt{2\pi}}e^{-0.2387^2/2} = 0.3877$$

$$N(d_1) = 1 - 0.3877(0.4361836 \times k + (-0.1201676) \times k^2 + 0.9372980 \times k^3) = 0.5943$$

Computer algorithm

The cumulative normal distribution function $CND(\cdot)$ returns values of $N(\cdot)$ to within six decimal places accuracy.

```
Function CND(x)
        a1 = 0.31938153, a2 = -0.356563782, a3 = 1.781477937
        a4 = -1.821255978, a5 = 1.330274429
        L = Abs(x)
        k = 1/(1 + 0.2316419 * L)
        CND = 1 - 1/Sqr(2 * Pi) * Exp(-L^2/2) * _
        (a1 * k + a2 * k^2 + a3 * k^3 + a4 * k^4 + a5 * k^5)
        If x < 0 Then
            CND = 1 - CND
        End If
End Function
```

T A B L E   A-1

The Cumulative Normal Distribution $N(x)$ When $x \le 0$

d	0.00	−0.01	−0.02	−0.03	−0.04	−0.05	−0.06	−0.07	−0.08	−0.09
−4.5	0.0000	0.0000	0.0000	0.0000	0.0000	0.0000	0.0000	0.0000	0.0000	0.0000
−4.4	0.0000	0.0000	0.0000	0.0000	0.0000	0.0000	0.0000	0.0000	0.0000	0.0000
−4.3	0.0000	0.0000	0.0000	0.0000	0.0000	0.0000	0.0000	0.0000	0.0000	0.0000
−4.2	0.0000	0.0000	0.0000	0.0000	0.0000	0.0000	0.0000	0.0000	0.0000	0.0000
−4.1	0.0000	0.0000	0.0000	0.0000	0.0000	0.0000	0.0000	0.0000	0.0000	0.0000
−4.0	0.0000	0.0000	0.0000	0.0000	0.0000	0.0000	0.0000	0.0000	0.0000	0.0000
−3.9	0.0000	0.0000	0.0000	0.0000	0.0000	0.0000	0.0000	0.0000	0.0000	0.0000
−3.8	0.0001	0.0001	0.0001	0.0001	0.0001	0.0001	0.0001	0.0001	0.0001	0.0001
−3.7	0.0001	0.0001	0.0001	0.0001	0.0001	0.0001	0.0001	0.0001	0.0001	0.0001
−3.6	0.0002	0.0002	0.0001	0.0001	0.0001	0.0001	0.0001	0.0001	0.0001	0.0001
−3.5	0.0002	0.0002	0.0002	0.0002	0.0002	0.0002	0.0002	0.0002	0.0002	0.0002
−3.4	0.0003	0.0003	0.0003	0.0003	0.0003	0.0003	0.0003	0.0003	0.0003	0.0002
−3.3	0.0005	0.0005	0.0005	0.0004	0.0004	0.0004	0.0004	0.0004	0.0004	0.0003
−3.2	0.0007	0.0007	0.0006	0.0006	0.0006	0.0006	0.0006	0.0005	0.0005	0.0005
−3.1	0.0010	0.0009	0.0009	0.0009	0.0008	0.0008	0.0008	0.0008	0.0007	0.0007
−3.0	0.0013	0.0013	0.0013	0.0012	0.0012	0.0011	0.0011	0.0011	0.0010	0.0010
−2.9	0.0019	0.0018	0.0018	0.0017	0.0016	0.0016	0.0015	0.0015	0.0014	0.0014
−2.8	0.0026	0.0025	0.0024	0.0023	0.0023	0.0022	0.0021	0.0021	0.0020	0.0019
−2.7	0.0035	0.0034	0.0033	0.0032	0.0031	0.0030	0.0029	0.0028	0.0027	0.0026
−2.6	0.0047	0.0045	0.0044	0.0043	0.0041	0.0040	0.0039	0.0038	0.0037	0.0036
−2.5	0.0062	0.0060	0.0059	0.0057	0.0055	0.0054	0.0052	0.0051	0.0049	0.0048
−2.4	0.0082	0.0080	0.0078	0.0075	0.0073	0.0071	0.0069	0.0068	0.0066	0.0064
−2.3	0.0107	0.0104	0.0102	0.0099	0.0096	0.0094	0.0091	0.0089	0.0087	0.0084
−2.2	0.0139	0.0136	0.0132	0.0129	0.0125	0.0122	0.0119	0.0116	0.0113	0.0110
−2.1	0.0179	0.0174	0.0170	0.0166	0.0162	0.0158	0.0154	0.0150	0.0146	0.0143
−2.0	0.0228	0.0222	0.0217	0.0212	0.0207	0.0202	0.0197	0.0192	0.0188	0.0183
−1.9	0.0287	0.0281	0.0274	0.0268	0.0262	0.0256	0.0250	0.0244	0.0239	0.0233
−1.8	0.0359	0.0351	0.0344	0.0336	0.0329	0.0322	0.0314	0.0307	0.0301	0.0294
−1.7	0.0446	0.0436	0.0427	0.0418	0.0409	0.0401	0.0392	0.0384	0.0375	0.0367
−1.6	0.0548	0.0537	0.0526	0.0516	0.0505	0.0495	0.0485	0.0475	0.0465	0.0455
−1.5	0.0668	0.0655	0.0643	0.0630	0.0618	0.0606	0.0594	0.0582	0.0571	0.0559
−1.4	0.0808	0.0793	0.0778	0.0764	0.0749	0.0735	0.0721	0.0708	0.0694	0.0681
−1.3	0.0968	0.0951	0.0934	0.0918	0.0901	0.0885	0.0869	0.0853	0.0838	0.0823
−1.2	0.1151	0.1131	0.1112	0.1093	0.1075	0.1056	0.1038	0.1020	0.1003	0.0985
−1.1	0.1357	0.1335	0.1314	0.1292	0.1271	0.1251	0.1230	0.1210	0.1190	0.1170
−1.0	0.1587	0.1562	0.1539	0.1515	0.1492	0.1469	0.1446	0.1423	0.1401	0.1379
−0.9	0.1841	0.1814	0.1788	0.1762	0.1736	0.1711	0.1685	0.1660	0.1635	0.1611
−0.8	0.2119	0.2090	0.2061	0.2033	0.2005	0.1977	0.1949	0.1922	0.1894	0.1867
−0.7	0.2420	0.2389	0.2358	0.2327	0.2296	0.2266	0.2236	0.2206	0.2177	0.2148
−0.6	0.2743	0.2709	0.2676	0.2643	0.2611	0.2578	0.2546	0.2514	0.2483	0.2451
−0.5	0.3085	0.3050	0.3015	0.2981	0.2946	0.2912	0.2877	0.2843	0.2810	0.2776
−0.4	0.3446	0.3409	0.3372	0.3336	0.3300	0.3264	0.3228	0.3192	0.3156	0.3121
−0.3	0.3821	0.3783	0.3745	0.3707	0.3669	0.3632	0.3594	0.3557	0.3520	0.3483
−0.2	0.4207	0.4168	0.4129	0.4090	0.4052	0.4013	0.3974	0.3936	0.3897	0.3859
−0.1	0.4602	0.4562	0.4522	0.4483	0.4443	0.4404	0.4364	0.4325	0.4286	0.4247
0.0	0.5000	0.4960	0.4920	0.4880	0.4840	0.4801	0.4761	0.4721	0.4681	0.4641

T A B L E   A-2

The Cumulative Normal Distribution $N(x)$ When $x \geq 0$

d	0.00	0.01	0.02	0.03	0.04	0.05	0.06	0.07	0.08	0.09
0.0	0.5000	0.5040	0.5080	0.5120	0.5160	0.5199	0.5239	0.5279	0.5319	0.5359
0.1	0.5398	0.5438	0.5478	0.5517	0.5557	0.5596	0.5636	0.5675	0.5714	0.5753
0.2	0.5793	0.5832	0.5871	0.5910	0.5948	0.5987	0.6026	0.6064	0.6103	0.6141
0.3	0.6179	0.6217	0.6255	0.6293	0.6331	0.6368	0.6406	0.6443	0.6480	0.6517
0.4	0.6554	0.6591	0.6628	0.6664	0.6700	0.6736	0.6772	0.6808	0.6844	0.6879
0.5	0.6915	0.6950	0.6985	0.7019	0.7054	0.7088	0.7123	0.7157	0.7190	0.7224
0.6	0.7257	0.7291	0.7324	0.7357	0.7389	0.7422	0.7454	0.7486	0.7517	0.7549
0.7	0.7580	0.7611	0.7642	0.7673	0.7704	0.7734	0.7764	0.7794	0.7823	0.7852
0.8	0.7881	0.7910	0.7939	0.7967	0.7995	0.8023	0.8051	0.8078	0.8106	0.8133
0.9	0.8159	0.8186	0.8212	0.8238	0.8264	0.8289	0.8315	0.8340	0.8365	0.8389
1.0	0.8413	0.8438	0.8461	0.8485	0.8508	0.8531	0.8554	0.8577	0.8599	0.8621
1.1	0.8643	0.8665	0.8686	0.8708	0.8729	0.8749	0.8770	0.8790	0.8810	0.8830
1.2	0.8849	0.8869	0.8888	0.8907	0.8925	0.8944	0.8962	0.8980	0.8997	0.9015
1.3	0.9032	0.9049	0.9066	0.9082	0.9099	0.9115	0.9131	0.9147	0.9162	0.9177
1.4	0.9192	0.9207	0.9222	0.9236	0.9251	0.9265	0.9279	0.9292	0.9306	0.9319
1.5	0.9332	0.9345	0.9357	0.9370	0.9382	0.9394	0.9406	0.9418	0.9429	0.9441
1.6	0.9452	0.9463	0.9474	0.9484	0.9495	0.9505	0.9515	0.9525	0.9535	0.9545
1.7	0.9554	0.9564	0.9573	0.9582	0.9591	0.9599	0.9608	0.9616	0.9625	0.9633
1.8	0.9641	0.9649	0.9656	0.9664	0.9671	0.9678	0.9686	0.9693	0.9699	0.9706
1.9	0.9713	0.9719	0.9726	0.9732	0.9738	0.9744	0.9750	0.9756	0.9761	0.9767
2.0	0.9772	0.9778	0.9783	0.9788	0.9793	0.9798	0.9803	0.9808	0.9812	0.9817
2.1	0.9821	0.9826	0.9830	0.9834	0.9838	0.9842	0.9846	0.9850	0.9854	0.9857
2.2	0.9861	0.9864	0.9868	0.9871	0.9875	0.9878	0.9881	0.9884	0.9887	0.9890
2.3	0.9893	0.9896	0.9898	0.9901	0.9904	0.9906	0.9909	0.9911	0.9913	0.9916
2.4	0.9918	0.9920	0.9922	0.9925	0.9927	0.9929	0.9931	0.9932	0.9934	0.9936
2.5	0.9938	0.9940	0.9941	0.9943	0.9945	0.9946	0.9948	0.9949	0.9951	0.9952
2.6	0.9953	0.9955	0.9956	0.9957	0.9959	0.9960	0.9961	0.9962	0.9963	0.9964
2.7	0.9965	0.9966	0.9967	0.9968	0.9969	0.9970	0.9971	0.9972	0.9973	0.9974
2.8	0.9974	0.9975	0.9976	0.9977	0.9977	0.9978	0.9979	0.9979	0.9980	0.9981
2.9	0.9981	0.9982	0.9982	0.9983	0.9984	0.9984	0.9985	0.9985	0.9986	0.9986
3.0	0.9987	0.9987	0.9987	0.9988	0.9988	0.9989	0.9989	0.9989	0.9990	0.9990
3.1	0.9990	0.9991	0.9991	0.9991	0.9992	0.9992	0.9992	0.9992	0.9993	0.9993
3.2	0.9993	0.9993	0.9994	0.9994	0.9994	0.9994	0.9994	0.9995	0.9995	0.9995
3.3	0.9995	0.9995	0.9995	0.9996	0.9996	0.9996	0.9996	0.9996	0.9996	0.9997
3.4	0.9997	0.9997	0.9997	0.9997	0.9997	0.9997	0.9997	0.9997	0.9997	0.9998
3.5	0.9998	0.9998	0.9998	0.9998	0.9998	0.9998	0.9998	0.9998	0.9998	0.9998
3.6	0.9998	0.9998	0.9999	0.9999	0.9999	0.9999	0.9999	0.9999	0.9999	0.9999
3.7	0.9999	0.9999	0.9999	0.9999	0.9999	0.9999	0.9999	0.9999	0.9999	0.9999
3.8	0.9999	0.9999	0.9999	0.9999	0.9999	0.9999	0.9999	0.9999	0.9999	0.9999
3.9	1.0000	1.0000	1.0000	1.0000	1.0000	1.0000	1.0000	1.0000	1.0000	1.0000
4.0	1.0000	1.0000	1.0000	1.0000	1.0000	1.0000	1.0000	1.0000	1.0000	1.0000
4.1	1.0000	1.0000	1.0000	1.0000	1.0000	1.0000	1.0000	1.0000	1.0000	1.0000
4.2	1.0000	1.0000	1.0000	1.0000	1.0000	1.0000	1.0000	1.0000	1.0000	1.0000
4.3	1.0000	1.0000	1.0000	1.0000	1.0000	1.0000	1.0000	1.0000	1.0000	1.0000
4.4	1.0000	1.0000	1.0000	1.0000	1.0000	1.0000	1.0000	1.0000	1.0000	1.0000
4.5	1.0000	1.0000	1.0000	1.0000	1.0000	1.0000	1.0000	1.0000	1.0000	1.0000

A.2   THE BIVARIATE NORMAL DENSITY FUNCTION

$$F(x,y) = \frac{1}{2\pi\sqrt{1-\rho^2}} \exp\left[-\frac{1}{2(1-\rho^2)}(x^2 - 2\rho xy + y^2)\right] \qquad \text{(A.1)}$$

The Cumulative Bivariate Normal Distribution Function

The standardized cumulative normal function returns the probability that one random variable is less than a and that a second random variable is less than b when the correlation between the two variables is ρ:

$$M(a,b;\ \rho) = \frac{1}{2\pi\sqrt{1-\rho^2}} \int_{-\infty}^{a} \int_{-\infty}^{b} \exp\left[-\frac{x^2 - 2\rho xy + y^2}{2(1-\rho^2)}\right] dx \quad dy$$

Drezner (1978) has developed a method for approximating the cumulative bivariate normal distribution function. This approximation produces values of $M(a,b;\ \rho)$ to within six decimal places accuracy.

$$\phi(a,b;\ \rho) = \frac{\sqrt{1-\rho^2}}{\pi} \sum_{i=1}^{5} \sum_{j=1}^{5} x_i x_j f(y_i, y_j),$$

where

$$f(y_i, y_j) = \exp[a_1(2y_i - a_1) + b_1(2y_j - b_1) + 2\rho(y_i - a_1)(y_j - b_1)]$$

$$a_1 = \frac{a}{\sqrt{2(1-\rho^2)}}, \qquad b_1 = \frac{b}{\sqrt{2(1-\rho^2)}}$$

$$\begin{aligned}
x_1 &= 0.24840615 & y_1 &= 0.10024215 \\
x_2 &= 0.39233107 & y_2 &= 0.48281397 \\
x_3 &= 0.21141819 & y_3 &= 1.0609498 \\
x_4 &= 0.033246660 & y_4 &= 1.7797294 \\
x_5 &= 0.00082485334 & y_5 &= 2.6697604
\end{aligned}$$

If the product of a, b, and ρ is nonpositive, compute the cumulative bivariate normal probability using the following rules:

1. If $a \le 0$, $b \le 0$, and $\rho \le 0$, then

$$M(a,b;\ \rho) = \phi(a,b;\ \rho)$$

2. If $a \le 0$, $b \ge 0$, and $\rho \ge 0$, then

$$M(a,b;\ \rho) = N(a) - \phi(a,-b;\ -\rho)$$

3. If $a \geq 0$, $b \leq 0$, and $\rho \geq 0$, then

$$M(a,b;\, \rho) = N(b) - \phi(-a,b;\, -\rho)$$

4. If $a \geq 0$, $b \geq 0$, and $\rho \leq 0$, then

$$M(a,b;\, \rho) = N(a) + N(b) - 1 + \phi(-a,-b;\, \rho)$$

In circumstances where the product of a, b, and ρ is positive, compute the cumulative bivariate normal function as

$$M(a,b;\, \rho) = M(a,0;\, \rho_1) + M(b,0;\, \rho_2) - \delta,$$

where $M(a,0;\, \rho_1)$ and $M(b,0;\, \rho_2)$ are computed from the rules where the product of a, b, and ρ is negative, and

$$\rho_1 = \frac{(\rho a - b)Sign(a)}{\sqrt{a^2 - 2\rho ab + b^2}}, \qquad \rho_2 = \frac{(\rho b - a)Sign(b)}{\sqrt{a^2 - 2\rho ab + b^2}}$$

$$\delta = \frac{1 - Sign(a) \times Sign(b)}{4}, \qquad Sign(x) = \begin{cases} +1 & \text{when} \quad x \geq 0 \\ -1 & \text{when} \quad x < 0 \end{cases}$$

Computer algorithm

The $CBND(a,b,rho)$ function returns the standardized bivariate normal probability that the first variable is less than a and the second variable is less than b where rho is the correlation between the variables.

Function $CBND(a,\ b,\ rho)$

```
x = Array(0.24840615, 0.39233107, 0.21141819, 0.03324666, 0.00082485334)
y = Array(0.10024215, 0.48281397, 1.0609498, 1.7797294, 2.6697604)
a1 = a/Sqr(2 * (1 - rho^2))
b1 = b/Sqr(2 * (1 - rho^2))
If a <= 0 And b <= 0 And rho <= 0 Then
    Sum = 0
    For i = 1 To 5
        For j = 1 To 5
            Sum = Sum + x(i) * x(j) * Exp(a1 * (2 * y(i) - a1) _
            + b1 * (2 * y(j) - b1) + 2 * rho * (y(i) - a1) * (y(j) - b1))
        Next
    Next
    CBND = Sqr(1 - rho^2)/Pi * Sum
ElseIf a <= 0 And b >= 0 And rho >= 0 Then
        CBND = CND(a) - CBND(a, -b, -rho)
ElseIf a >= 0 And b <= 0 And rho >= 0 Then
        CBND = CND(b) - CBND(-a, b, -rho)
ElseIf a >= 0 And b >= 0 And rho <= 0 Then
```

$$CBND = CND(a) + CND(b) - 1 + CBND(-a, -b, rho)$$

ElseIf $a*b*rho > 0$ Then

$$rho1 = (rho*a - b)*Sgn(a)/Sqr(a\hat{}2 - 2*rho*a*b + b\hat{}2)$$
$$rho2 = (rho*b - a)*Sgn(b)/Sqr(a\hat{}2 - 2*rho*a*b + b\hat{}2)$$
$$delta = (1 - Sgn(a)*Sgn(b))/4$$
$$CBND = CBND(a, 0, rho1) + CBND(b, 0, rho2) - delta$$

     End If

End Function

Those who wish to retype or program the cumulative bivariate function on their own can check the result against Table A–3.

T A B L E A-3

Bivariate Normal Probabilities

a	b	ρ	$M(a,b;\rho)$
0.0	0.0	0.0	0.250000
0.0	0.0	−0.5	0.166667
0.0	0.0	0.5	0.333333
0.0	−0.5	0.0	0.154269
0.0	−0.5	−0.5	0.081660
0.0	−0.5	0.5	0.226878
0.0	0.5	0.0	0.345731
0.0	0.5	−0.5	0.273122
0.0	0.5	0.5	0.418340
−0.5	0.0	0.0	0.154269
−0.5	0.0	−0.5	0.081660
−0.5	0.0	0.5	0.226878
−0.5	−0.5	0.0	0.095195
−0.5	−0.5	−0.5	0.036298
−0.5	−0.5	0.5	0.163319
−0.5	0.5	0.0	0.213342
−0.5	0.5	−0.5	0.145218
−0.5	0.5	0.5	0.272239
0.5	0.0	0.0	0.345731
0.5	0.0	−0.5	0.273122
0.5	0.0	0.5	0.418340
0.5	−0.5	0.0	0.213342
0.5	−0.5	−0.5	0.145218
0.5	−0.5	0.5	0.272239
0.5	0.5	0.0	0.478120
0.5	0.5	−0.5	0.419223
0.5	0.5	0.5	0.546244

B

⑥ PARTIAL DERIVATIVES OF THE BLACK–SCHOLES

This appendix shows in detail how to find the partial derivatives of the generalized version of the Black–Scholes formula. We repeat the formula for easy reference:

$$c = Se^{(b-r)T}N(d_1) - Xe^{-rT}N(d_2)$$

$$p = Xe^{-rT}N(-d_2) - Se^{(b-r)T}N(-d_1)$$

$$d_1 = \frac{\ln(S/X) + (b + \sigma^2/2)T}{\sigma\sqrt{T}}$$

$$d_2 = \frac{\ln(S/X) + (b - \sigma^2/2)T}{\sigma\sqrt{T}} = d_1 - \sigma\sqrt{T}$$

$b = r$:   The Black–Scholes stock option model.

$b = r - q$:   The Merton (1973) stock option model with continuous dividend yield q.

$b = 0$:   The Black (1976) futures option model.

$b = r - r_f$:   The Garman and Kohlhagen (1983) currency option model.

To find the different partial derivatives, the following relationships are useful.

$$d_2 = d_1 - \sigma\sqrt{T}$$

$$
\begin{aligned}
d_2^2 &= d_1^2 - 2d_1\sigma\sqrt{T} + \sigma^2 T \\
&= d_1^2 - 2[\ln(S/X) + (b + \sigma^2/2)T] + \sigma^2 T \\
&= d_1^2 - 2\ln(Se^{bT}/X)
\end{aligned}
$$

$$n(d_2) = \frac{1}{\sqrt{2\pi}} e^{-d_2^2/2}$$

$$
\begin{aligned}
n(d_2) &= \frac{1}{\sqrt{2\pi}} e^{-d_1^2/2 + \ln(Se^{bT}/X)} \\
&= \frac{1}{\sqrt{2\pi}} e^{-d_1^2/2} e^{\ln(Se^{bT}/X)} \\
&= n(d_1)Se^{bT}/X
\end{aligned}
$$

$$n(d_1) = \frac{1}{\sqrt{2\pi}} e^{-d_1^2/2}$$

$$n(d_1) = n(d_2)X/Se^{bT}$$

Partial Derivatives

$$N(x) = \frac{1}{\sqrt{2\pi}} \int_{-\infty}^{x} \exp(-z^2/2)dz$$

$$\frac{\partial N(x)}{\partial S} = n(x)\frac{\partial x}{\partial S}$$

Delta

$$\Delta_{call} = \frac{\partial c}{\partial S} \quad = \quad e^{(b-r)T}N(d_1) + Se^{(b-r)T}\frac{\partial N(d_1)}{\partial S} - Xe^{-rT}\frac{\partial N(d_2)}{\partial S}$$

$$= \quad e^{(b-r)T}N(d_1) + Se^{(b-r)T}\frac{\partial N(d_1)}{\partial d_1}\frac{\partial d_1}{\partial S} - Xe^{-rT}\frac{\partial N(d_2)}{\partial d_2}\frac{\partial d_2}{\partial S}$$

$$= \quad e^{(b-r)T}N(d_1) + Se^{(b-r)T}n(d_1)\frac{\partial d_1}{\partial S} - Xe^{-rT}n(d_2)\frac{\partial d_2}{\partial S}$$

$$= \quad e^{(b-r)T}N(d_1) + Se^{(b-r)T}n(d_1)\frac{\partial d_1}{\partial S} - Xe^{-rT}n(d_1)Se^{bT}/X\frac{\partial d_1}{\partial S}$$

$$= \quad e^{(b-r)T}N(d_1) > 0$$

$$\Delta_{put} = \frac{\partial p}{\partial S} \quad = \quad Xe^{-rT}\frac{\partial N(-d_2)}{\partial S} - e^{(b-r)T}N(-d_1) - Se^{(b-r)T}\frac{\partial N(-d_1)}{\partial S}$$

$$= \quad Xe^{-rT}n(-d_2)\frac{-\partial d_2}{\partial S} - e^{(b-r)T}N(-d_1) - Se^{(b-r)T}n(-d_1)\frac{-\partial d_1}{\partial S}$$

$$= \quad Xe^{-rT}n(-d_1)Se^{bT}/X\frac{\partial d_1}{\partial S} - e^{(b-r)T}N(-d_1) + Se^{(b-r)T}n(-d_1)\frac{\partial d_1}{\partial S}$$

$$= \quad -e^{(b-r)T}N(-d_1) < 0$$

Gamma

$$\Gamma_{call} = \frac{\partial^2 c}{\partial S^2} = \frac{\partial \Delta_{call}}{\partial S} \quad = \quad \frac{\partial e^{(b-r)T}N(d_1)}{\partial S}$$

$$= \quad \frac{n(d_1)e^{(b-r)T}}{S\sigma\sqrt{T}} > 0$$

$$\Gamma_{put} = \frac{\partial^2 p}{\partial S^2} = \frac{\partial \Delta_{put}}{\partial S} \quad = \quad \frac{-\partial e^{(b-r)T}N(-d_1)}{\partial S}$$

$$= \quad \frac{n(d_1)e^{(b-r)T}}{S\sigma\sqrt{T}} > 0$$

Strike

$$
\frac{\partial c}{\partial X} = Se^{(b-r)T}\frac{\partial N(d_1)}{\partial X} - e^{-rT}N(d_2) - Xe^{-rT}\frac{\partial N(d_2)}{\partial X}
$$

$$
= Se^{(b-r)T}\frac{\partial N(d_1)}{\partial d_1}\frac{\partial d_1}{\partial X} - e^{-rT}N(d_2) - Xe^{-rT}\frac{\partial N(d_2)}{\partial d_2}\frac{\partial d_2}{\partial X}
$$

$$
= Se^{(b-r)T}n(d_1)\frac{\partial d_1}{\partial X} - e^{-rT}N(d_2) - Xe^{-rT}n(d_2)\frac{\partial d_2}{\partial X}
$$

$$
= Se^{(b-r)T}n(d_1)\frac{\partial d_1}{\partial X} - e^{-rT}N(d_2) - Xe^{-rT}n(d_1)Se^{bT}/X\frac{\partial d_1}{\partial X}
$$

$$
= -e^{-rT}N(d_2) < 0
$$

$$
\frac{\partial p}{\partial X} = e^{-rT}N(-d_2) + Xe^{-rT}\frac{\partial N(-d_2)}{\partial X} - Se^{(b-r)T}\frac{\partial N(-d_1)}{\partial X}
$$

$$
= e^{-rT}N(-d_2) + Xe^{-rT}n(-d_2)\frac{\partial d_2}{\partial X} - Se^{(b-r)T}n(-d_1)\frac{\partial d_1}{\partial X}
$$

$$
= e^{-rT}N(-d_2) + Xe^{-rT}n(-d_1)Se^{bT}/X\frac{\partial d_1}{\partial X} - Se^{(b-r)T}n(-d_1)\frac{\partial d_1}{\partial X}
$$

$$
= e^{-rT}N(-d_2) > 0
$$

$$
\frac{\partial^2 c}{\partial X^2} = \frac{-\partial e^{-rT}N(d_2)}{\partial X}
$$

$$
= \frac{n(d_2)e^{-rT}}{X\sigma\sqrt{T}} > 0
$$

$$
\frac{\partial^2 p}{\partial X^2} = \frac{\partial e^{-rT}N(-d_2)}{\partial X}
$$

$$
= \frac{n(d_2)e^{-rT}}{X\sigma\sqrt{T}} > 0
$$

Rho
When $b <> 0$

$$\rho_{call} = \frac{\partial c}{\partial r} = TSe^{(b-r)T}N(d_1) - TSe^{(b-r)T}N(d_1) + Se^{(b-r)T}\frac{\partial N(d_1)}{\partial r}$$

$$+ TXe^{-rT}N(d_2) - Xe^{-rT}\frac{\partial N(d_2)}{\partial r}$$

$$= Se^{(b-r)T}n(d_1)\frac{\partial d_1}{\partial r} + TXe^{-rT}N(d_2)$$

$$- Xe^{-rT}n(d_1)Se^{bT}/X\frac{\partial d_1}{\partial r}$$

$$= TXe^{-rT}N(d_2) > 0$$

$$\rho_{put} = \frac{\partial p}{\partial r} = -TXe^{-rT}N(-d_2) + Xe^{-rT}\frac{\partial N(-d_2)}{\partial r}$$

$$- TSe^{(b-r)T}N(-d_1) + TSe^{(b-r)T}N(-d_1) - Se^{(b-r)T}\frac{\partial N(-d_1)}{\partial r}$$

$$= -TXe^{-rT}N(-d_2) < 0$$

When $b = 0$

$$\rho_{call} = \frac{\partial c}{\partial r} = -TSe^{(b-r)T}N(d_1) + Se^{(b-r)T}\frac{\partial N(d_1)}{\partial r}$$

$$+ TXe^{-rT}N(d_2) - Xe^{-rT}\frac{\partial N(d_2)}{\partial r}$$

$$= -TSe^{(b-r)T}N(d_1) + Se^{(b-r)T}n(d_1)\frac{\partial d_1}{\partial r}$$

$$+ TXe^{-rT}N(d_2) - Xe^{-rT}n(d_1)Se^{bT}/X\frac{\partial d_1}{\partial r}$$

$$= -TSe^{(b-r)T}N(d_1) + TXe^{-rT}N(d_2)$$

$$= -Tc < 0$$

$$\rho_{put} = \frac{\partial p}{\partial r} = -TXe^{-rT}N(-d_2) + Xe^{-rT}\frac{\partial N(-d_2)}{\partial r}$$

$$+ TSe^{(b-r)T}N(-d_1) - Se^{(b-r)T}\frac{\partial N(-d_1)}{\partial r}$$

$$= -Tp < 0$$

Cost of carry

$$
\begin{aligned}
\frac{\partial c}{\partial b} &= TSe^{(b-r)T}N(d_1) + Se^{(b-r)T}\frac{\partial N(d_1)}{\partial b} - Xe^{-rT}\frac{\partial N(d_2)}{\partial b} \\
&= TSe^{(b-r)T}N(d_1) + Se^{(b-r)T}n(d_1)\frac{\partial d_1}{\partial b} - Xe^{-rT}n(d_1)Se^{bT}/X\frac{\partial d_1}{\partial b} \\
&= TSe^{(b-r)T}N(d_1) > 0
\end{aligned}
$$

$$
\begin{aligned}
\frac{\partial p}{\partial b} &= Xe^{-rT}\frac{\partial N(-d_2)}{\partial b} - TSe^{(b-r)T}N(-d_1) - Se^{(b-r)T}\frac{\partial N(-d_1)}{\partial b} \\
&= -TSe^{(b-r)T}N(-d_1) > 0
\end{aligned}
$$

Vega

$$
\begin{aligned}
Vega_{call} = \frac{\partial c}{\partial \sigma} &= Se^{(b-r)T}\frac{\partial N(d_1)}{\partial \sigma} - Xe^{-rT}\frac{\partial N(d_2)}{\partial \sigma} \\
&= Se^{(b-r)T}n(d_1)\frac{\partial d_1}{\partial \sigma} - Xe^{-rT}n(d_2)\frac{\partial d_2}{\partial \sigma} \\
&= Se^{(b-r)T}n(d_1)\frac{\partial d_1}{\partial \sigma} - Xe^{-rT}n(d_1)Se^{bT}/X\frac{\partial d_2}{\partial \sigma} \\
&= Se^{(b-r)T}n(d_1)\left[\frac{\partial d_1}{\partial \sigma} - \frac{\partial d_2}{\partial \sigma}\right] \\
&= Se^{(b-r)T}n(d_1)\sqrt{T} > 0
\end{aligned}
$$

$$
\begin{aligned}
Vega_{put} = \frac{\partial p}{\partial \sigma} &= Xe^{-rT}\frac{\partial N(-d_2)}{\partial \sigma} - Se^{(b-r)T}\frac{\partial N(-d_1)}{\partial \sigma} \\
&= Xe^{-rT}n(-d_2)\left[-\frac{\partial d_2}{\partial \sigma}\right] - Se^{(b-r)T}n(-d_1)\left[-\frac{\partial d_1}{\partial \sigma}\right] \\
&= Se^{(b-r)T}n(d_1)\left[\frac{\partial d_1}{\partial \sigma} - \frac{\partial d_2}{\partial \sigma}\right] \\
&= Se^{(b-r)T}n(d_1)\sqrt{T} > 0
\end{aligned}
$$

$$
\frac{\partial d_1}{\partial \sigma} - \frac{\partial d_2}{\partial \sigma} = \left[-\frac{\ln(Se^{bT}/X)}{\sigma^2\sqrt{T}} + \frac{1}{2}\sqrt{T}\right] - \left[-\frac{\ln(Se^{bT}/X)}{\sigma^2\sqrt{T}} - \frac{1}{2}\sqrt{T}\right] = \sqrt{T}
$$

Theta

$$\Theta_{call} = -\frac{\partial c}{\partial T} \quad = \quad -(b-r)S^{(b-r)T}N(d_1) - Se^{(b-r)T}\frac{\partial N(d_1)}{\partial T}$$

$$-rXe^{-rT}N(d_2) + Xe^{-rT}\frac{\partial N(d_2)}{\partial T}$$

$$= \quad -(b-r)S^{(b-r)T}N(d_1) - Se^{(b-r)T}n(d_1)\frac{\partial d_1}{\partial T}$$

$$-rXe^{-rT}N(d_2) + Xe^{-rT}n(d_1)Se^{bT}/X\frac{\partial d_2}{\partial T}$$

$$= \quad Se^{(b-r)T}n(d_1)\left[\frac{\partial d_2}{\partial T} - \frac{\partial d_1}{\partial T}\right]$$

$$-(b-r)S^{(b-r)T}N(d_1) - rXe^{-rT}N(d_2)$$

$$= \quad -\frac{Se^{(b-r)T}n(d_1)\sigma}{2\sqrt{T}} - (b-r)S^{(b-r)T}N(d_1)$$

$$-rXe^{-rT}N(d_2) \leq \geq 0$$

$$\Theta_{put} = -\frac{\partial p}{\partial T} \quad = \quad rXe^{-rT}N(-d_2) - Xe^{-rT}\frac{\partial N(-d_2)}{\partial T}$$

$$+(b-r)S^{(b-r)T}N(-d_1) + Se^{(b-r)T}\frac{\partial N(-d_1)}{\partial T}$$

$$= \quad rXe^{-rT}N(-d_2) + (b-r)S^{(b-r)T}N(-d_1)$$

$$\times Se^{(b-r)T}n(d_1)\left[\frac{\partial d_2}{\partial T} - \frac{\partial d_1}{\partial T}\right]$$

$$= \quad -\frac{Se^{(b-r)T}n(d_1)\sigma}{2\sqrt{T}} + (b-r)S^{(b-r)T}N(-d_1)$$

$$+rXe^{-rT}N(-d_2) \leq \geq 0$$

$$\frac{\partial d_2}{\partial T} - \frac{\partial d_1}{\partial T} \quad = \quad \left[-\frac{\ln(S/X)}{2\sigma T^{3/2}} + \frac{b}{2\sigma\sqrt{T}} - \frac{\sigma}{4\sqrt{T}}\right]$$

$$-\left[-\frac{\ln(S/X)}{2\sigma T^{3/2}} + \frac{b}{2\sigma\sqrt{T}} + \frac{\sigma}{4\sqrt{T}}\right] = -\frac{\sigma}{2\sqrt{T}}$$

C

THE OPTION-PRICING SOFTWARE

C.1 HARDWARE REQUIREMENTS

The spreadsheets require a Windows compatible computer or a Macintosh that can run Microsoft Excel 5.0 (or later versions). The source code is also included in a text file for those who do not have access to Excel or who wish to port the code to another language (e.g., C++ or Pascal).

C.2 COMPUTER CODE AND READY-TO-USE SPREADSHEETS

This book contains a large collection of option-pricing formulas. The book also includes a floppy disk with source code and ready-to-use spreadsheets for most of the formulas presented in the book. These ready-to-use spreadsheets can be used by anyone—regardless of his or her knowledge of computer languages. Beginning to price options requires only minimum knowledge of spreadsheets. All one has to do is type in the input variables for the relevant formula. The computer will do the rest.

The various spreadsheets use small computer programs that are written in Visual Basic for Applications (also available in Excel). The source code is hopefully informative to programmers of option pricing formulas, students taking courses in finance (financial engineering in particular), or anyone who wants some knowledge of or hints about how the option-pricing models are implemented. Most people attain a more profound understanding of mathematical formulas after having implemented them on a computer or calculator.

All codes are made as general as possible to facilitate porting of the code to other programming languages. The computer algorithms are therefore not written in with maximum efficiency in mind. Visual Basic is chosen basically because it is easy to learn and understand. Further, Visual Basic is available to all computer users with access to Excel, version 5.0 or later. The code should appeal to a wide audience, not only to highly skilled programmers.

For programmers with experience in other programming languages, it is worth taking a look at terminology particular to Visual Basic.

Declaration of variables. Visual Basic does not require the variables to be declared before they are used (C++, for instance, requires that all variables are initially declared). However, it is a good idea to declare all variables for maximum speed and to reduce possible programming errors. All variables are thus declared in the computer code included on the disk that comes with this book.

Power. To take the power of a number, Visual Basic uses the symbol "^". Example: 4^2 corresponds to 4^2. Further, Visual Basic uses "$Exp()$" for the exponential function. Example: $S * Exp(-rT)$ corresponds to Se^{-rT}.

Line break. To instruct the computer that the command continues on the next line, Visual Basic uses a space followed by the character "_". In C++ for instance, the code for a command continues until it is terminated by ";".

Square root. Visual Basic applies the $Sqr()$ command. Example: $Sqr(T)$ is equal to $\sqrt{T}$.

Natural logarithm. Visual Basic uses the $Log()$ command. Example: $Log(S/X)$ is equal to $\ln(S/X)$.

C.3   COMPUTER FUNCTIONS

This section gives a short overview of the Visual Basic functions included on the disk.

Throughout, setting the $AmeEurFlag$="a" gives American option values while $AmeEurFlag$ ="e" gives European values. Similarly, setting the $CallPutFlag$="c" returns a call value while $CallPutFlag$ ="p" returns a put value. Some of the symbols used for the input variables in the computer code are somewhat different from the symbols used in the rest of the book. The equivalent computer symbols are:

$\delta = delta$	Barrier's curvature in double barrier option.
$\Delta t = dt$	Size of time step in a tree model.
$\eta = eta$	Binary variable, with range $\{1, -1\}$.
$\phi = phi$	Binary variable, with range $\{1, -1\}$.
$\theta = theta$	Mean-reversion level.

$\kappa = kappa$	Speed of mean reversion ("gravity").
$\rho = rho$	Correlation coefficient.
$\sigma = v$	Volatility of the relative price change of the underlying asset.
$\tau = tau$	Time to bond maturity in the Vasicek model.

Further, notice that the input for the risk-free rate r, cost of carry b, and dividend yield q should be continuously compounded in all the functions below. The functions are organized in the same manner as in the table of options pricing formulas in the Option Pricing Formulas Overview Section.

C.3.1   Plain Vanilla Options

GBlackScholes(CallPutFlag,S,X,T,r,b,v) The generalized Black–Scholes model.

GDelta(CallPutFlag,S,X,T,r,b,v) Delta for the generalized Black–Scholes model.

GGamma(S,X,T,r,b,v) Gamma for the generalized Black–Scholes model.

GVega(S,X,T,r,b,v) Vega for the generalized Black–Scholes model.

GTheta(CallPutFlag,S,X,T,r,b,v) Theta for the generalized Black–Scholes model.

GRho(CallPutFlag,S,X,T,r,b,v) Rho for the generalized Black–Scholes model.

GCarry(CallPutFlag,S,X,T,r,b,v) The generalized Black–Scholes model's sensitivity to a small change in cost of carry.

JumpDiffusion(CallPutFlag,S,X,T,r,v,lambda,gamma) The jump diffusion model.

RollGeskeWhaley(S,X,t1,T2,r,D,v) The Roll-Geske-Whaley exact formula for American call options with cash dividend.

BAWAmericanApprox(CallPutFlag,S,X,T,r,b,v) The Barone-Adesi and Whaley American option approximation.

BSAmericanApprox(CallPutFlag,S,X,T,r,b,v) The Bjerksund and Stensland American option approximation.

MiltersenSchwartz(CallPutFlag,Pt,FT,Xe,t1,T2,vS,ve,vf,rhoSe,rhoSf,rhoef, Kappae,Kappaf) The Miltersen and Schwartz commodity option pricing model.

C.3.2   Exotic Options

Executive(CallPutFlag,S,X,T,r,b,v,lambda) Executive stock option.

ForwardStartOption(CallPutFlag,S,alpha,t1,T,r,b,v) Forward start option.

TimeSwitchOption(CallPutFlag,S,X,A,T,m,dt,r,b,v) Time switch option.

SimpleChooser(S,X,t1,T2,r,b,v) Simple chooser option.

ComplexChooser(S,Xc,Xp,t,Tc,Tp,r,b,v) Complex chooser option.

OptionsOnOptions(TypeFlag,S,X1,X2,t1,T2,r,b,v) Options on plain vanilla options. By specifying the *TypeFlag* the function will return:

> "cc" a call on call option.
> "cp" a call on put option.
> "pc" a put on call option.
> "pp" a put on put option.

ExtendibleWriter(CallPutFlag,S,X1,X2,t1,T2,r,b,v) Writer extendible options.

TwoAssetCorrelation(CallPutFlag,S1,S2,X1,X2,T,b1,b2,r,v1,v2,rho) Two asset correlation option.

EuropeanExchangeOption(S1,S2,Q1,Q2,T,r,b1,b2,v1,v2,rho) European option to exchange one asset for another.

AmericanExchangeOption(S1,S2,Q1,Q2,T,r,b1,b2,v1,v2,rho) American option to exchange one asset for another.

ExchangeExchangeOption(TypeFlag,S1,S2,Q,t1,T2,r,b1,b2,v1,v2,rho) Exchange options on exchange options. By specifying the *TypeFlag* the function will return:

> 1 an option to exchange $Q * S2$ for the option to exchange $S2$ for $S1$.
> 2 an option to exchange the option to exchange $S2$ for $S1$ in return for $Q * S2$.
> 3 an option to exchange $Q * S2$ for the option to exchange $S1$ for $S2$.
> 4 an option to exchange the option to exchange $S1$ for $S2$ in return for $Q * S2$.

OptionsOnTheMaxMin(TypeFlag,S1,S2,X,T,r,b1,b2,v1,v2,rho) Options on the maximum or minimum of two risky assets. By specifying the *TypeFlag* the function will return:

> "cmax" a call on the maximum.
> "cmin" a call on the minimum.
> "pmax" a put on the maximum.
> "pmin" a put on the minimum.

SpreadApproximation(CallPutFlag,F1,F2,X,T,r,v1,v2,rho) Spread option approximation.

FloatingStrikeLookback(CallPutFlag,S,SMin,SMax,T,r,b,v) Floating strike lookback options.

FixedStrikeLookback(CallPutFlag,S,SMin,SMax,X,T,r,b,v) Fixed strike look-back option.

PartialFloatLB(CallPutFlag,S,SMin,SMax,t1,T2,r,b,v,lambda) Partial-time floating strike lookback options.

PartialFixedLB(CallPutFlag,S,X,t1,T2,r,b,v) Partial-time fixed strike lookback options.

ExtremeSpreadOption(TypeFlag,S,SMin,SMax,t1,T,r,b,v) Extreme and reverse extreme options. By specifying the *TypeFlag* the function will return:

1 an extreme spread call.
2 an extreme spread put.
3 a reverse extreme spread call.
4 a reverse extreme spread put.

StandardBarrier(TypeFlag,S,X,H,K,T,r,b,v) Standard barrier options. By specifying the *TypeFlag* the function returns:

"cdi" a call down-and-in.
"cui" a call up-and-in.
"pdi" a put down-and-in.
"pui" a put up-and-in.
"cdo" a call down-and-out.
"cuo" a call up-and-out.
"pdo" a put down-and-out.
"puo" a put up-and-out.

DoubleBarrier(TypeFlag,S,X,L,U,T,r,b,v,delta1,delta2) Double barrier options. By specifying the *TypeFlag* the function returns:

"co" a call up-and-out-down-and-out.
"po" a put up-and-out-down-and-out.
"ci" a call up-and-in-down-and-in.
"po" a put up-and-in-down-and-in.

PartialTimeBarrier(TypeFlag,S,X,H,t1,T2,r,b,v) Partial-time single asset barrier options. By specifying the *TypeFlag* the function will return:

"cuoA" a call up-and-out type A.
"cdoA" a call down-and-out type A.
"puoA" a put up-and-out type A.
"pdoA" a put down-and-out type A.
"coB1" a call out type B1.
"poB1" a put out type B1.
"cuoB2" a call up-and-out type B2.

"cdoB2" a call down-and-out type B2.
"puoB2" a put up-and-out type B2.
"pdoB2" a put down-and-out type B2.

TwoAssetBarrier(TypeFlag,S1,S2,X,H,T,r,b1,b2,v1,v2,rho) Two asset barrier options. By specifying the *TypeFlag* the function returns:

"cdi" a call down-and-in.
"cui" a call up-and-in.
"pdi" a put down-and-in.
"pui" a put up-and-in.
"cdo" a call down-and-out.
"cuo" a call up-and-out.
"pdo" a put down-and-out.
"puo" a put up-and-out.

PartialTimeTwoAssetBarrier(TypeFlag,S1,S2,X,H,t1,T2,r,b1,b2,v1,v2,rho) Partial-time two asset barrier options. By specifying the *TypeFlag* the function will return:

"cdi" a call down-and-in.
"cui" a call up-and-in.
"pdi" a put down-and-in.
"pui" a put up-and-in.
"cdo" a call down-and-out.
"cuo" a call up-and-out.
"pdo" a put down-and-out.
"puo" a put up-and-out.

LookBarrier(TypeFlag,S,X,H,t1,T,r,b,v) Look-barrier options. By specifying the *TypeFlag* the function will return:

"cuo" a call up-and-out.
"cui" a call up-and-in.
"pdo" a put down-and-out.
"pdi" a put down-and-in.

SoftBarrier(TypeFlag,S,X,L,U,T,r,b,v) Soft barrier options. By specifying the *TypeFlag* the function returns:

"cdi" a call down-and-in.
"cdo" a call down-and-out.
"pui" a put up-and-in.
"puo" a put up-and-out.

GapOption(CallPutFlag,S,X1,X2,T,r,b,v) Gap options.

CashOrNothing(CallPutFlag,S,X,K,T,r,b,v) Cash-or-nothing options.

TwoAssetCashOrNothing(TypeFlag,S1,S2,X1,X2,K,T,r,b1,b2,v1,v2,rho) Two asset cash-or-nothing options.

AssetOrNothing(CallPutFlag,S,X,T,r,b,v) Asset-or-nothing options.

SuperShare(S,XL,XH,T,r,b,v) Supershare options.

BinaryBarrier(TypeFlag,S,X,H,K,T,r,b,v,eta,phi) 28 different binary barrier options.

GeometricAverageRateOption(CallPutFlag,S,SA,X,T,T2,r,b,v) Geometric average options.

TurnbullWakemanAsian(CallPutFlag,S,SA,X,T,T2,tau,r,b,v) The Turnbull and Wakeman arithmetic average rate option approximation.

LevyAsian(CallPutFlag,S,SA,X,T,T2,r,b,v) The Levy arithmetic average rate option approximation.

ForEquOptInDomCur(CallPutFlag,E,S,X,T,r,q,vS,vE,rho) Foreign equity options struck in domestic currency.

Quanto(CallPutFlag,Ep,S,X,T,r,rf,q,vS,vE,rho) Fixed exchange rate foreign equity options (Quantos).

EquityLinkedFXO(CallPutFlag,E,S,X,T,r,rf,q,vS,vE,rho) Equity linked foreign exchange options.

TakeoverFXoption(v,b,E,X,T,r,rf,vV,vE,rho) Takeover foreign exchange options.

C.3.3 Numerical Methods in Options Pricing

CRRBinomial(AmeEurFlag,CallPutFlag,S,X,T,r,b,v,n) Standard binomial tree model.

BarrierBinomial(AmeEurFlag,TypeFlag,S,X,H,T,r,b,v,n) Barrier options in binomial trees:

> "cuo" a call up-and-out.
> "cdo" a call down-and-out.
> "puo" a put up-and-out.
> "pdo" a put down-and-out.

ConvertibleBond(AmeEurFlag,S,X,T2,t1,r,k,q,v,F,Coupon,n) Convertible bond in a binomial tree, where F is the face value.

TrinomialTree(AmeEurFlagAsString,CallPutFlag,S,X,T,r,b,v,n) Trinomial tree model.

ThreeDimensionalBinomial(TypeFlag,AmeEurFlag,CallPutFlag,S1,S2,Q1,Q2,X1,X2,T,r,b1,b2,v1,v2,rho,n) Three dimensional binomial tree for valuation of options that depends on two assets. By specifying the *TypeFlag* the function returns:

1 a spread option.

2 an options on the maximum of two assets.

3 an options on the minimum of two assets.

4 a dual-strike option.

5 a reverse dual-strike option.

6 a portfolio option.

7 an exchange option.

ImpliedTrinomialTree(ReturnFlag,STEPn,STATEi,S,X,T,r,b,v,Skew,nSteps)
Implied trinomial tree model. By specifying the *ReturnFlag* the function
returns:

"UPM" a matrix of implied up transition probabilities.

"DPM" a matrix of implied down transition probabilities.

"LVM" a matrix of implied local volatilities.

"ADM" a matrix of Arrow-Debreu prices at a single node.

"DPni" the implied down transition probability at a single node.

"ADni" the Arrow-Debreu price at a single node (at time-step *STEPn* and
state *STATEn*).

"LVni" the local volatility at a single node.

"c" the value of a European call option.

"p" the value of a European put option.

MonteCarloStandardOption(CallPutFlag,S,X,T,r,b,v,nSteps,
nSimulations) Monte Carlo simulation for plain vanilla European options.

MonteCarloAsianSpreadOption(CallPutFlag,S1,S2,X,T,r,b1,b2,v1,v2e, rho,
nSteps,nSimulations) Example of Monte Carlo simulation of European type
Asian spread option.

C.3.4 Interest-rate Options

Swaption(CallPutFlag,t1,m,F,X,T,r,v) Modified Black-76 European swaption model.

VasicekBondOption(CallPutFlag,F,X,tau,T,r,theta,kappa,v) Vasicek yield
based model for European options on zero coupon bonds.

VasicekBondPrice(t1,T,r,theta,kappa,v) Vasicek yield based model for the
value of zero coupon bonds.

C.3.5 Distributions

CND(x) The standard cumulative normal distribution function.

CBND(a,b,rho) The standard cumulative bivariate normal distribution
function.

C.4 EXCEL FILES

The accompanying floppy disk contains three Excel files:

- "Analy.xls" contains all closed-form analytical option formulas.
- "Tree.xls" contains all tree models.
- "Monte.xls" contains examples of Monte Carlo simulation.

Each file/workbook starts with ready-to-use models and ends with the computer code.

C.4.1 Computation Time

- When working with a CPU-intensive numerical model, it can sometimes be advantageous to set the calculation option in Excel to manual.
- When making a change in the computer code, Excel will recompile the entire code. This will take some time and slow down the computations. After the first recalculation, the workbook should be up to speed again.

BIBLIOGRAPHY

AASE, K. K. (1988): "Contingent Claims Valuation when the Security Price is a Combination of an Ito Process and a Random Point Process," *Stochastic Processes and their Applications*, 28, 185–220.

AMIN, K. I. (1993): "Jump Diffusion Option Valuation in Discrete Time," *Journal of Finance*, 48, 1833–1864.

AMIN, K. I., AND R. A. JARROW (1992): "Pricing Options on Risky Assets in a Stochastic Interest Rate Economy," *Mathematical Finance*, 2, 217–237.

AMIN, K. I., V. NG, AND S. C. PIRRONG (1995): "Valuing Energy Derivatives," in *Managing Energy Price Risk*. Risk Publications and Enron, pp. 57–70, London.

BALL, C. A., AND W. N. TOROUS (1983): "A Simplified Jump Process for Common Stock Returns," *Journal of Financial and Quantitative Analysis*, 18(1), 53–66.

——— (1985): "On Jumps in Common Stock Prices and Their Impact on Call Option Pricing," *Journal of Finance*, 40, 155–173.

BARLE, S., AND N. CAKICI (1995): "Growing a Smiling Tree," *Risk Magazine*, 8(10).

BARONE-ADESI, G., AND R. E. WHALEY (1987): "Efficient Analytic Approximation of American Option Values," *Journal of Finance*, 42(2), 301–320.

BARRAQUAND, J., AND D. MARTINEAU (1995): "Numerical Valuation of High Dimensional Multivariate American Securities," *Journal of Financial and Quantitative Analysis*, 30(3), 383–405.

BATES, D. S. (1991): "The Crash of '87: Was It Expected? The Evidence from Options Markets," *Journal of Finance*, 46(3), 1009–1044.

BECKERS, S. (1983): "Variances of Security Price Returns Based on High, Low, and Closing Prices," *Journal of Business*, 56, 97–109.

BERMIN, H. P. (1996a): "Combining Lookback Options and Barrier Options: The Case of Look-Barrier Options," *Working Paper, Department of Economics, Lund University, Sweden*.

——— (1996b): "Exotic Lookback Options: The Case of Extreme Spread Options," *Working Paper, Department of Economics, Lund University, Sweden*.

——— (1996c): "Time and Path Dependent Options: The Case of Time Dependent Inside and Outside Barrier Options," *Paper presented at the Third Nordic Symposium on Contingent Claims Analysis in Finance, Iceland, May*.

BHAGAVATULA, R. S., AND P. P. CARR (1995): "Valuing Double Barrier Options with Time-Dependent Parameters," Discussion paper, Cornell University: Johnson Graduate School of Management.

BJERKSUND, P., AND G. STENSLAND (1993a): "American Exchange Options and a Put-Call Tranformation: A Note," *Journal of Business Finance and Accounting*, 20(5), 761–764.

——— (1993b): "Closed-Form Approximation of American Options," *Scandinavian Journal of Management*, 9, 87–99.

——— (1994): "An American Call on the Difference of Two Assets," *International Review of Economics and Finance*, 3(1), 1–26.

——— (1996): "Implementation of the Black-Derman-Toy Interest Rate Model," *Journal of Fixed Income*, 6, 67–75.

BLACK, F. (1976): "The Pricing of Commodity Contracts," *Journal of Financial Economics*, 3, 167–179.

BLACK, F., E. DERMAN, AND W. TOY (1990): "A One-Factor Model of Interest Rates and Its Application to Treasury Bond Options," *Financial Analysts Journal*, pp. 33–39.

BLACK, F., AND P. KARASINSKI (1991): "Bond and Option Pricing when Short Rates are Lognormal," *Financial Analysts Journal*, pp. 52–59.

BLACK, F., AND M. SCHOLES (1973): "The Pricing of Options and Corporate Liabilities," *Journal of Political Economy*, 81, 637–654.

BOUAZIZ, L., E. BRIYS, AND M. GROUHY (1994): "The Pricing of Forward Starting Asian Options," *Journal of Banking and Finance*, 18, 823–839.

BOYLE, P. P. (1977): "Options: A Monte Carlo Approach," *Journal of Financial Economics*, 4, 323–338.

——— (1986): "Option Valuation Using a Three Jump Process," *International Options Journal*, 3, 7–12.

——— (1988): "A Lattice Framework for Option Pricing with Two State Variables," *Journal of Financial and Quantitative Analysis*, 23, 1–12.

BOYLE, P. P., J. EVNINE, AND S. GIBBS (1989): "Numerical Evaluation of Multivariate Contingent Claims," *Review of Financial Studies*, 2, 241–50.

BOYLE, P. P., AND S. H. LAU (1994): "Bumping Up Against the Barrier with the Binomial Method," *Journal of Derivatives*, 1, 6–14.

BOYLE, P. P., AND Y. K. TSE (1990): "An Algorithm for Computing Values of Options on the Maximum or Minimum of Several Assets," *Journal of Financial and Quantitative Analysis*, 25, 215–27.

BRENNER, M., AND M. G. SUBRAHMANYAM (1988): "A Simple Solution to Compute the Implied Standard Deviation," *Financial Analysts Journal*, pp. 80–83.

––––––– (1994): "A Simple Approach to Option Valuation and Hedging in the Black-Scholes Model," *Financial Analysts Journal*, pp. 25–28.

BROADIE, M., P. GLASSERMAN, AND S. KOU (1995): "A Continuity Correction for Discrete Barrier Options," *Working paper*.

BROTHERTON-RATCLIFFE (1994): "Monte Carlo Monitoring," *Risk Magazine*, December.

BROTHERTON-RATCLIFFE, R., AND B. IBEN (1993): "Yield Curve Applications of Swap Products," in *Advanced Strategies in Financial Risk Management, Robert J. Schwartz and Clifford W. Smith, Jr.,* New York Institute of Finance.

BUCHEN, P., AND M. KELLY (1996): "The Maximum Entropy Distribution of an Asset Inferred from Option Prices," *Journal of Financial and Quantitative Analysis*, 31, 143–159.

CAKS, J. (1977): "The Coupon Effect on Yield to Maturity," *Journal of Finance*, March, 103–115.

CARR, P. P. (1988): "The Valuation of Sequential Exchange Opportunities," *Journal of Finance*, 43, 1235–1256.

CARR, P. P., AND J. BOWIE (1994): "Static Simplicity," *Risk Magazine*, 7(8).

CARR, P. P. (1994): "European Put Call Symmetry," *Working Paper, Cornell University*.

CARR, P. P., AND K. ELLIS (1995): "Static Hedging of Exotic Options," *Working Paper, Cornell University*.

CHEUK, T. H., AND T. C. VORST (1996): "Complex Barrier Options," *Journal of Derivatives*, 4, 8–22.

CHO, H. Y., AND K. W. LEE (1995): "An Extension of the Three-Jump Process Model for Contingent Claim Valuation," *Journal of Derivatives*, 3, 102–108.

CHRISS, N. (1996): "Transatlantic Trees," *Risk Magazine*, 9(7).

CONZE, A., AND VISWANATHAN (1991): "Path Dependent Options: The Case of Lookback Options," *Journal of Finance*, 46, 1893–1907.

CORRADO, C. J., AND T. W. MILLER (1996a): "A Note on a Simple, Accurate Formula to Compute Implied Standard Deviations," *Journal of Banking and Finance*, 20, 595–603.

——— (1996b): "Volatility Without Tears," *Risk Magazine*, 9(7).

CORTAZAR, G., AND E. S. SCHWARTZ (1994): "The Valuation of Commodity-Contingent Claims," *Journal of Derivatives*, 1, 27–39.

COX, J. C., S. A. ROSS, AND M. RUBINSTEIN (1979): "Option Pricing: A Simplified Approach," *Journal of Financial Economics*, 7, 229–263.

COX, J. C., AND M. RUBINSTEIN (1985): "Innovations in Options Markets," *Options Markets,* Chap. 8. Prentice-Hall, New Jersey.

CURRAN, M. (1992): "Beyond Average Intelligence," *Risk Magazine*, 5(10).

——— (1994a): "Strata Gems," *Risk Magazine*, March.

——— (1994b): "Valuing Asian and Portfolio Options by Conditioning on the Geometric Mean Price," *Management Science*, 40(12), 1705–1711.

DERMAN, E., D. ERGENER, AND I. KANI (1995): "Static Options Replication," *Journal of Derivatives*, 2, 78–95.

DERMAN, E., AND I. KANI (1994): "Riding on a Smile," *Risk Magazine*, 7(2).

DERMAN, E., I. KANI, AND N. CHRISS (1996): "Implied Trinomial Trees of the Volatility Smile," *Journal of Derivatives*, 3(4), 7–22.

DERMAN, E., P. KARASINSKI, AND J. S. WECKER (1990): "Understanding Guaranteed Exchange-Rate Contracts in Foreign Stock Investments," *International Equity Strategies,* Goldman Sachs, June.

DRAVID, A., M. RICHARDSON, AND T. S. SUN (1993): "Pricing Foreign Index Contingent Claims: An Application to Nikkei Index Warrants," *Journal of Derivatives*, 1(1), 33–51.

DREZNER, Z. (1978): "Computation of the Bivariate Normal Integral," *Mathematics of Computation*, 32, 277–279.

DUFFIE, D., AND P. GLYNN (1992): "Efficient Monte Carlo Estimation of Security Prices," Discussion paper, Graduate School of Business, Stanford University.

DUPIRE, B. (1994): "Pricing with a Smile," *Risk Magazine*, 7(1).

FEINSTEIN, S. (1988): "A Source of Unbiased Implied Volatility Forcasts," Working Paper 88-9, Federal Reserve Bank of Atlanta.

FRENCH, D. W. (1984): "The Weekend Effect on the Distribution of Stock Prices," *Journal of Financial Economics*, 13, 547–559.

FRENCH, K. R. (1980): "Stock Returns and the Weekend Effect," *Journal of Financial Economics*, 8, 55–69.

FRENCH, K. R., AND R. ROLL (1986): "Stock Return Variances," *Journal of Financial Economics*, 17, 5–26.

GARMAN, M. B. (1989): "Recollection in Tranquility," *Risk Magazine*, 2(3).

GARMAN, M. B., AND S. W. KOHLHAGEN (1983): "Foreign Currency Option Values," *Journal of International Money and Finance*, 2, 231–237.

GARMAN, M. B., AND M. J. KLASS (1980): "On the Estimation of Security Price Volatilities from Historical Data," *Journal of Business*, 53(1), 67–78.

GEMAN, H., AND M. YOR (1993): "Bessel Processes, Asian Options, and Perpetuities," *Mathematical Finance*, 3(4), 349–375.

GEMAN, H., AND A. EYDELAND (1995): "Domino Effect," *Risk Magazine*, 8(4).

GEMAN, H., AND M. YOR (1996): "Pricing and Hedging Double-Barrier Options: A Probabilistic Approach," *Mathematical Finance*, 6(4), 365–378.

GESKE, R. (1977): "The Valuation of Corporate Liabilities as Compound Options," *Journal of Financial and Quantitative Analysis*, pp. 541–552.

——— (1979a): "A Note on an Analytical Formula for Unprotected American Call Options on Stocks with Known Dividends," *Journal of Financial Economics*, 7, 375–80.

——— (1979b): "The Valuation of Compound Options," *Journal of Financial Economics*, 7, 63–81.

GIBBONS, M. R., AND P. HESS (1981): "Day of the Week Effect and Asset Returns," *Journal of Business*, 54, 579–596.

GIBSON, R., AND E. S. SCHWARTZ (1990): "Stochastic Convenience Yield and the Pricing of Oil Contingent Claims," *Journal of Finance*, 45, 959–976.

GOLDMAN, B. M., H. B. SOSIN, AND M. A. GATTO (1979): "Path Dependent Options: Buy at the Low, Sell at the High." *Journal of Finance*, 34(5), 1111–1127.

GOLDMAN-SACHS (1993): "Valuing Convertible Bonds as Derivatives," *Quantitative Strategies Research Notes*.

HAKANSSON, N. (1991): "Supershares," Discussion paper, Institute of Business and Economic Research, University of California at Berkeley.

HAKANSSON, N. H. (1976): "The Purchasing Power Fund: A New Kind of Financial Intermediary," *Financial Analysts Journal*, 32, 49–59.

HART, I., AND M. ROSS (1994): "Striking Continuity," *Risk Magazine*, 7(6).

HAUG, E. G. (1993): "Opportunities and Perils of Using Option Sensitivities," *Journal of Financial Engineering*, 2(3), 253–269.

——— (1996): "Implisitt Korrelasjon i Valutamarkedet," *Beta*, 9(1), 39–43.

HAUG, E. G., AND J. HAUG (1996): "Implied Forward Volatility," Paper presented at the Third Nordic Symposium on Contingent Claims Analysis in Finance, Iceland, May.

HAYKOV, J. M. (1993): "A Better Control Variate for Pricing Standard Asian Options," *Journal of Financial Engineering*, 2(3), 207–216.

HEENK, B. A., A. G. Z. KEMNA, AND A. C. F. VORST (1990): "Asian Options on Oil Spreads," *Review of Futures Markets*, 9, 510–528.

HEYNEN, R. C., AND H. M. KAT (1994a): "Crossing Barriers," *Risk Magazine*, 7.

——— (1994b): "Partial Barrier Options," *Journal of Financial Engineering*, 3, 253–274.

——— (1994c): "Selective Memory," *Risk Magazine*, 7(11).

——— (1996a): "Brick by Brick," *Risk Magazine*, 9(6).

——— (1996b): "Discrete Partial Barrier Options with a Moving Barrier," *Journal of Financial Engineering*, 5(3), 199–210.

HO, T. S. Y., AND S.-B. LEE (1986): "Term Structure Movements and Pricing Interest Rate Contingent Claims," *Journal of Finance*, 41, 1011–29.

HODGES, S. D., AND M. J. P. SELBY (1987): "On the Evaluation of Compound Options," *Management Science*, 33(3), 347–355.

HULL, J., AND A. WHITE (1990): "Pricing Interest Rate Derivative Securities," *Review of Financial Studies*, 3(4), 573–92.

——— (1992): "In the Common Interest," *Risk Magazine*, 5(3).

——— (1993): "The Pricing of Options on Interest-Rate Caps and Floors Using the Hull-White Model," *Journal of Financial Engineering*, 2, pp. 287–96.

IKEDA, M., AND N. KUNITOMO (1992): "Pricing Options with Curved Boundaries," *Mathematical Finance*, 2, 275–298.

JACKWERTH, J. C., AND M. RUBINSTEIN (1996): "Recovering Probability Distributions from Option Prices," *Journal of Finance*, 51, 1611–1631.

JAMSHIDIAN, F. (1989): "An Exact Bond Option Formula," *Journal of Finance*, 44, 205–9.

——— (1991): "Forward Induction and Construction of Yield Curve Diffusion Models," *Journal of Fixed Income*, pp. 62–74.

——— (1996): "Sorting Out Swaptions," *Risk Magazine*, 9(3).

JENNERGREN, L. P., AND B. NASLUND (1993): "A Comment on Valuation of Executive Stock Options and the FASB Proposal," *The Accounting Review*, 68(1), 179–183.

JOHNSON, H. (1987): "Options on the Maximum or the Minimum of Several Assets," *Journal of Financial and Quantitative Analysis*, 22(3), 277–283.

KAT, H., AND L. VERDONK (1995): "Tree Surgery," *Risk Magazine*, 8(2).

KEMNA, A., AND A. VORST (1990): "A Pricing Method for Options Based on Average Asset Values," *Journal of Banking and Finance*, 14, 113–129.

KIRK, E. (1995): "Correlation in the Energy Markets," in *Managing Energy Price Risk*. London: Risk Publications and Enron, pp. 71–78.

KUNITOMO, N. (1992): "Improving the Parkinson Method of Estimating Security Price Volatilities," *Journal of Business*, 65, 295–302.

LEVY, E. (1992): "Pricing European Average Rate Currency Options," *Journal of International Money and Finance*, 11, 474–491.

LEVY, E., AND S. TURNBULL (1992): "Average Intelligence," *Risk Magazine*, 5(2).

LONGSTAFF, F. A. (1990): "Pricing Options with Extendible Maturities: Analysis and Applications," *Journal of Finance*, 45(3), 935–957.

MANASTER, S., AND G. KOEHLER (1982): "The Calculation of Implied Variances from the Black-Scholes Model," *Journal of Finance*, 37(1), 227–230.

MARGRABE, W. (1978): "The Value of an Option to Exchange One Asset for Another," *Journal of Finance*, 33(1), 177–186.

MARSH, T. A., AND E. R. ROSENFIELD (1986): "Non-Trading, Market Making, and Estimates of Stock Price Volatility," *Journal of Financial Economics*, 15, 359–372.

MERTON, R. C. (1973): "Theory of Rational Option Pricing," *Bell Journal of Economics and Management Science*, 4, 141–183.

——— (1976): "Option Pricing When Underlying Stock Returns are Discontinuous," *Journal of Financial Economics*, 3, 125–144.

MILTERSEN, K., K. SANDMANN, AND D. SONDERMANN (1997): "Closed Form Solutions for Term Structure Derivatives with Log-Normal Interest Rates," *Journal of Finance*, 52(1), pp. 409–30.

MILTERSEN, K., AND E. S. SCHWARTZ (1997): "Pricing of Options on Commodity Futures with Stochastic Term Structures of Convenience Yields and Interest Rates," Working Paper, The John E. Anderson Graduate School of Management at UCLA, Los Angeles.

MORO, B. (1995): "The Full Monte," *Risk Magazine*, February.

NELKEN, I. (1993): "Square Deals," *Risk Magazine*, 6(4).

PARKINSON, M. (1980): "The Extreme Value Method for Estimating the Variance of the Rate of Return," *Journal of Business*, 53(1), 61–65.

PEARSON, N. D. (1995): "An Efficient Approach for Pricing Spread Options," *Journal of Derivatives*, 3, 76–91.

PECHTL, A. (1995): "Classified Information," *Risk Magazine*, 8.

REIMER, M., AND M. SANDEMANN (1995): "A Discrete Time Approach for European and American Barrier Options," Working Paper.

REINER, E. (1992): "Quanto Mechanics," *Risk Magazine*, 5, 59–63.

REINER, E., AND M. RUBINSTEIN (1991a): "Breaking Down the Barriers," *Risk Magazine*, 4(8).

——— (1991b): "Unscrambling the Binary Code," *Risk Magazine*, 4(9).

REISMANN, H. (1992): "Movements of the Term Structure of Commodity Futures and Pricing of Commodity Claims," Working Paper, Faculty of I. E. and Management, Technion-Israel Institute of Technology, Israel.

RENDLEMAN, R. J., AND B. J. BARTTER (1979): "Two-State Option Pricing," *Journal of Finance*, 34, 1093–1110.

—— (1980): "The Pricing of Options on Debt Securities," *Journal of Financial and Quantitative Analysis*, 15, 11–24.

RICH, D. R. (1994): "The Mathematical Foundation of Barrier Option-Pricing Theory," *Advances in Futures and Options Research*, 7, 267–311.

RICH, D. R., AND D. M. CHANCE (1993): "An Alternative Approach to the Pricing of Options on Multiple Assets," *Journal of Financial Engineering*, 2(3), 271–285.

RITCHKEN, P. (1995): "On Pricing Barrier Options," *Journal of Derivatives*, 3, 19–28.

ROGERS, L. C. G., AND S. E. SATCHELL (1991): "Estimating Variance from High, Low and Closing Prices," *The Annals of Applied Probability*, 1, 504–512.

ROLL, R. (1977): "An Analytic Valuation Formula for Unprotected American Call Options on Stocks with Known Dividends," *Journal of Financial Economics*, 5, 251–58.

RUBINSTEIN, M. (1990): "Pay Now, Choose Later," *Risk Magazine*.

—— (1991a): "Double Trouble," *Risk Magazine*, 5(1).

—— (1991b): "One for Another," *Risk Magazine*, 4(7).

—— (1991c): "Options for the Undecided," *Risk Magazine*, 4(4).

—— (1991d): "Somewhere over the Rainbow," *Risk Magazine*, 4(10).

—— (1994a): "Implied Binomial Trees," *Journal of Finance*, 49, 771–818.

—— (1994b): "Return to OZ," *Risk Magazine*, 7(11).

—— (1995a): "As Simple as One, Two, Three," *Risk Magazine*, 8(1).

—— (1995b): "SuperShares," in *The Handbook of Equity Derivatives*. Burr Ridge, IL: Irwin.

SCHAEFER, S., AND E. SCHWARTZ (1987): "Time Dependent Variance and the Pricing of Bond Options," *Journal of Finance*, 42, 1113–28.

SCHNABEL, J. A., AND J. Z. WEI (1994): "Valuing Takeover-Contingent Foreign Exchange Call Options," *Advances in Futures and Options Research*, 7, 223–236.

SCHWARTZ, E. S. (1997): "The Stochastic Behavior of Commodity Prices: Implications for Valuation and Hedging," Finance Working Paper 1-97, The John E. Anderson Graduate School of Management at UCLA, Los

Angeles, Forthcoming in the Journal of Finance, July 1997.

SHIMKO, D. (1994): "Options on Futures Spreads: Hedging, Speculation, and Valuation," *The Journal of Futures Markets*, 14(2), 183–213.

SMITH, D. R. (1991): "A Simple Method for Pricing Interest Rate Swaptions," *Financial Analysts Journal*, May-June, 72–76.

STULZ, R. M. (1982): "Options on the Minimum or the Maximum of Two Risky Assets," *Journal of Financial Economics*, 10, 161–185.

TURNBULL, S. M., AND L. M. WAKEMAN (1991): "A Quick Algorithm for Pricing European Average Options," *Journal of Financial and Quantitative Analysis*, 26, 377–389.

VASICEK, O. (1977): "An Equilibrium Characterization of the Term Structure," *Journal of Financial Economics*, 5, 177–88.

WHALEY, R. E. (1981): "On the Valuation of American Call Options on Stocks with Known Dividends," *Journal of Financial Economics*, 9, 207–11.

WILCOX, D. (1991): "Spread Options Enchance Risk Management Choices," *NYMEX Energy in the News*, Fall, 9–13.

ZHANG, P. G. (1994): "Flexible Asian Options," *Journal of Financial Engineering*, 3(1), 65–83.

——— (1995a): "Flexible Arithmetic Asian Options," *Journal of Derivatives*, 2(3), 53–63.

——— (1995b): "Correlation Digital Options," *Journal of Financial Engineering*, 4, 75–96.

INDEX